6,000 MILES TO FREEDOM

Two Boys and Their Flight from the Taliban

Written by Stéphane Marchetti
and illustrated by Cyrille Pomès

graphic mundi

For Sacha and Lou.

Thanks to all the kids who trusted me with their stories.
Their courage moved me deeply.

Thanks to Thomas Dandois, Alexis Monchovet,
Olivier Boccon-Gibod, and Emmanuel Duparcq.

Special thanks to Mélanie Brelot for her unwavering
support throughout the writing of this book.

Stéphane Marchetti

Library of Congress Cataloging-in-Publication Data

Names: Marchetti, Stéphane, 1978– author.
Title: 6,000 miles to freedom : two boys and their flight from the Taliban / written by Stéphane Marchetti ; and illustrated by Cyrille Pomès ; translated by Hannah Chute.
Description: University Park, Pennsylvania : Graphic Mundi, [2022] | Includes bibliographical references and index.
Summary: "A narrative account, in graphic novel format, of the traumatic experiences faced by children fleeing war and poverty in Afghanistan, as well as the isolation they often feel as refugees in the West"—Provided by publisher.
Identifiers: LCCN 2021052968 | ISBN 9781637790212 (hardback)
Subjects: LCSH: Refugees—Afghanistan—Comic books, strips, etc. | Refugees—England—Comic books, strips, etc. | Refugee children—Afghanistan—Comic books, strips, etc.
Classification: LCC HV640.5.A28 M365 2022
LC record available at https://lccn.loc.gov/2021052968

Printed in Lithuania by BALTO Print
Published by
The Pennsylvania State University Press,
University Park, PA 16802–1003

graphic mundi
drawing our worlds together

Graphic Mundi is an imprint of
The Pennsylvania State University Press.

Translated by Hannah Chute.

Originally published as *9603 Kilomètres: L'Odyssée de deux enfants*, Futuropolis, Paris © 2020.

The Pennsylvania State University Press is a member of the Association of University Presses.

It is the policy of The Pennsylvania State University Press to use acid-free paper. Publications on uncoated stock satisfy the minimum requirements of American National Standard for Information Sciences—Permanence of Paper for Printed Library Material, ANSI Z39.48–1992.

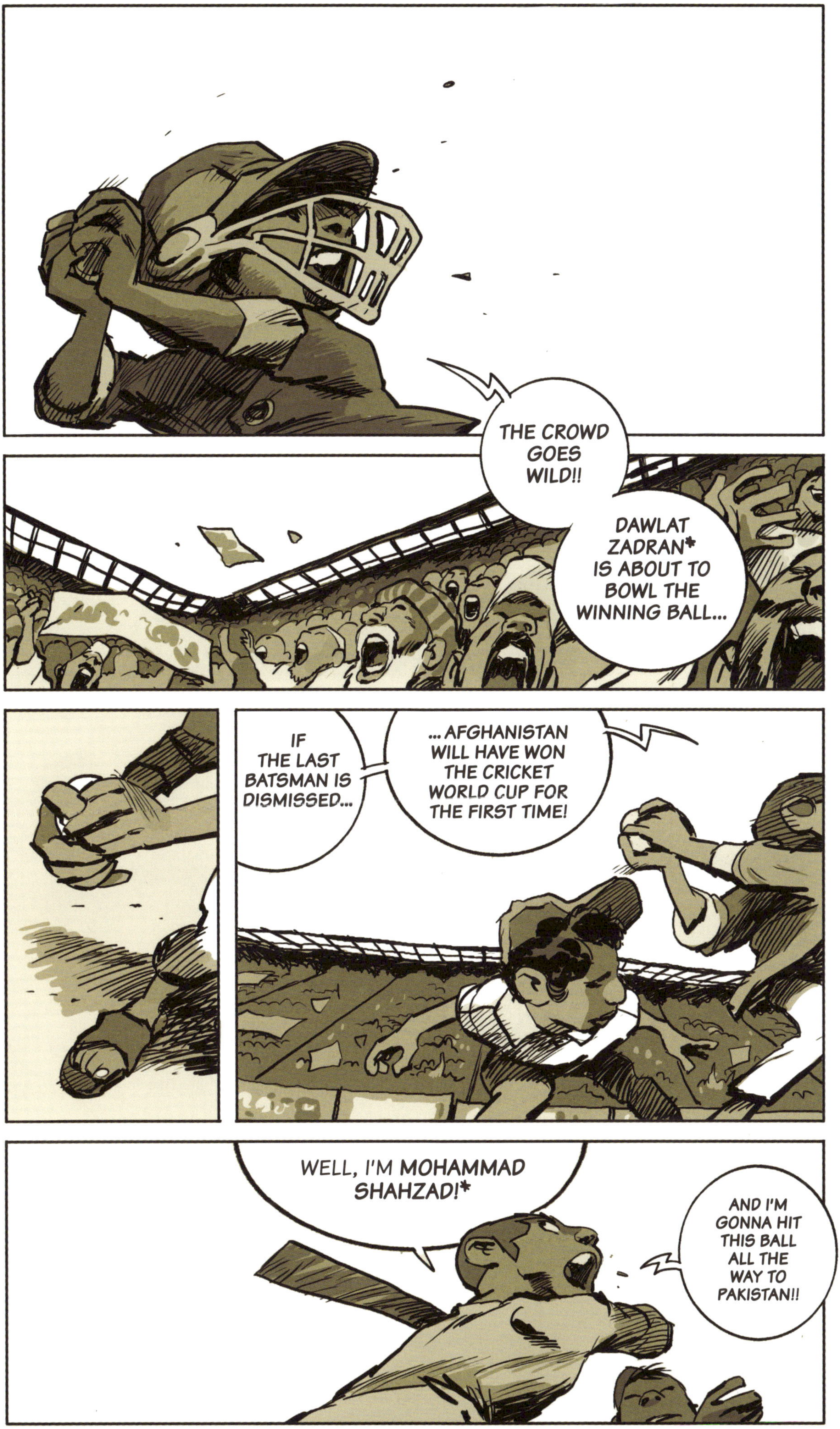
THE CROWD GOES WILD!!
DAWLAT ZADRAN* IS ABOUT TO BOWL THE WINNING BALL...
IF THE LAST BATSMAN IS DISMISSED...
...AFGHANISTAN WILL HAVE WON THE CRICKET WORLD CUP FOR THE FIRST TIME!
WELL, I'M MOHAMMAD SHAHZAD!*
AND I'M GONNA HIT THIS BALL ALL THE WAY TO PAKISTAN!!

*AFGHAN CRICKETERS.

KHOST PROVINCE, SOUTHEASTERN AFGHANISTAN. LATE SUMMER 2014.
ADEL! YOU GONNA BOWL OR WHAT?!
YOU'RE TAKING FOREVER...
DAWLAT ZADRAN FOCUSES...
... DAWLAT ZADRAN IS ABOUT TO GET HIS ASS KICKED!
BOWL!!
HE LOOKS AT HIS CHEERING FANS, HE...
COME ON, RAFI! WE WAITED A WHOLE HOUR WHEN BALOO WENT TO PISS!
IT WASN'T THAT LONG...
WHO CARES, JUST PLAY!!
YEAH, IT WAS!
JACKASS.
WHAT DID YOU SAY?

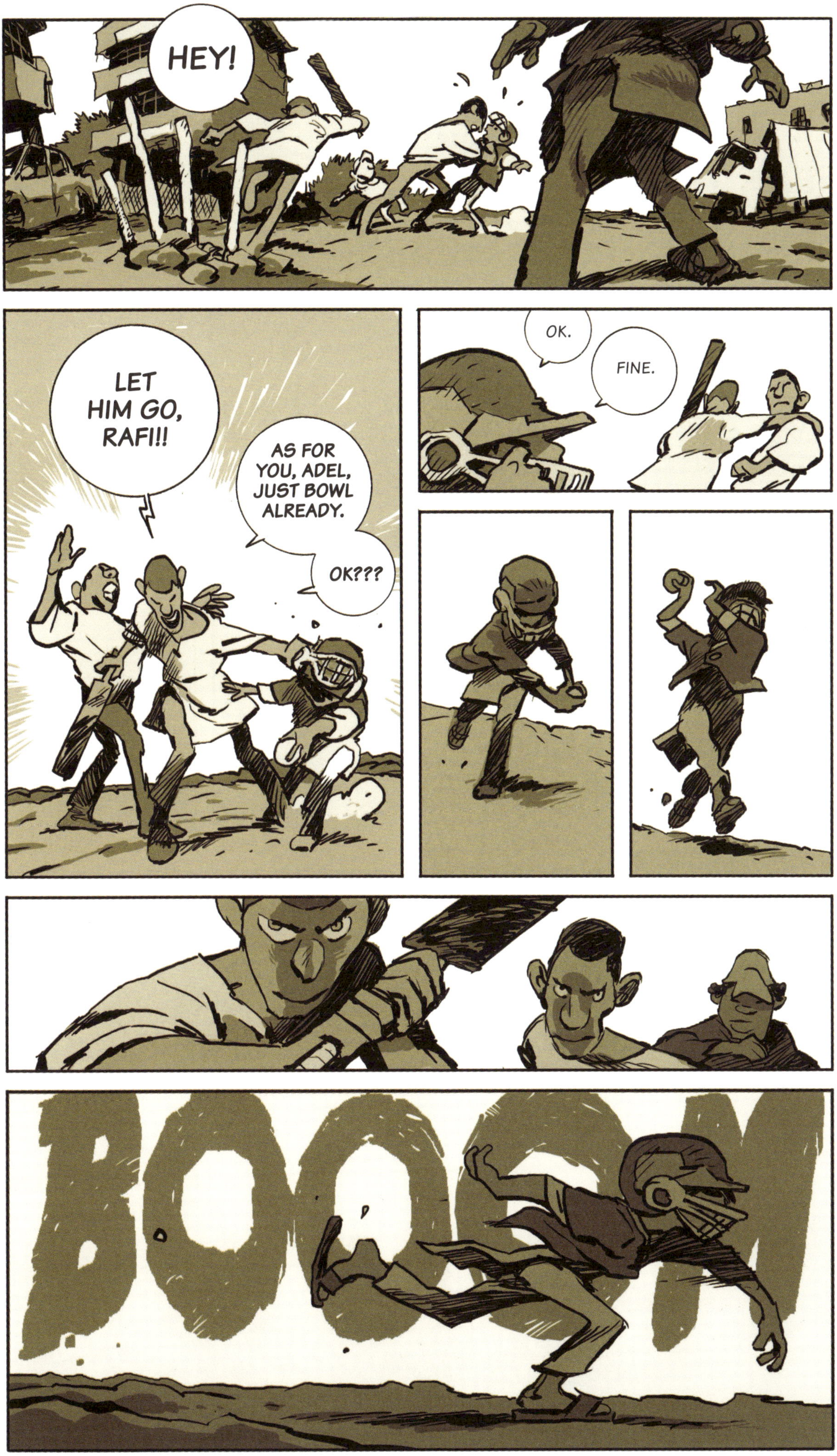
HEY!
LET HIM GO, RAFI!!
AS FOR YOU, ADEL, JUST BOWL ALREADY.
OK???
OK.
FINE.
BOOOM

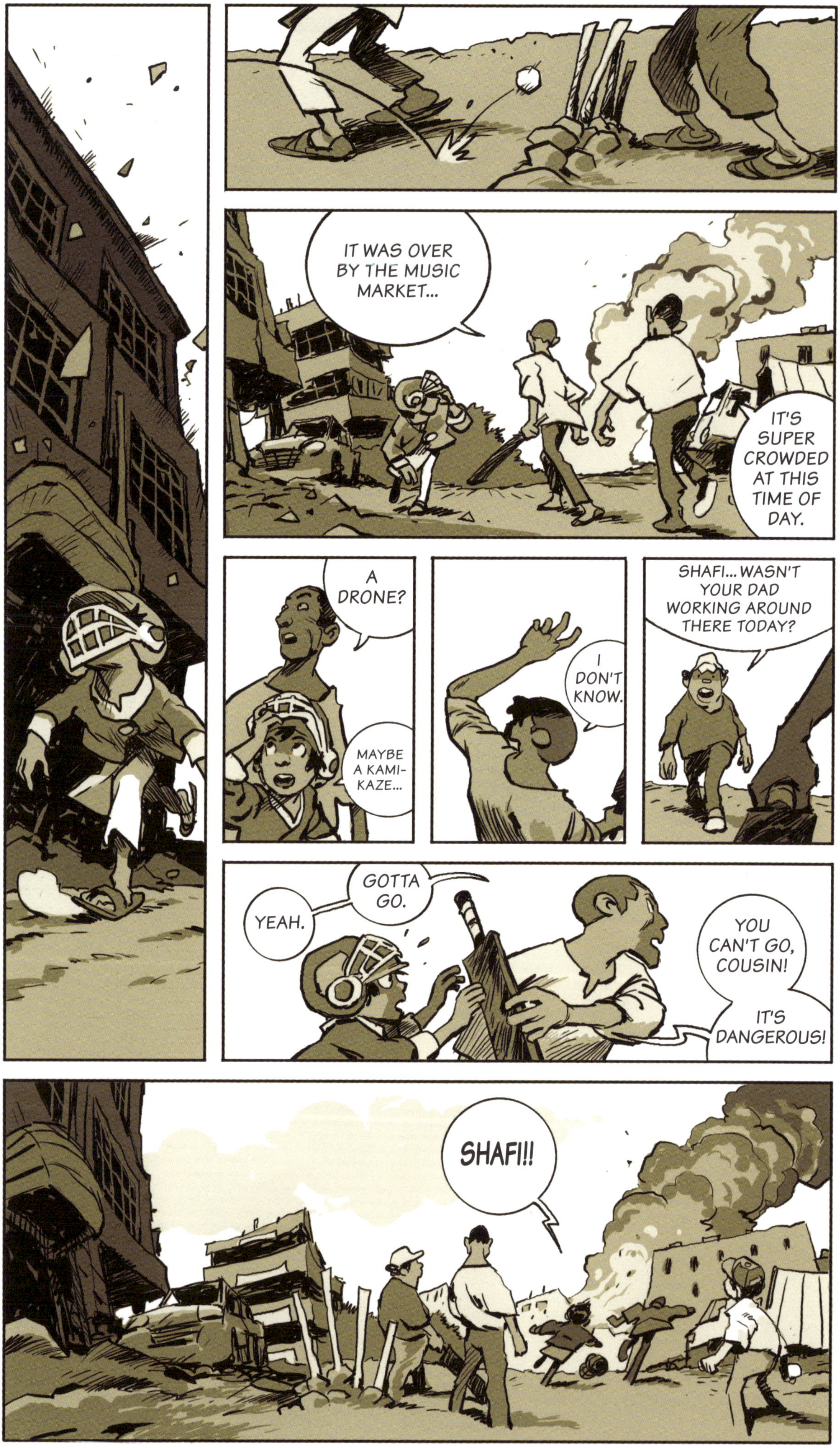
IT WAS OVER BY THE MUSIC MARKET...
IT'S SUPER CROWDED AT THIS TIME OF DAY.
A DRONE?
MAYBE A KAMI-KAZE...
I DON'T KNOW.
SHAFI... WASN'T YOUR DAD WORKING AROUND THERE TODAY?
YEAH.
GOTTA GO.
YOU CAN'T GO, COUSIN!
IT'S DANGEROUS!
SHAFI!!

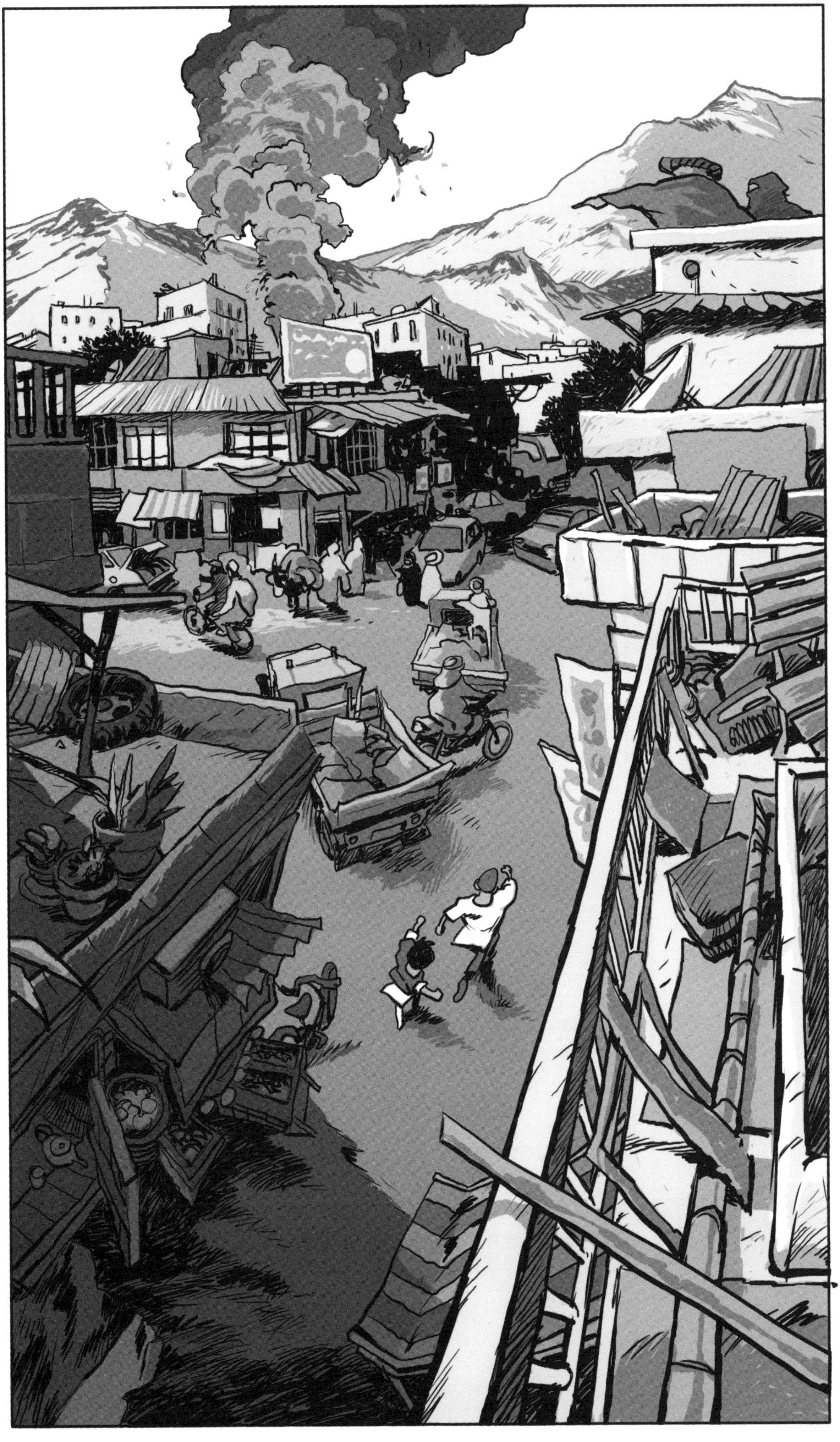

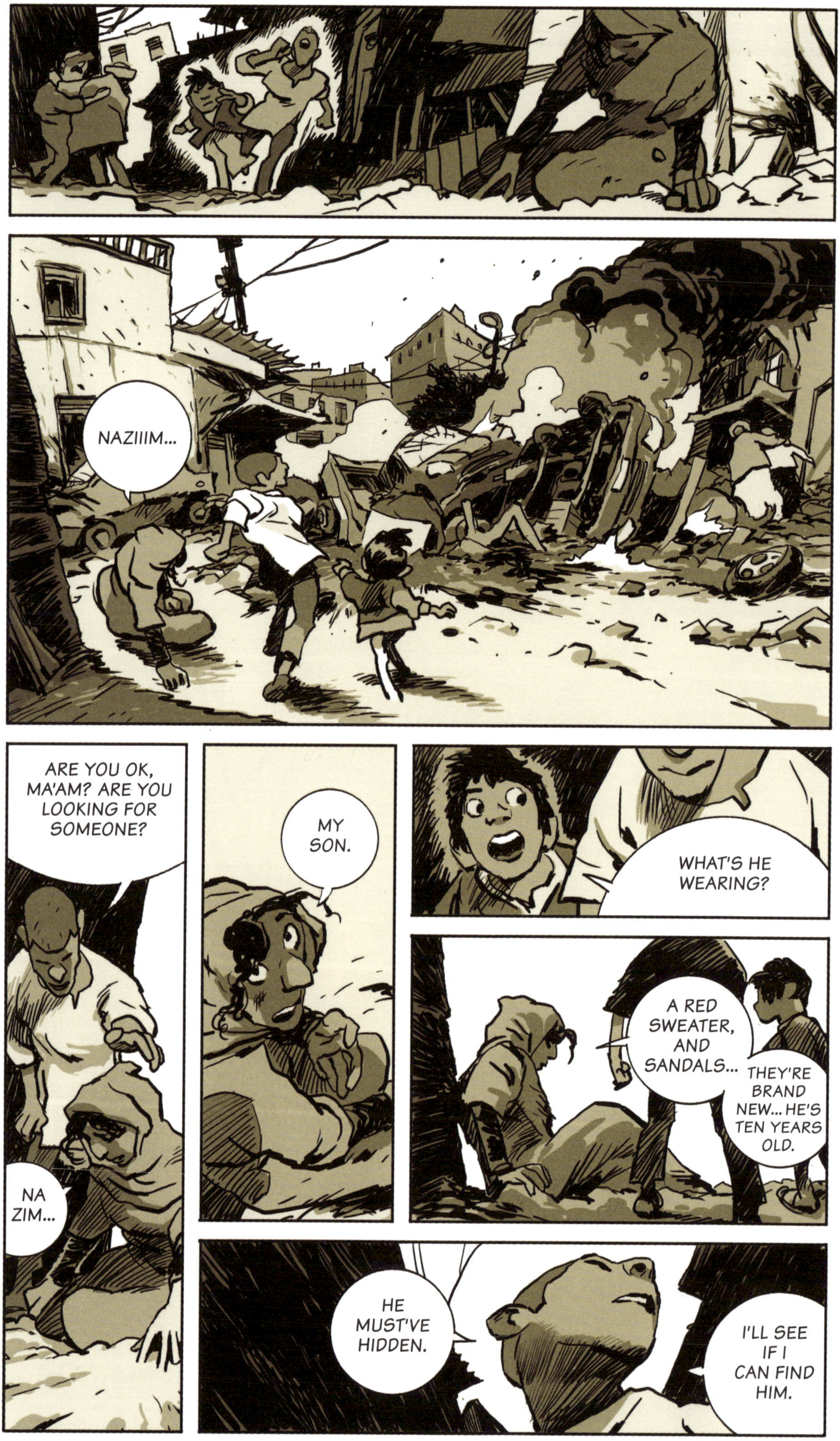
NAZIIIM...
ARE YOU OK, MA'AM? ARE YOU LOOKING FOR SOMEONE?
NA ZIM...
MY SON.
WHAT'S HE WEARING?
A RED SWEATER, AND SANDALS...
THEY'RE BRAND NEW... HE'S TEN YEARS OLD.
HE MUST'VE HIDDEN.
I'LL SEE IF I CAN FIND HIM.

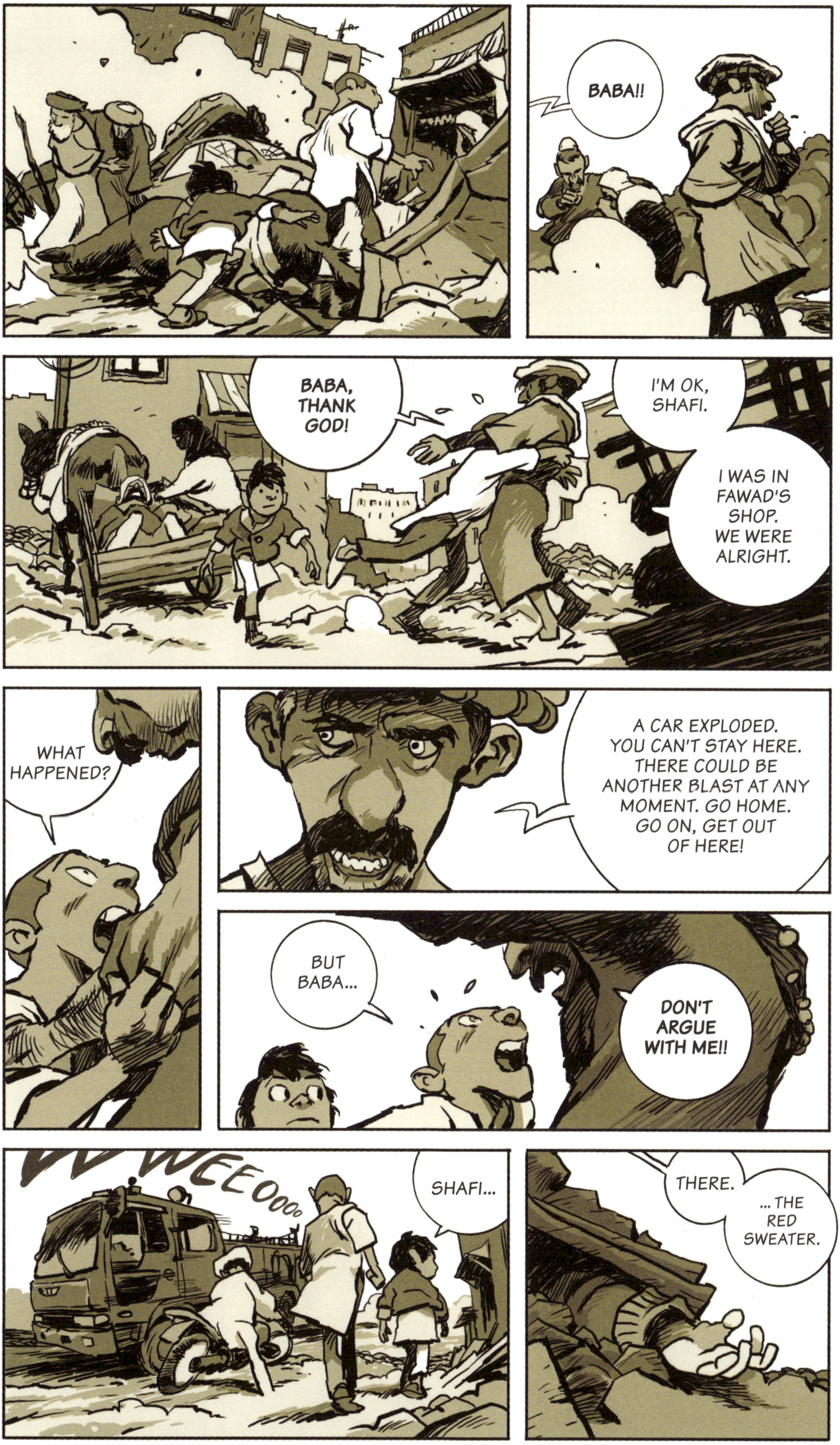
BABA!!
BABA, THANK GOD!
I'M OK, SHAFI.
I WAS IN FAWAD'S SHOP. WE WERE ALRIGHT.
WHAT HAPPENED?
A CAR EXPLODED. YOU CAN'T STAY HERE. THERE COULD BE ANOTHER BLAST AT ANY MOMENT. GO HOME. GO ON, GET OUT OF HERE!
BUT BABA...
DON'T ARGUE WITH ME!!
WEEOooo
SHAFI...
THERE.
...THE RED SWEATER.

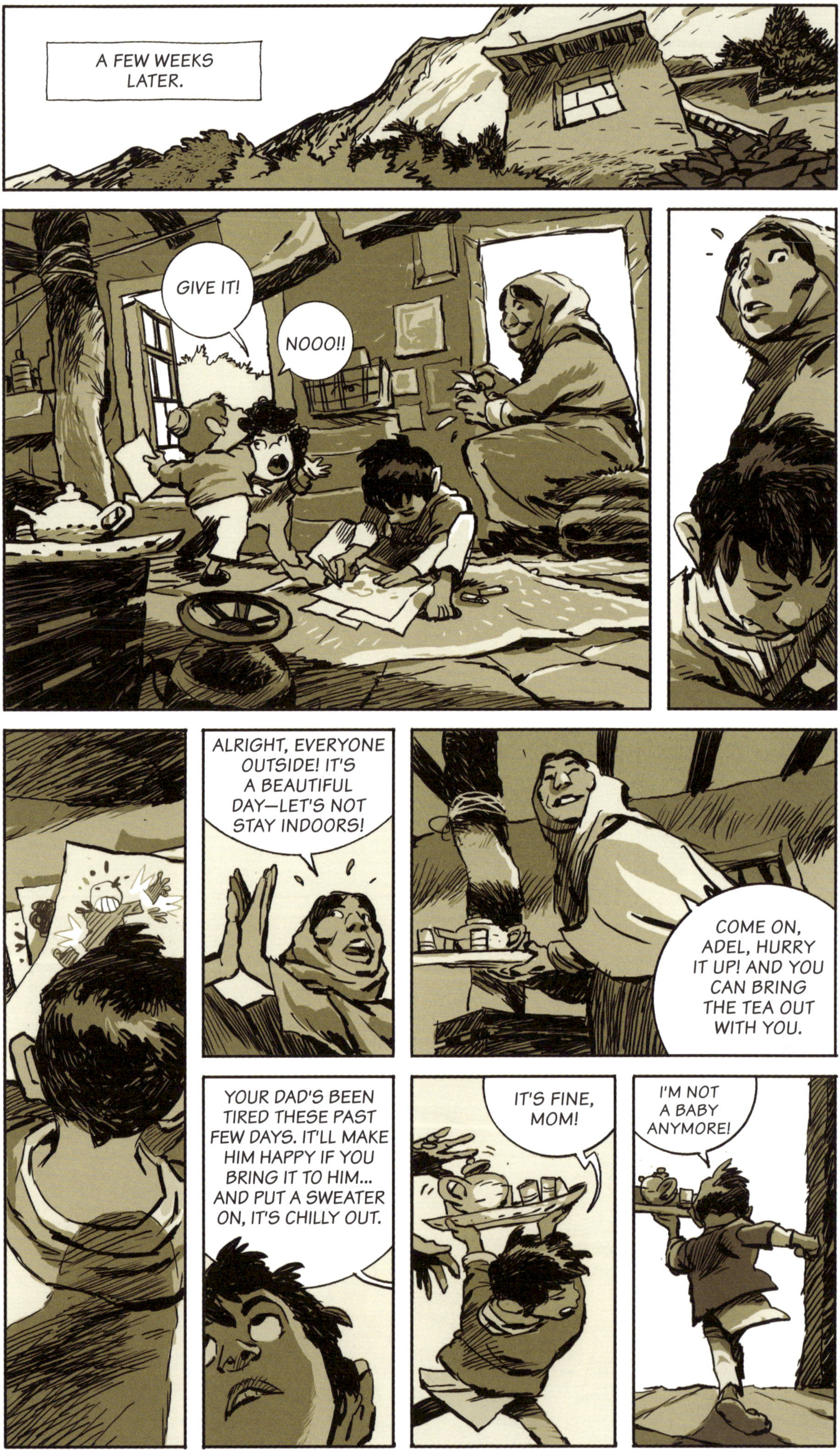
A FEW WEEKS LATER.
GIVE IT!
NOOO!!
ALRIGHT, EVERYONE OUTSIDE! IT'S A BEAUTIFUL DAY—LET'S NOT STAY INDOORS!
COME ON, ADEL, HURRY IT UP! AND YOU CAN BRING THE TEA OUT WITH YOU.
YOUR DAD'S BEEN TIRED THESE PAST FEW DAYS. IT'LL MAKE HIM HAPPY IF YOU BRING IT TO HIM... AND PUT A SWEATER ON, IT'S CHILLY OUT.
IT'S FINE, MOM!
I'M NOT A BABY ANYMORE!

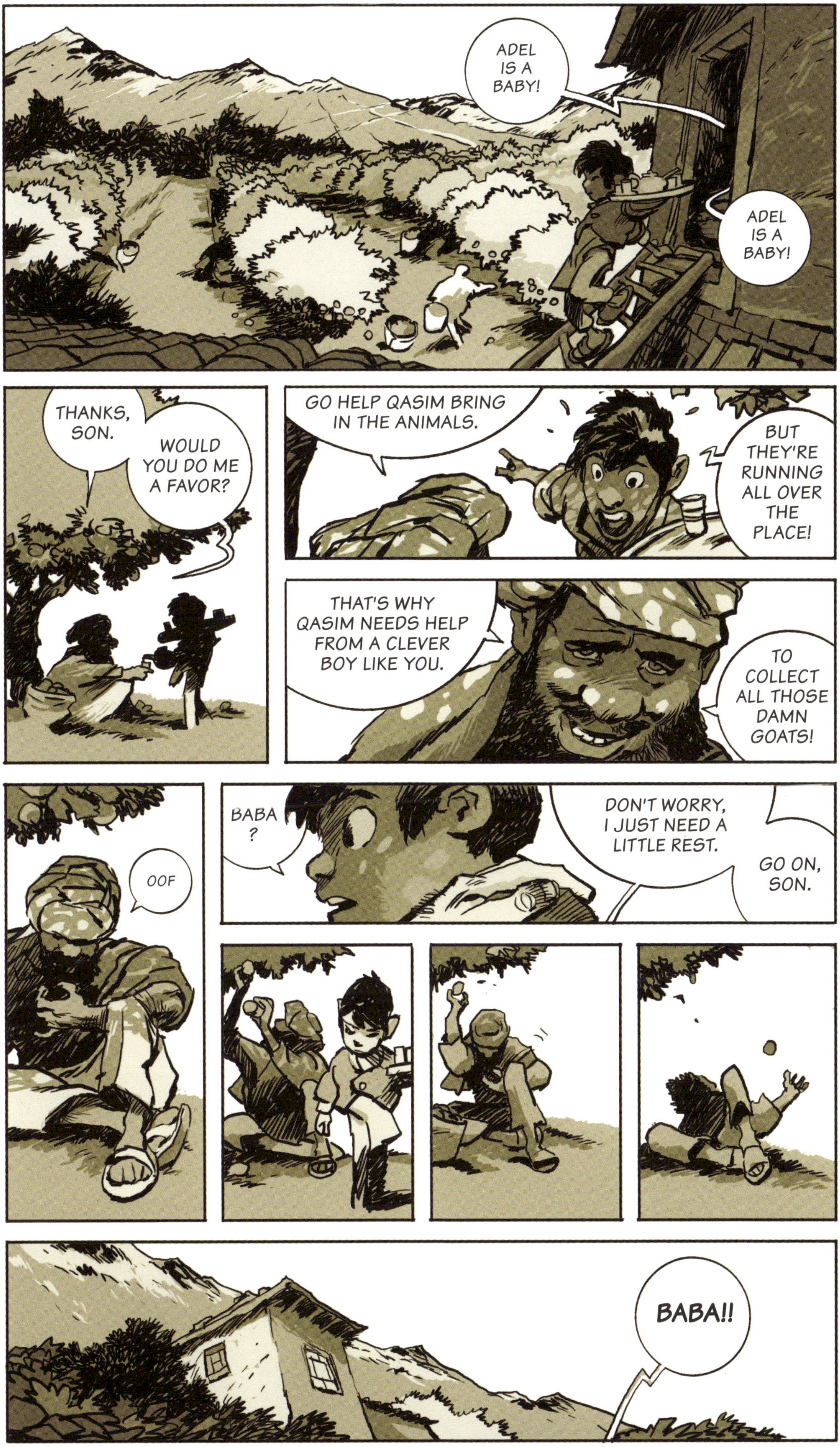
ADEL IS A BABY!
ADEL IS A BABY!
THANKS, SON.
WOULD YOU DO ME A FAVOR?
GO HELP QASIM BRING IN THE ANIMALS.
BUT THEY'RE RUNNING ALL OVER THE PLACE!
THAT'S WHY QASIM NEEDS HELP FROM A CLEVER BOY LIKE YOU.
TO COLLECT ALL THOSE DAMN GOATS!
OOF
BABA ?
DON'T WORRY, I JUST NEED A LITTLE REST.
GO ON, SON.
BABA!!

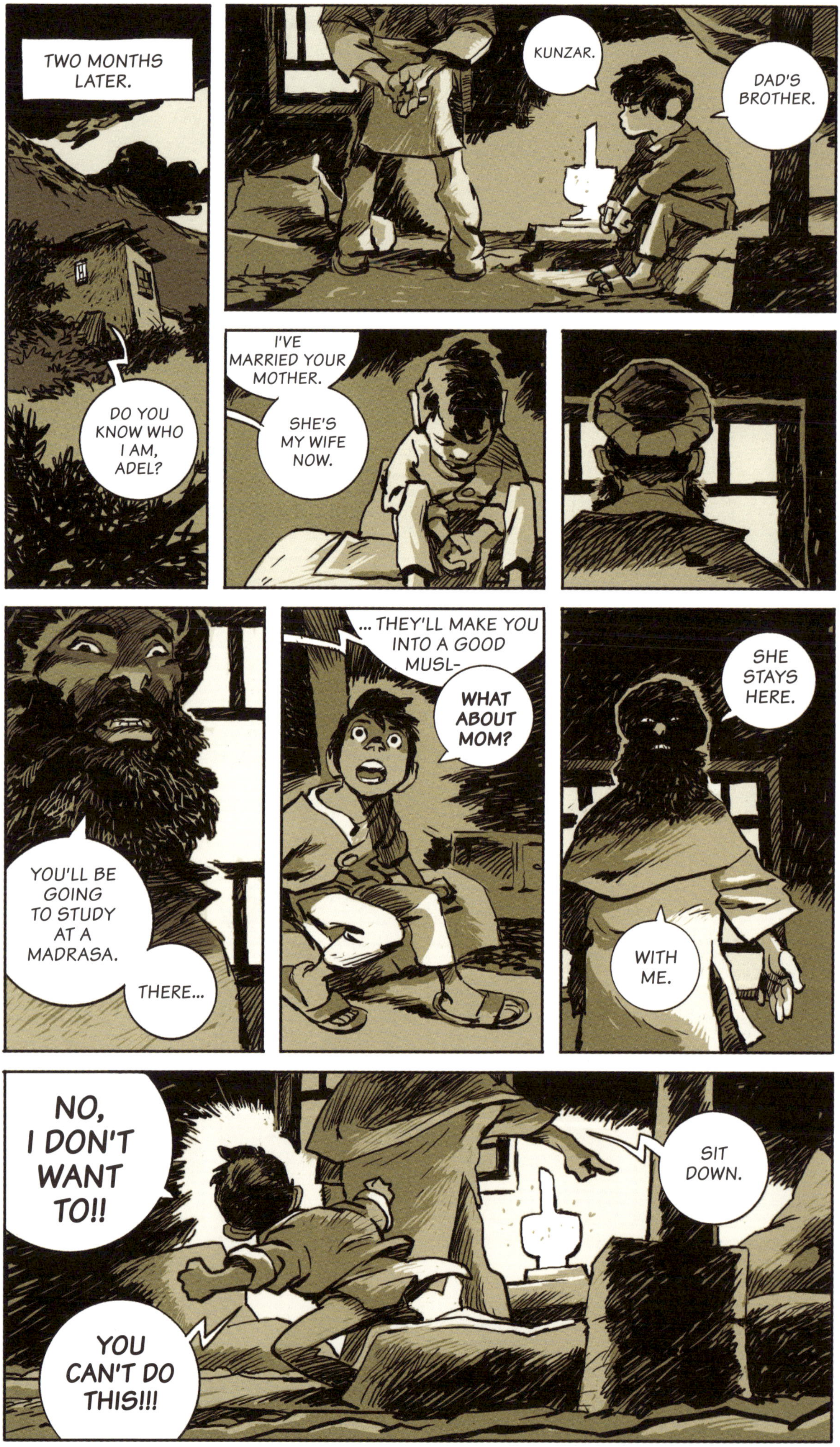
TWO MONTHS LATER.
KUNZAR.
DAD'S BROTHER.
DO YOU KNOW WHO I AM, ADEL?
I'VE MARRIED YOUR MOTHER.
SHE'S MY WIFE NOW.
YOU'LL BE GOING TO STUDY AT A MADRASA.
THERE...
...THEY'LL MAKE YOU INTO A GOOD MUSL-
WHAT ABOUT MOM?
SHE STAYS HERE.
WITH ME.
NO, I DON'T WANT TO!!
YOU CAN'T DO THIS!!!
SIT DOWN.

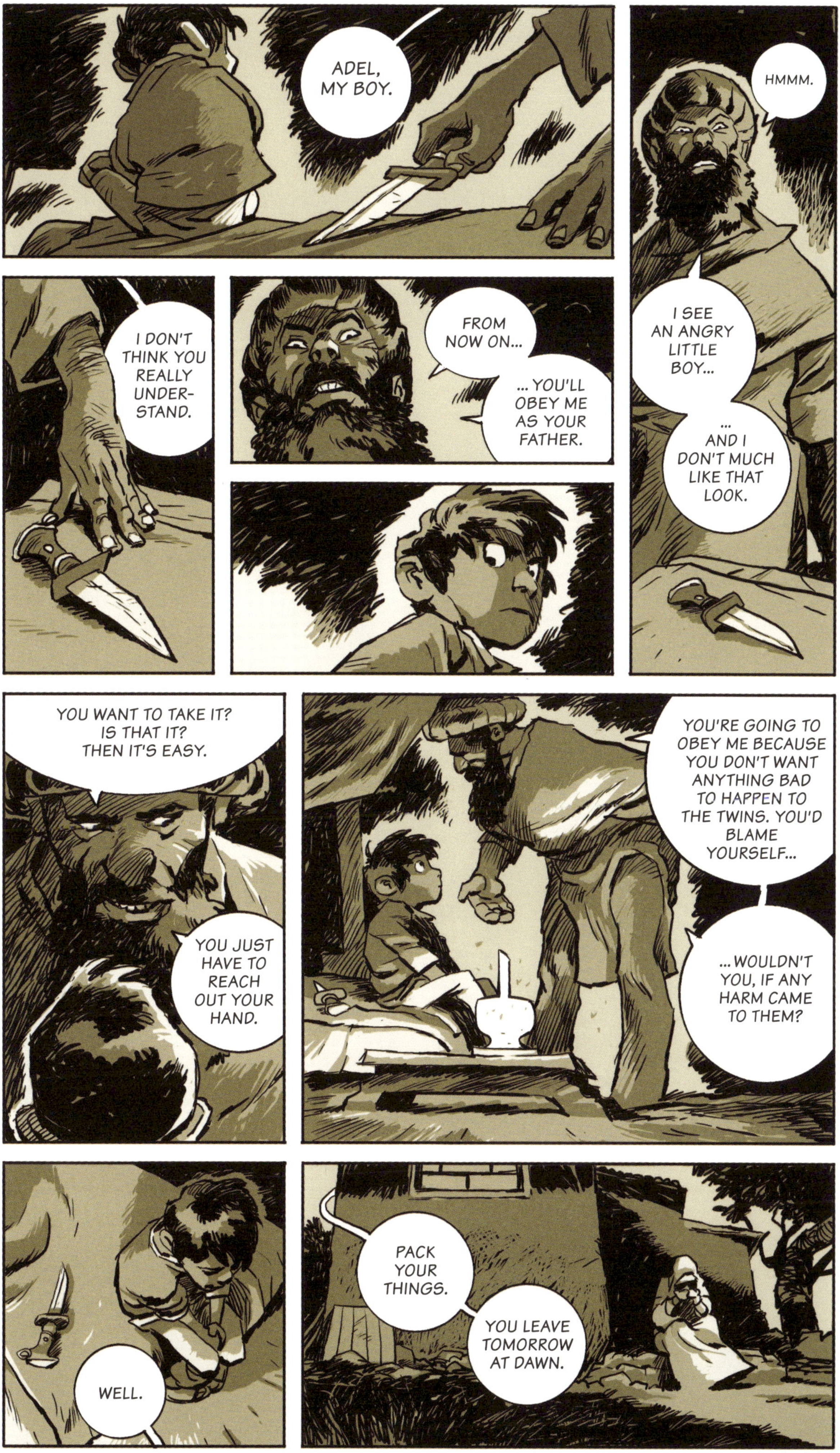
ADEL, MY BOY.
HMMM.
I DON'T THINK YOU REALLY UNDER-STAND.
FROM NOW ON...
... YOU'LL OBEY ME AS YOUR FATHER.
I SEE AN ANGRY LITTLE BOY...
... AND I DON'T MUCH LIKE THAT LOOK.
YOU WANT TO TAKE IT? IS THAT IT? THEN IT'S EASY.
YOU JUST HAVE TO REACH OUT YOUR HAND.
YOU'RE GOING TO OBEY ME BECAUSE YOU DON'T WANT ANYTHING BAD TO HAPPEN TO THE TWINS. YOU'D BLAME YOURSELF...
...WOULDN'T YOU, IF ANY HARM CAME TO THEM?
WELL.
PACK YOUR THINGS.
YOU LEAVE TOMORROW AT DAWN.

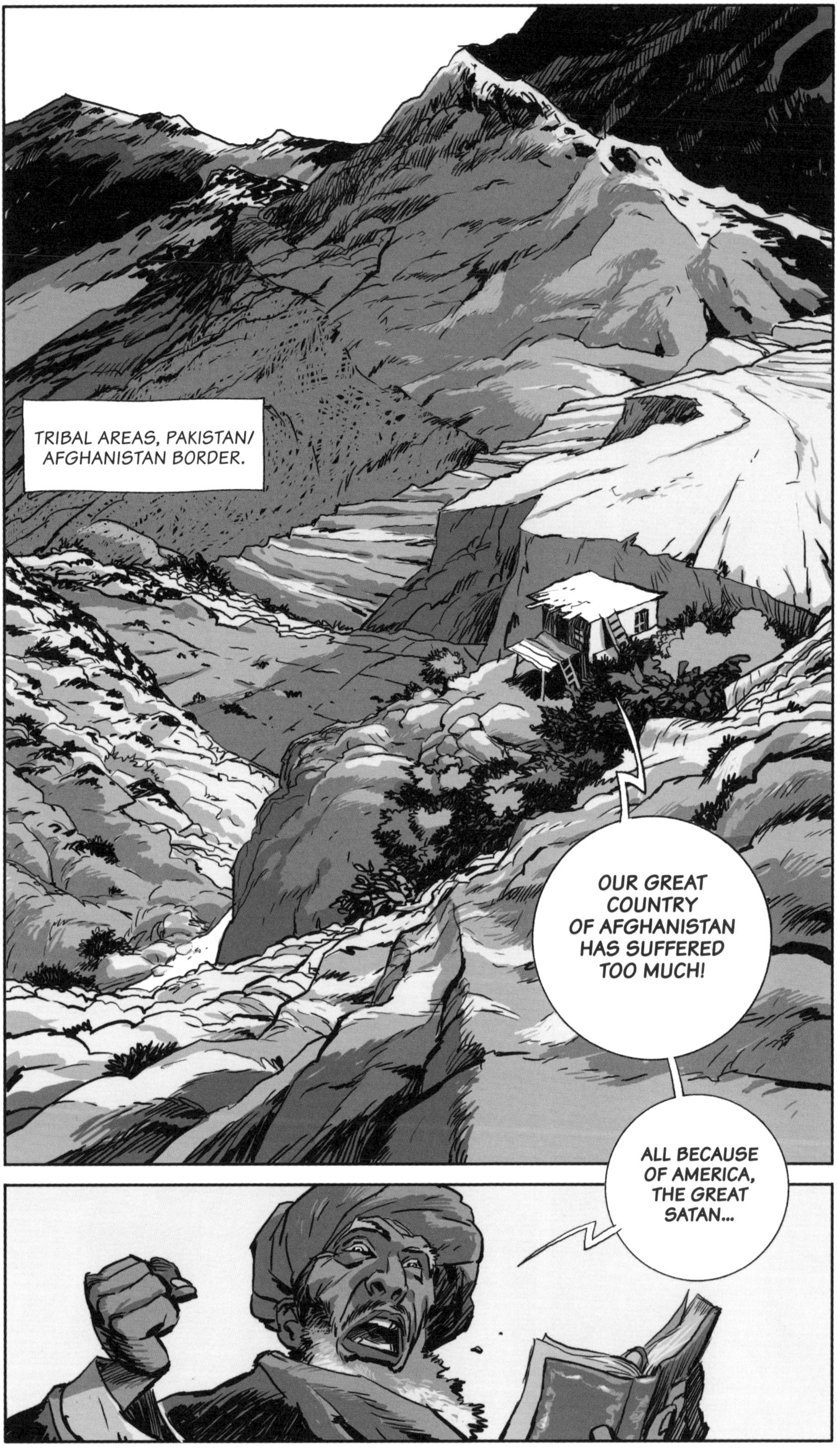
TRIBAL AREAS, PAKISTAN/ AFGHANISTAN BORDER.
OUR GREAT COUNTRY OF AFGHANISTAN HAS SUFFERED TOO MUCH!
ALL BECAUSE OF AMERICA, THE GREAT SATAN...

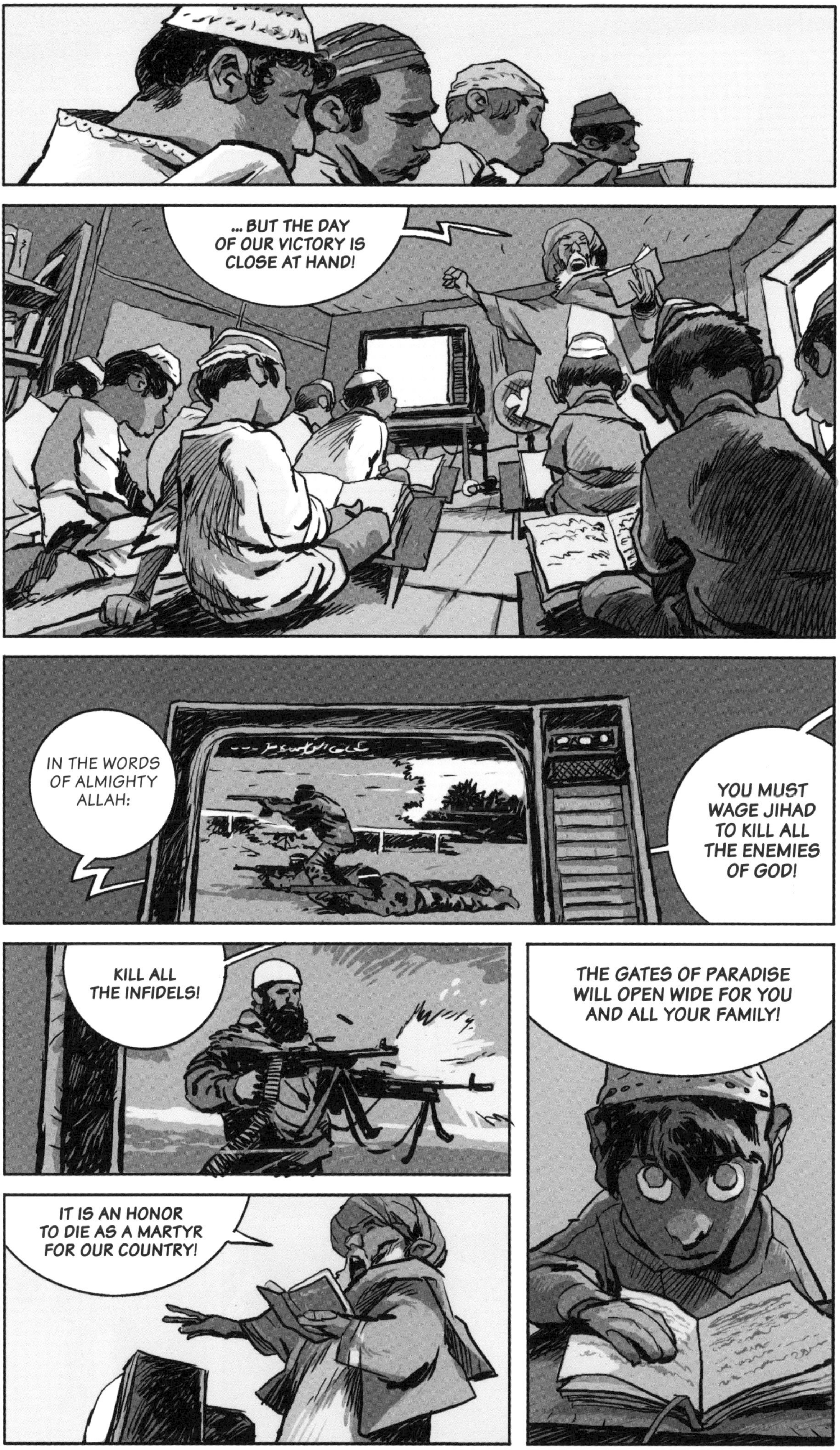
...BUT THE DAY OF OUR VICTORY IS CLOSE AT HAND!
IN THE WORDS OF ALMIGHTY ALLAH:
YOU MUST WAGE JIHAD TO KILL ALL THE ENEMIES OF GOD!
KILL ALL THE INFIDELS!
THE GATES OF PARADISE WILL OPEN WIDE FOR YOU AND ALL YOUR FAMILY!
IT IS AN HONOR TO DIE AS A MARTYR FOR OUR COUNTRY!

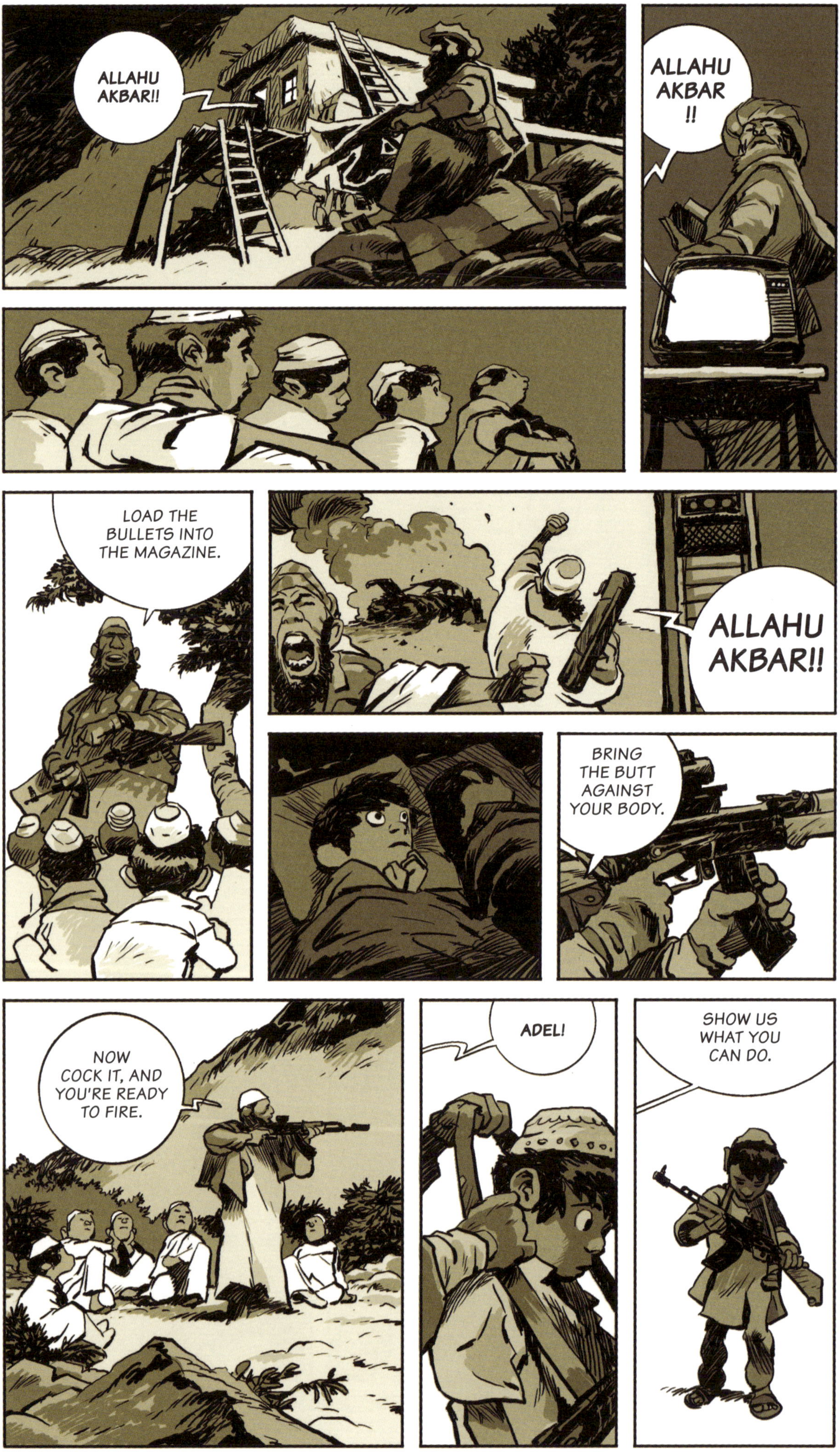
ALLAHU AKBAR!!
ALLAHU AKBAR !!
LOAD THE BULLETS INTO THE MAGAZINE.
ALLAHU AKBAR!!
BRING THE BUTT AGAINST YOUR BODY.
NOW COCK IT, AND YOU'RE READY TO FIRE.
ADEL!
SHOW US WHAT YOU CAN DO.

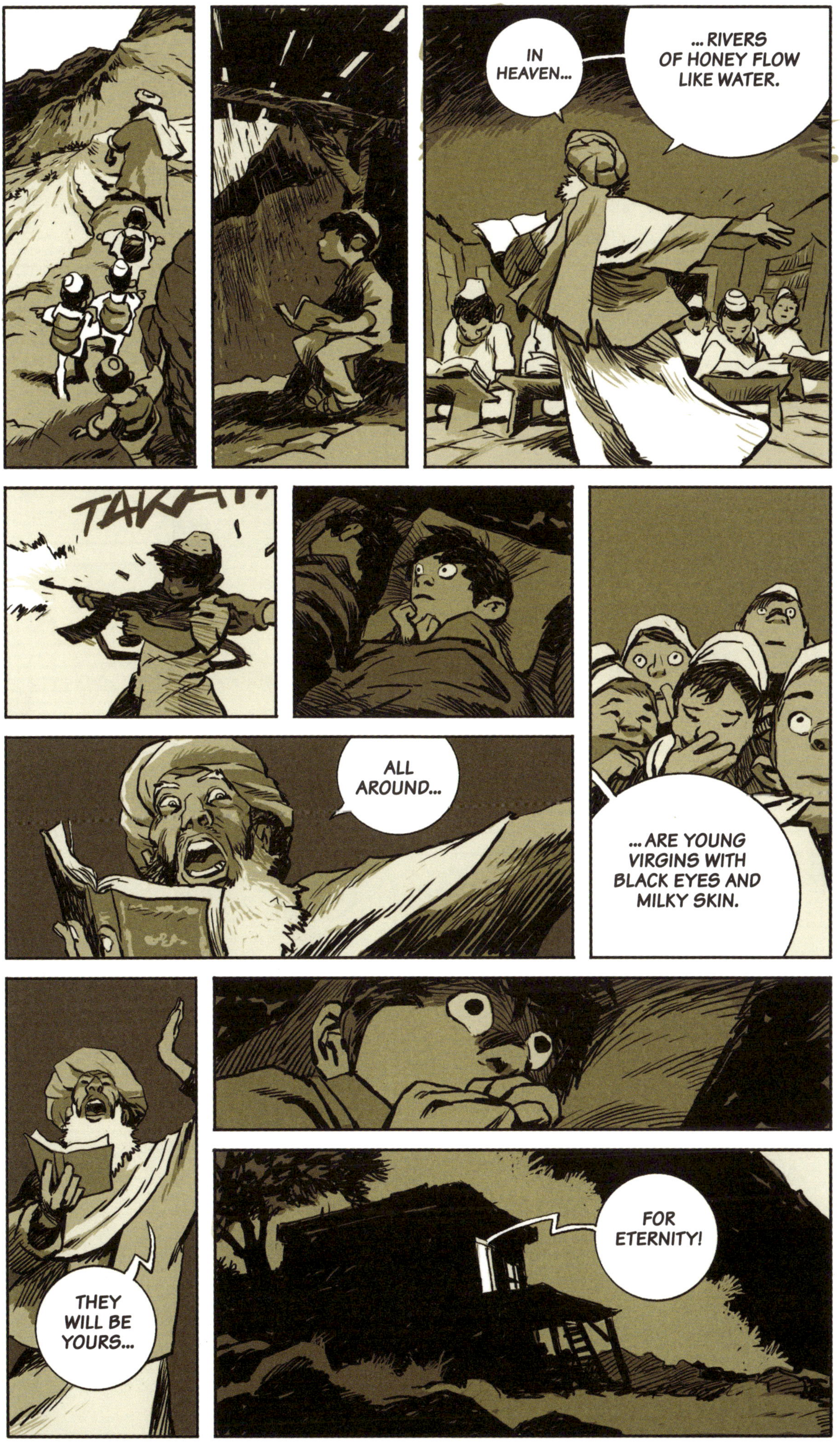
IN HEAVEN...
... RIVERS OF HONEY FLOW LIKE WATER.
ALL AROUND...
... ARE YOUNG VIRGINS WITH BLACK EYES AND MILKY SKIN.
THEY WILL BE YOURS...
FOR ETERNITY!

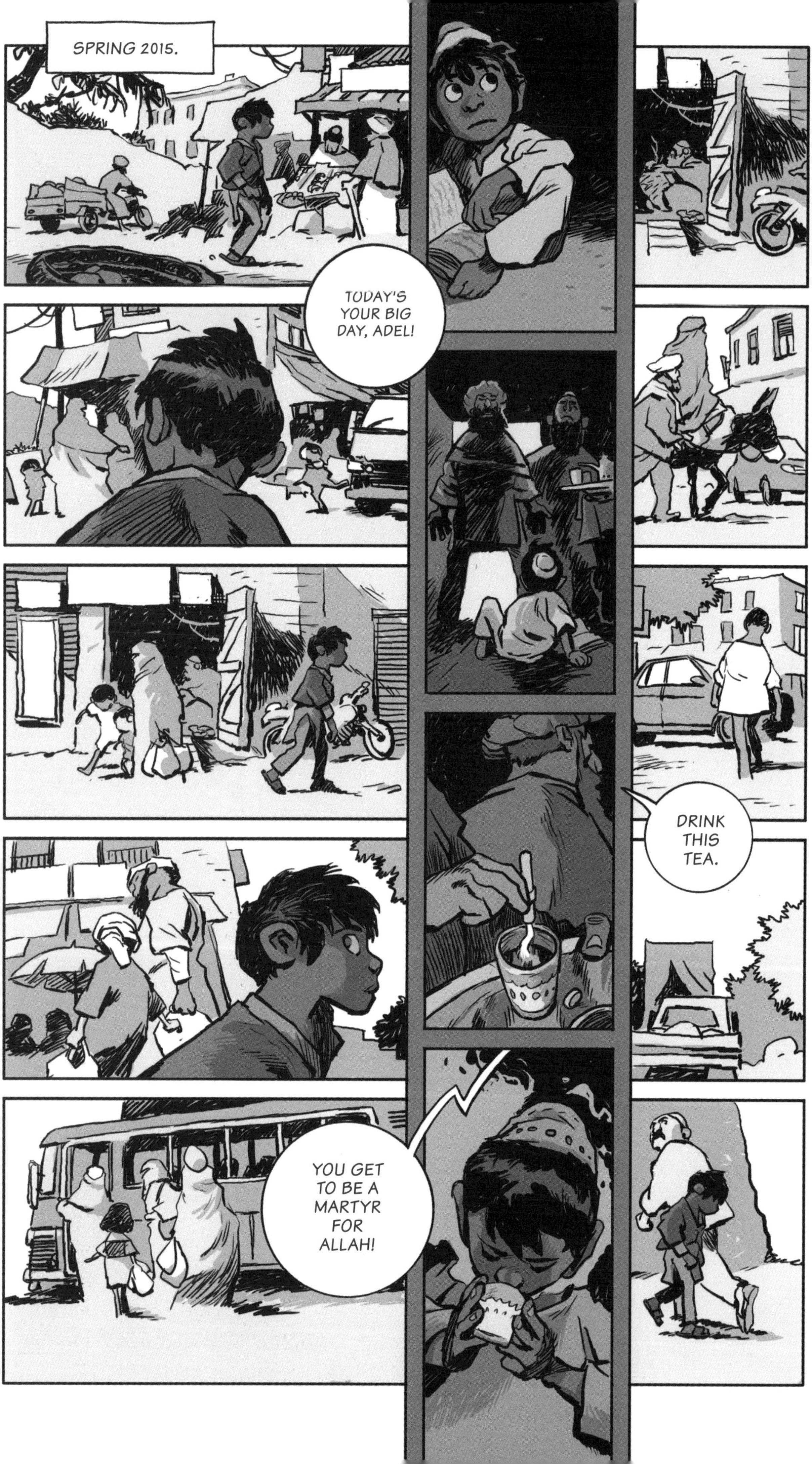
SPRING 2015.
TODAY'S YOUR BIG DAY, ADEL!
DRINK THIS TEA.
YOU GET TO BE A MARTYR FOR ALLAH!

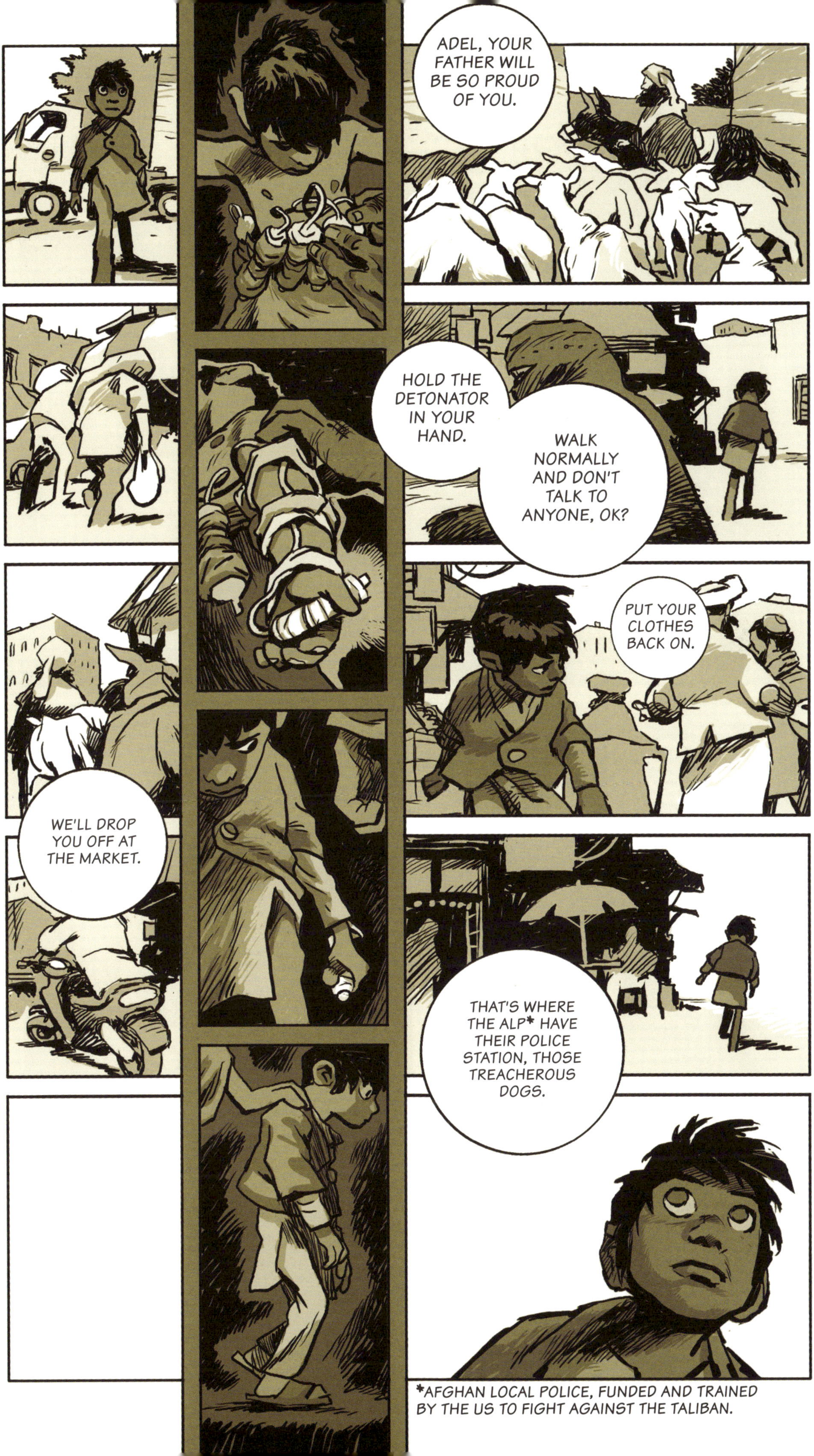
ADEL, YOUR FATHER WILL BE SO PROUD OF YOU.
HOLD THE DETONATOR IN YOUR HAND.
WALK NORMALLY AND DON'T TALK TO ANYONE, OK?
PUT YOUR CLOTHES BACK ON.
WE'LL DROP YOU OFF AT THE MARKET.
THAT'S WHERE THE ALP* HAVE THEIR POLICE STATION, THOSE TREACHEROUS DOGS.

*AFGHAN LOCAL POLICE, FUNDED AND TRAINED BY THE US TO FIGHT AGAINST THE TALIBAN.

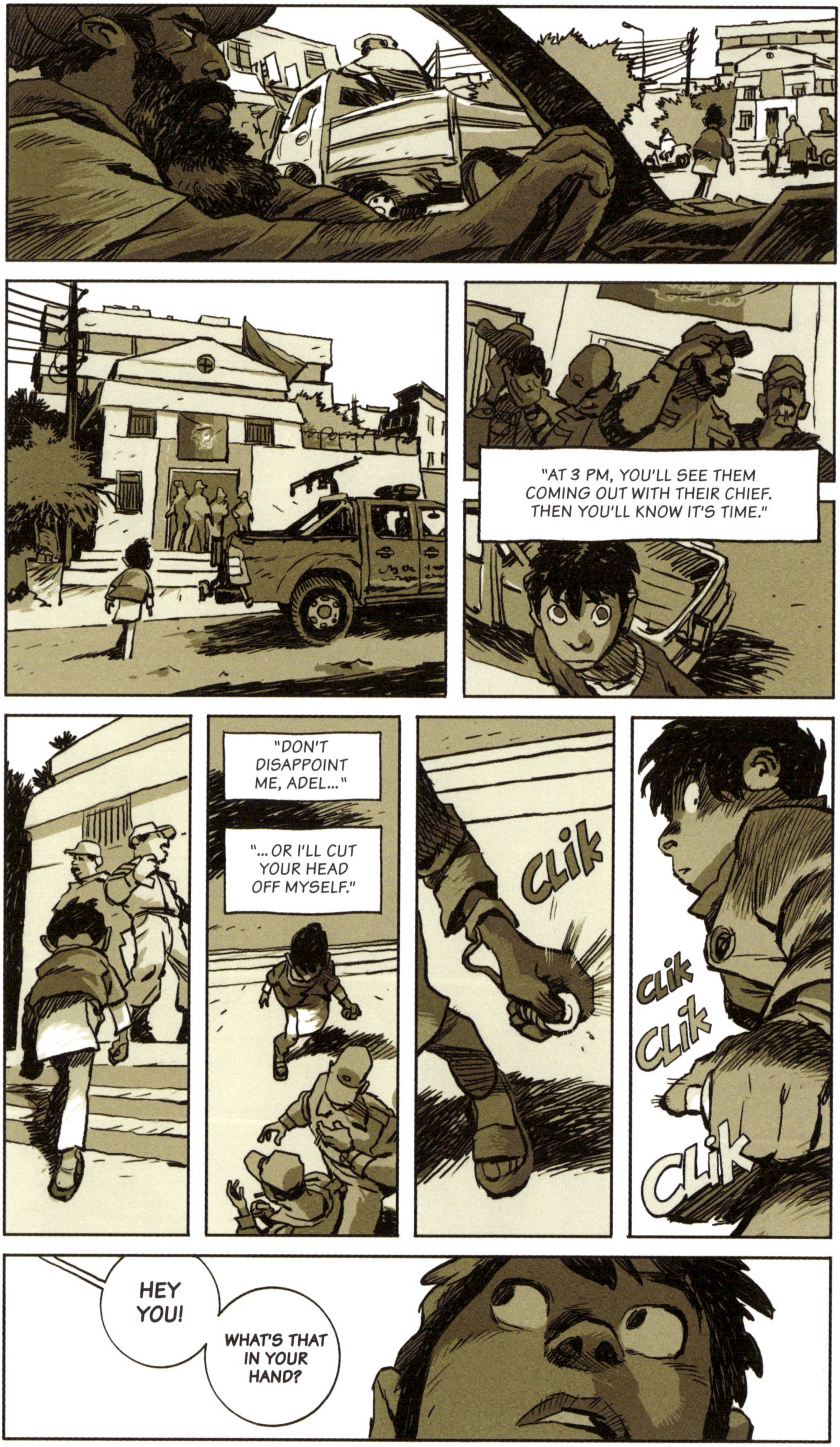
"AT 3 PM, YOU'LL SEE THEM COMING OUT WITH THEIR CHIEF. THEN YOU'LL KNOW IT'S TIME."
"DON'T DISAPPOINT ME, ADEL..."
"...OR I'LL CUT YOUR HEAD OFF MYSELF."
CLIK
CLIK
CLIK
CLIK
HEY YOU!
WHAT'S THAT IN YOUR HAND?

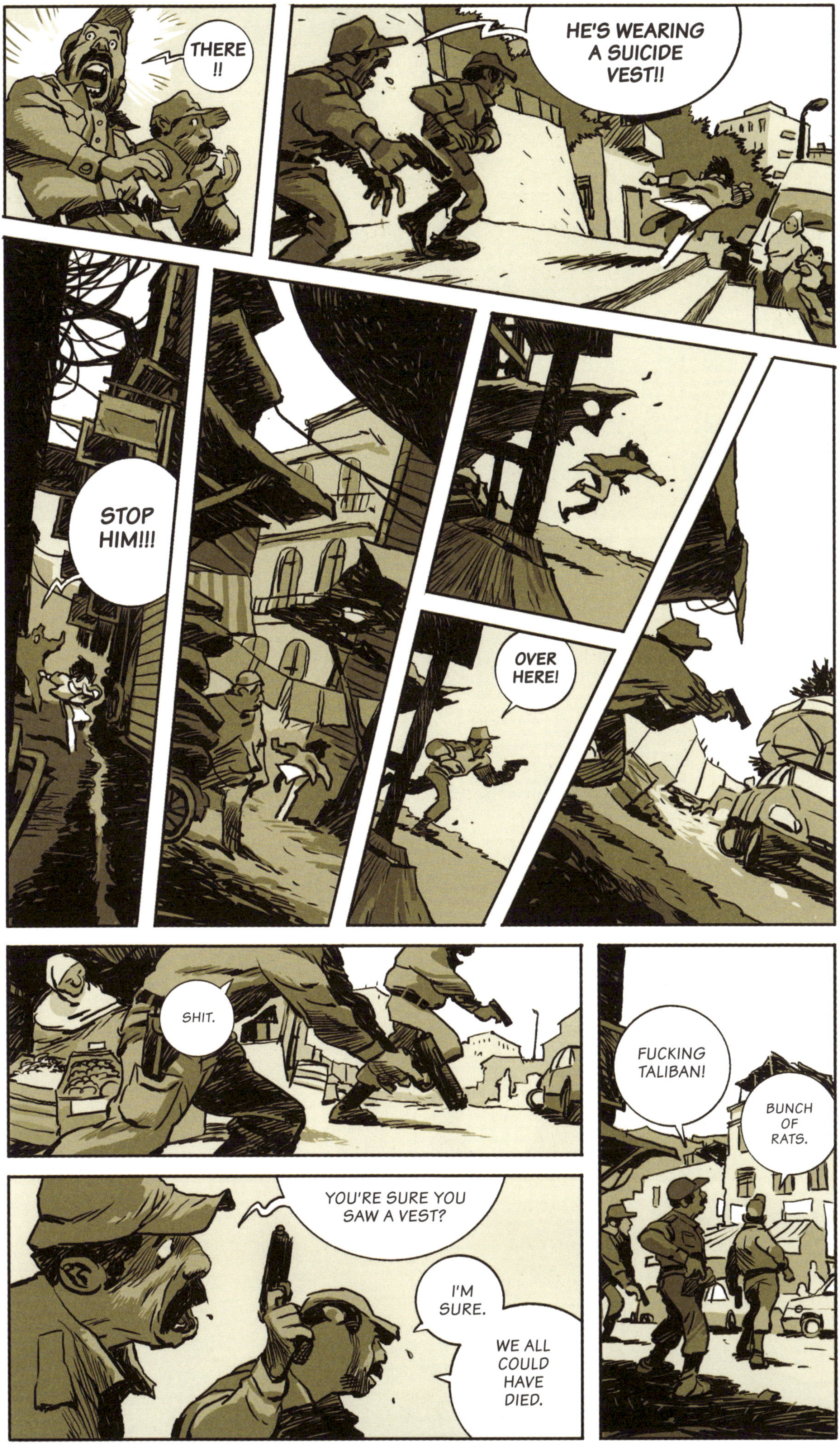
THERE !!
HE'S WEARING A SUICIDE VEST!!
STOP HIM!!!
OVER HERE!
SHIT.
FUCKING TALIBAN!
BUNCH OF RATS.
YOU'RE SURE YOU SAW A VEST?
I'M SURE.
WE ALL COULD HAVE DIED.

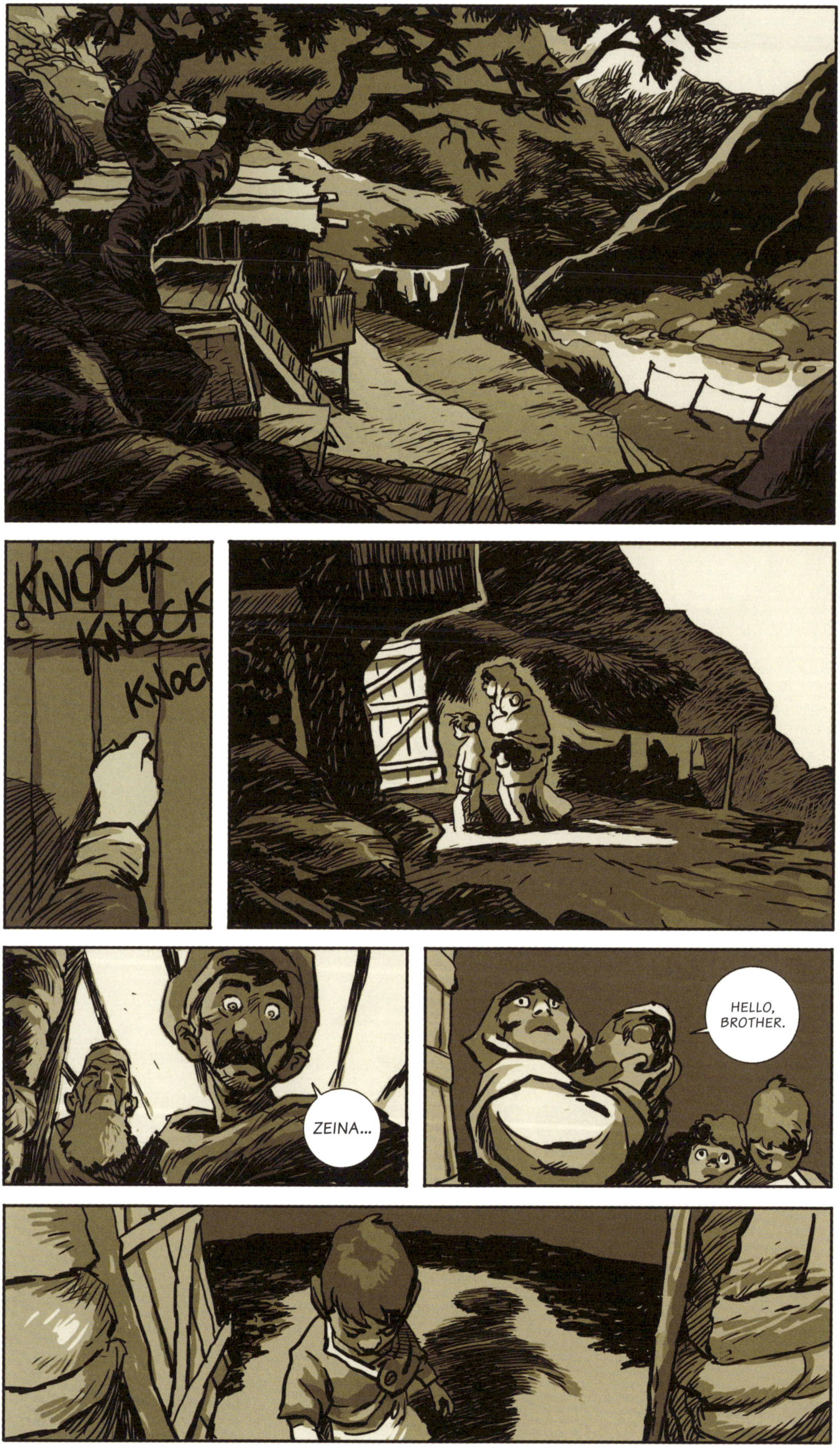
KNOCK
KNOCK
KNOCK
ZEINA...
HELLO, BROTHER.

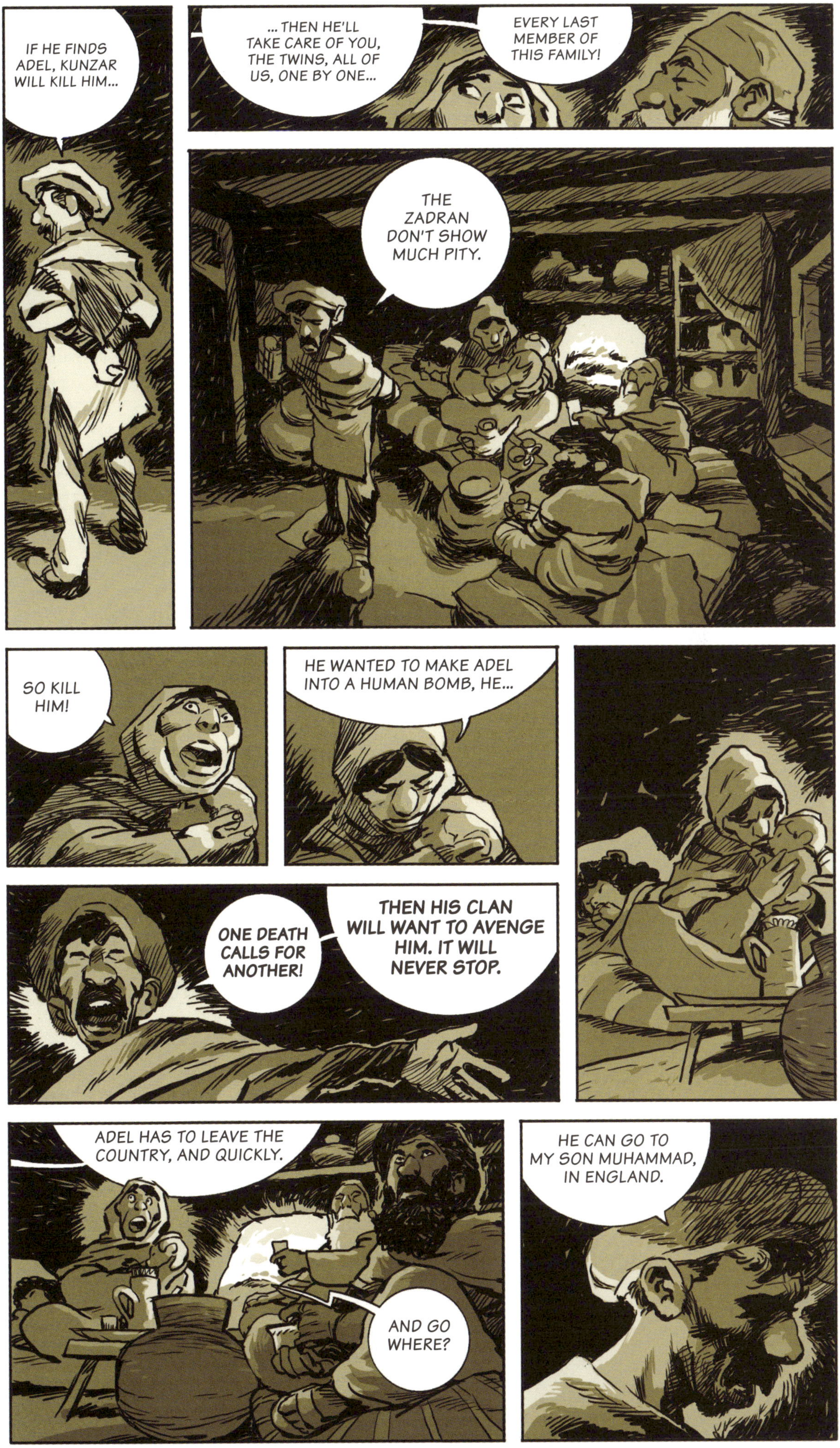
IF HE FINDS ADEL, KUNZAR WILL KILL HIM...
... THEN HE'LL TAKE CARE OF YOU, THE TWINS, ALL OF US, ONE BY ONE...
EVERY LAST MEMBER OF THIS FAMILY!
THE ZADRAN DON'T SHOW MUCH PITY.
SO KILL HIM!
HE WANTED TO MAKE ADEL INTO A HUMAN BOMB, HE...
ONE DEATH CALLS FOR ANOTHER!
THEN HIS CLAN WILL WANT TO AVENGE HIM. IT WILL NEVER STOP.
ADEL HAS TO LEAVE THE COUNTRY, AND QUICKLY.
AND GO WHERE?
HE CAN GO TO MY SON MUHAMMAD, IN ENGLAND.

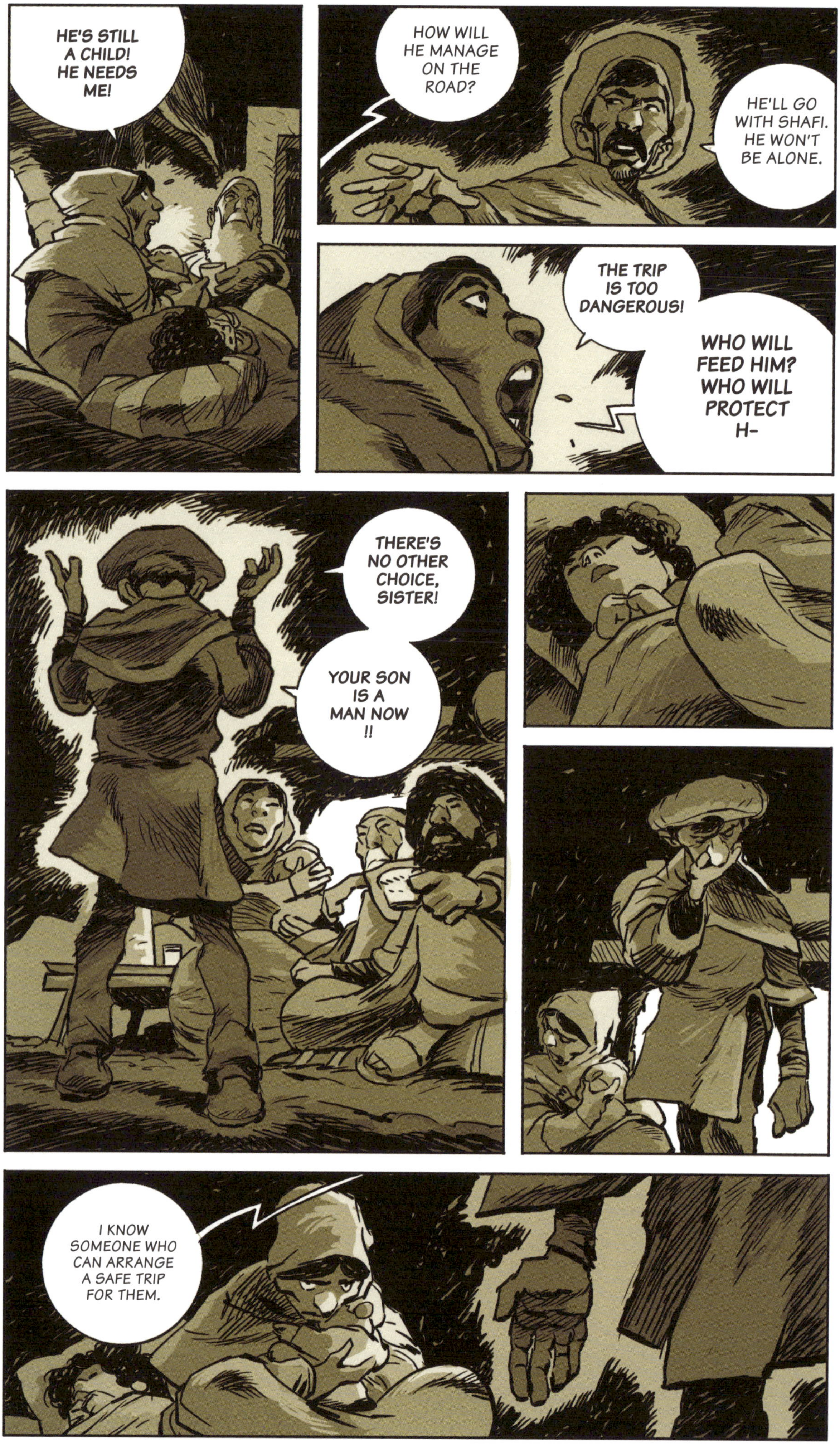
HE'S STILL A CHILD! HE NEEDS ME!
HOW WILL HE MANAGE ON THE ROAD?
HE'LL GO WITH SHAFI. HE WON'T BE ALONE.
THE TRIP IS TOO DANGEROUS!
WHO WILL FEED HIM? WHO WILL PROTECT H-
THERE'S NO OTHER CHOICE, SISTER!
YOUR SON IS A MAN NOW !!
I KNOW SOMEONE WHO CAN ARRANGE A SAFE TRIP FOR THEM.

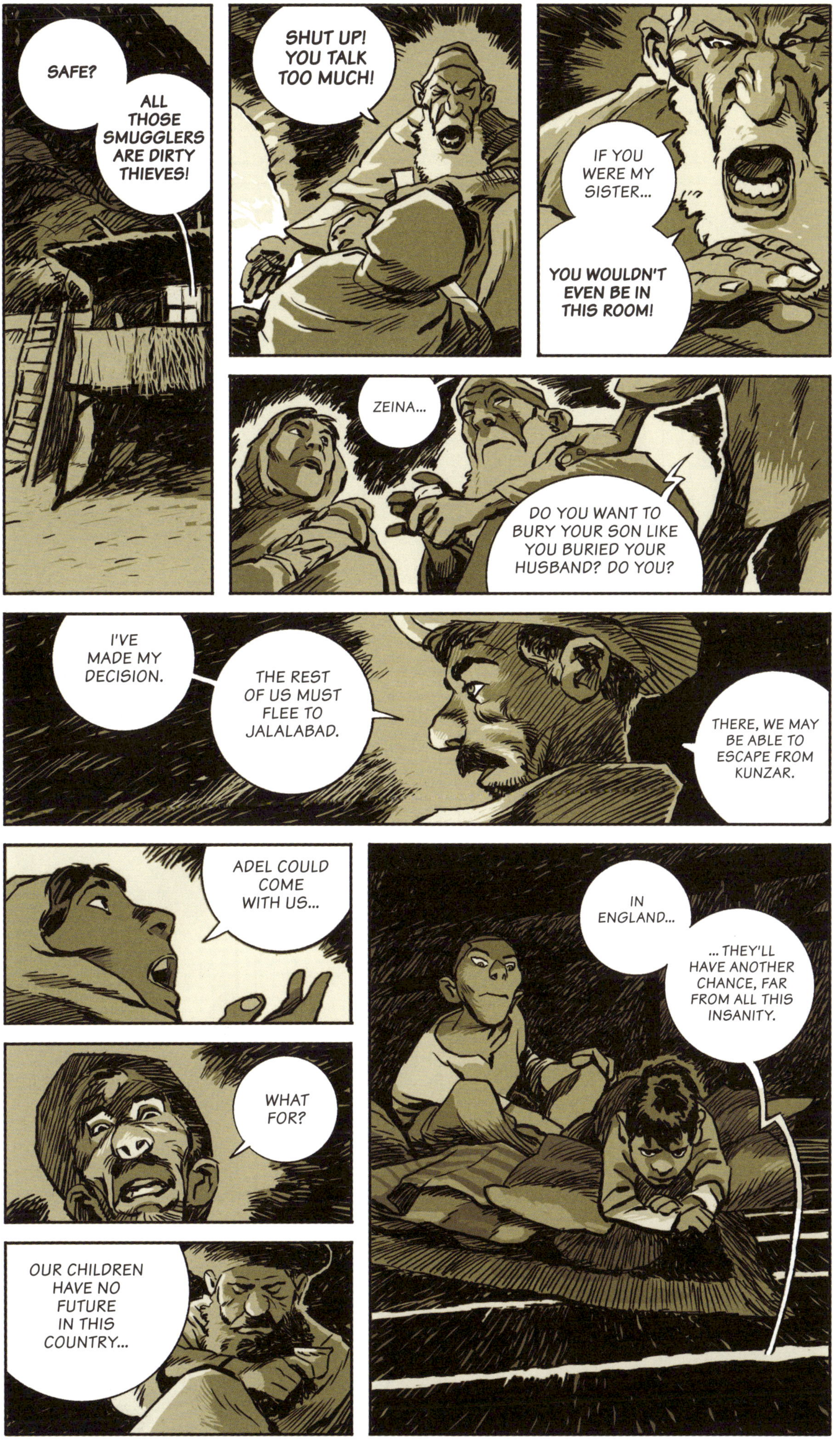
SAFE?
ALL THOSE SMUGGLERS ARE DIRTY THIEVES!
SHUT UP! YOU TALK TOO MUCH!
IF YOU WERE MY SISTER...
YOU WOULDN'T EVEN BE IN THIS ROOM!
ZEINA...
DO YOU WANT TO BURY YOUR SON LIKE YOU BURIED YOUR HUSBAND? DO YOU?
I'VE MADE MY DECISION.
THE REST OF US MUST FLEE TO JALALABAD.
THERE, WE MAY BE ABLE TO ESCAPE FROM KUNZAR.
ADEL COULD COME WITH US...
WHAT FOR?
OUR CHILDREN HAVE NO FUTURE IN THIS COUNTRY...
IN ENGLAND...
... THEY'LL HAVE ANOTHER CHANCE, FAR FROM ALL THIS INSANITY.

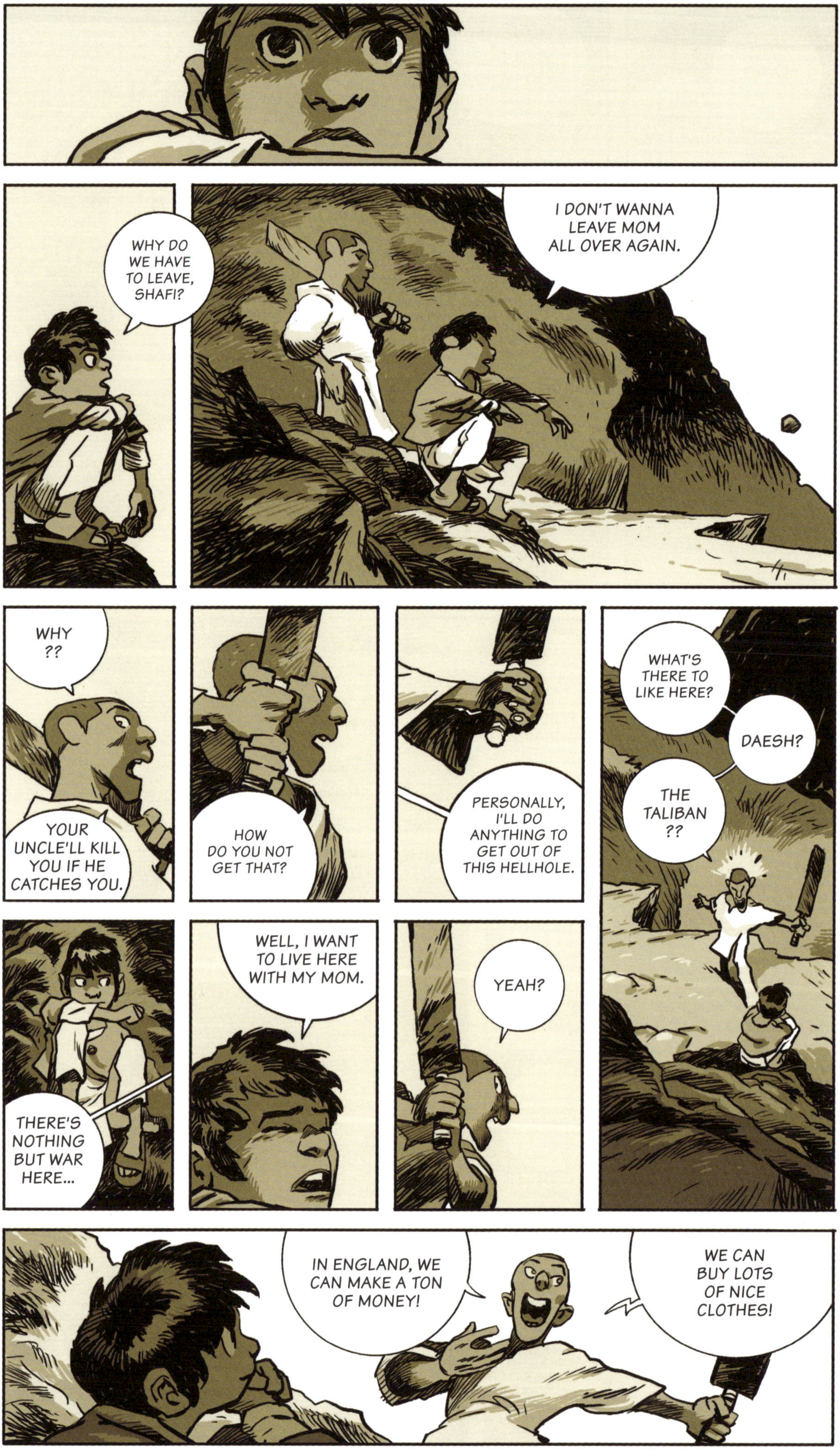
WHY DO WE HAVE TO LEAVE, SHAFI?
I DON'T WANNA LEAVE MOM ALL OVER AGAIN.
WHY ??
YOUR UNCLE'LL KILL YOU IF HE CATCHES YOU.
HOW DO YOU NOT GET THAT?
PERSONALLY, I'LL DO ANYTHING TO GET OUT OF THIS HELLHOLE.
WHAT'S THERE TO LIKE HERE?
DAESH?
THE TALIBAN ??
THERE'S NOTHING BUT WAR HERE...
WELL, I WANT TO LIVE HERE WITH MY MOM.
YEAH?
IN ENGLAND, WE CAN MAKE A TON OF MONEY!
WE CAN BUY LOTS OF NICE CLOTHES!

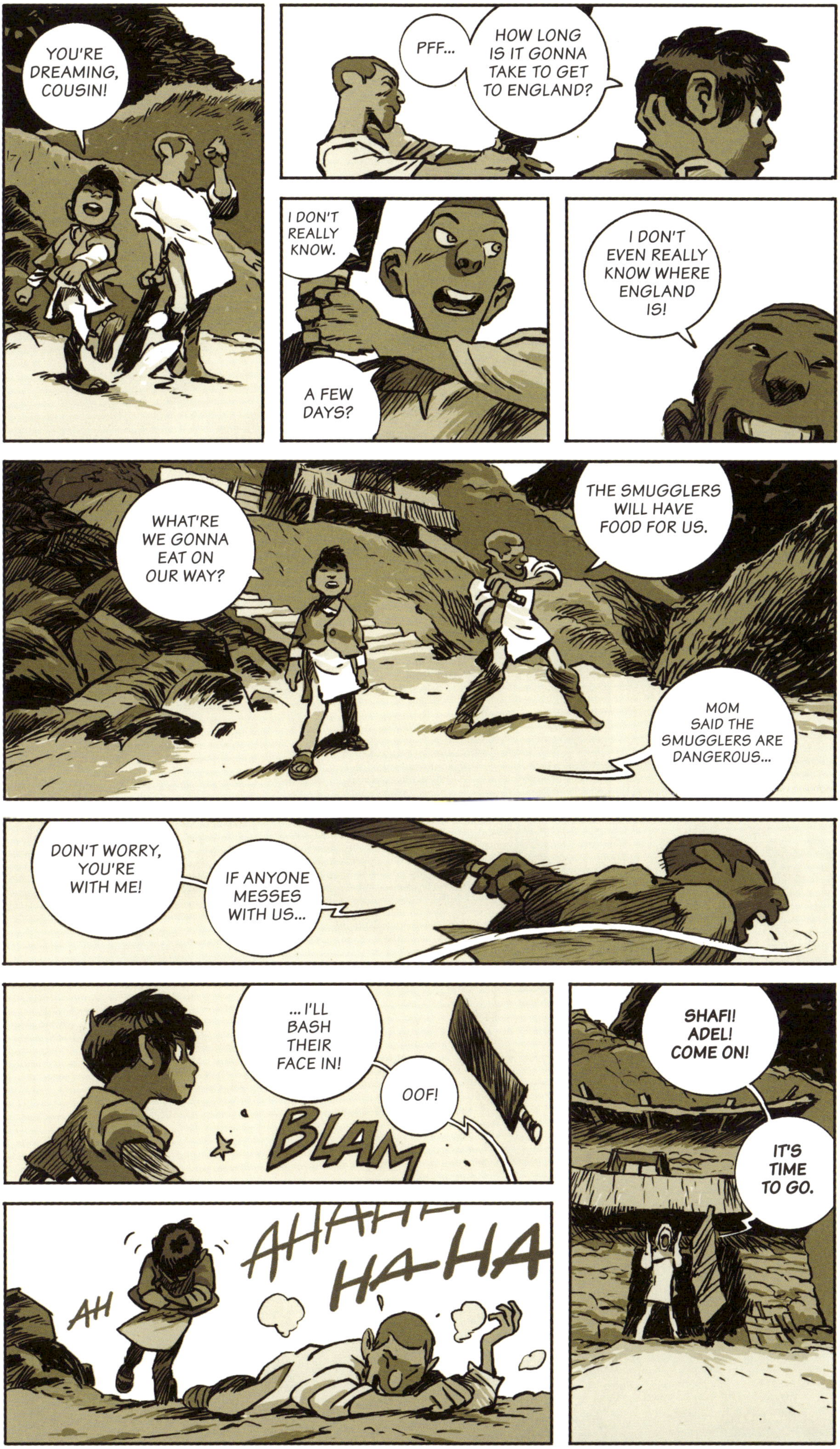
YOU'RE DREAMING, COUSIN!
PFF...
HOW LONG IS IT GONNA TAKE TO GET TO ENGLAND?
I DON'T REALLY KNOW.
A FEW DAYS?
I DON'T EVEN REALLY KNOW WHERE ENGLAND IS!
WHAT'RE WE GONNA EAT ON OUR WAY?
THE SMUGGLERS WILL HAVE FOOD FOR US.
MOM SAID THE SMUGGLERS ARE DANGEROUS...
DON'T WORRY, YOU'RE WITH ME!
IF ANYONE MESSES WITH US...
...I'LL BASH THEIR FACE IN!
OOF!
BLAM
AHAHA
HA-HA
AH
SHAFI! ADEL! COME ON!
IT'S TIME TO GO.

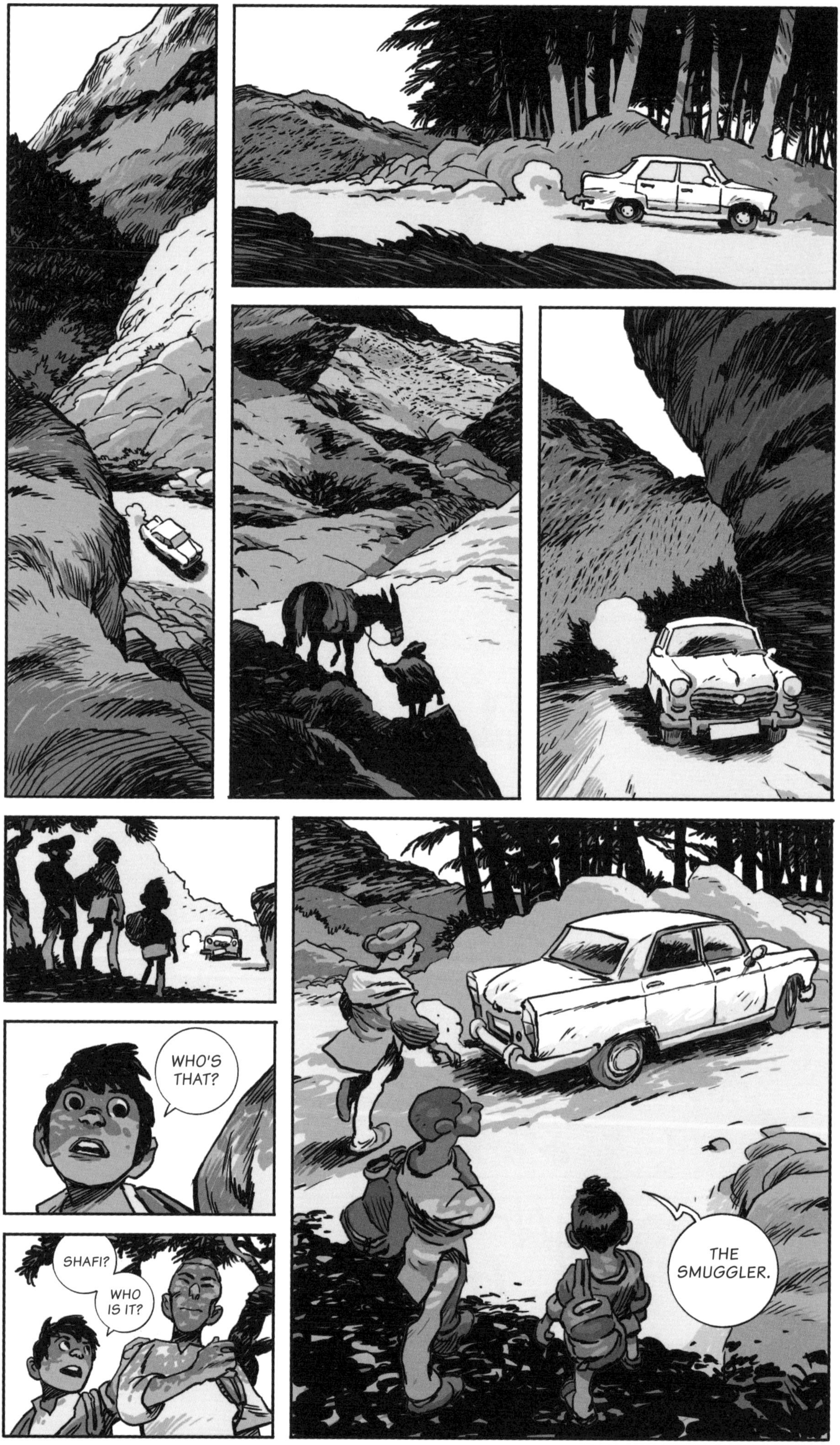
WHO'S THAT?
THE SMUGGLER.
SHAFI?
WHO IS IT?

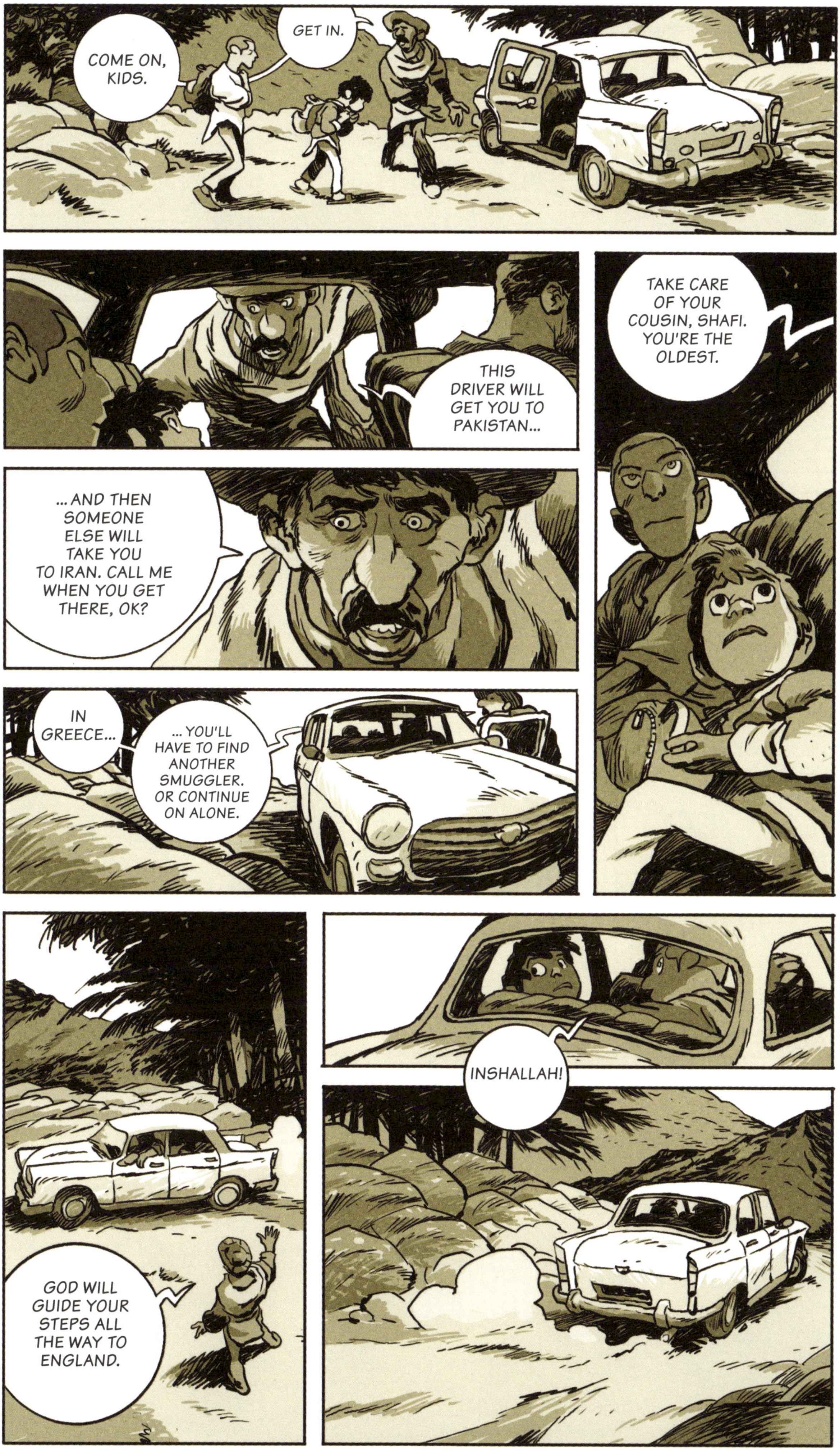
COME ON, KIDS.
GET IN.
THIS DRIVER WILL GET YOU TO PAKISTAN...
TAKE CARE OF YOUR COUSIN, SHAFI. YOU'RE THE OLDEST.
...AND THEN SOMEONE ELSE WILL TAKE YOU TO IRAN. CALL ME WHEN YOU GET THERE, OK?
IN GREECE...
...YOU'LL HAVE TO FIND ANOTHER SMUGGLER. OR CONTINUE ON ALONE.
GOD WILL GUIDE YOUR STEPS ALL THE WAY TO ENGLAND.
INSHALLAH!

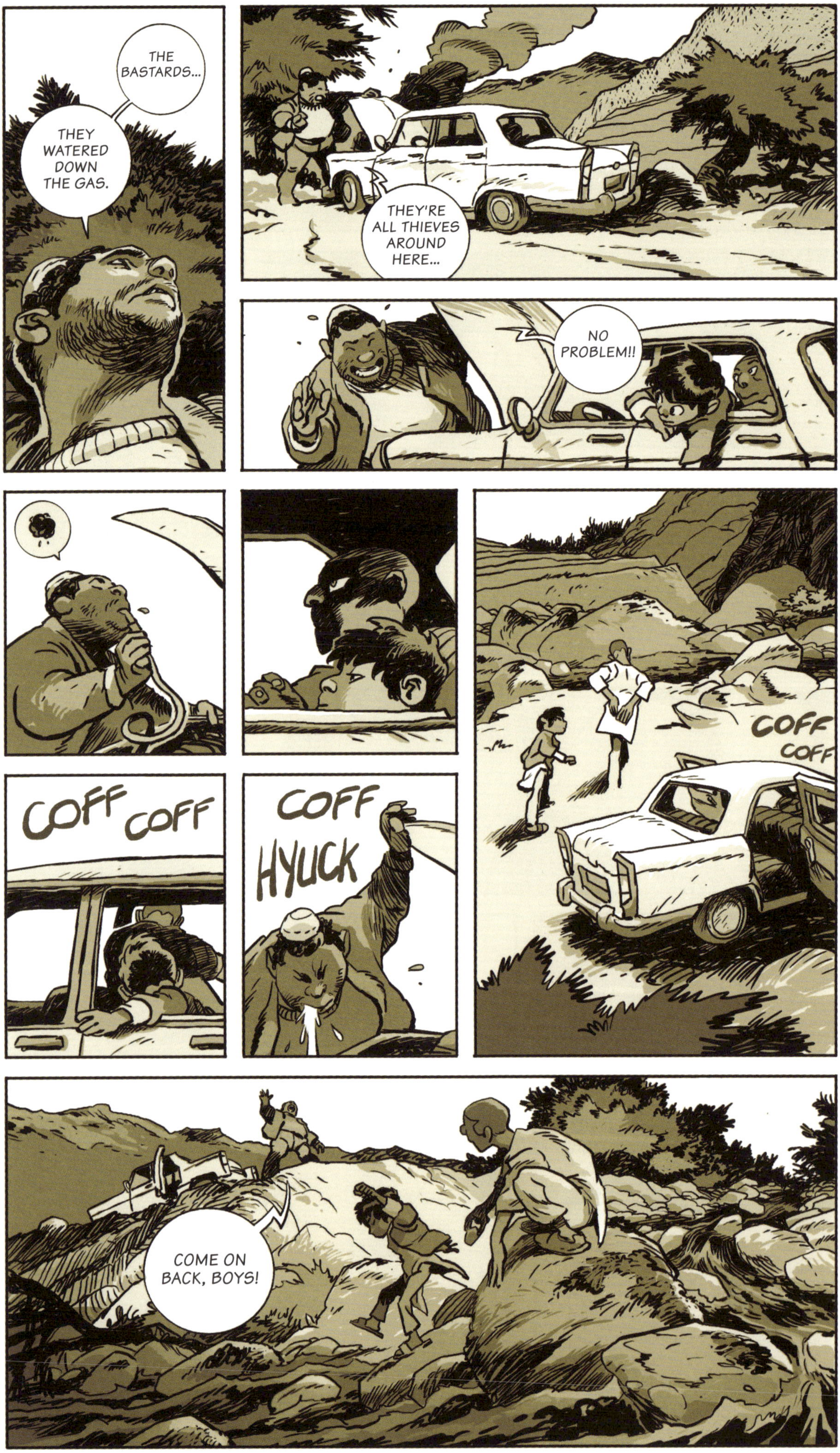
THE BASTARDS...
THEY WATERED DOWN THE GAS.
THEY'RE ALL THIEVES AROUND HERE...
NO PROBLEM!!
COFF COFF
COFF COFF
COFF
HYUCK
COME ON BACK, BOYS!

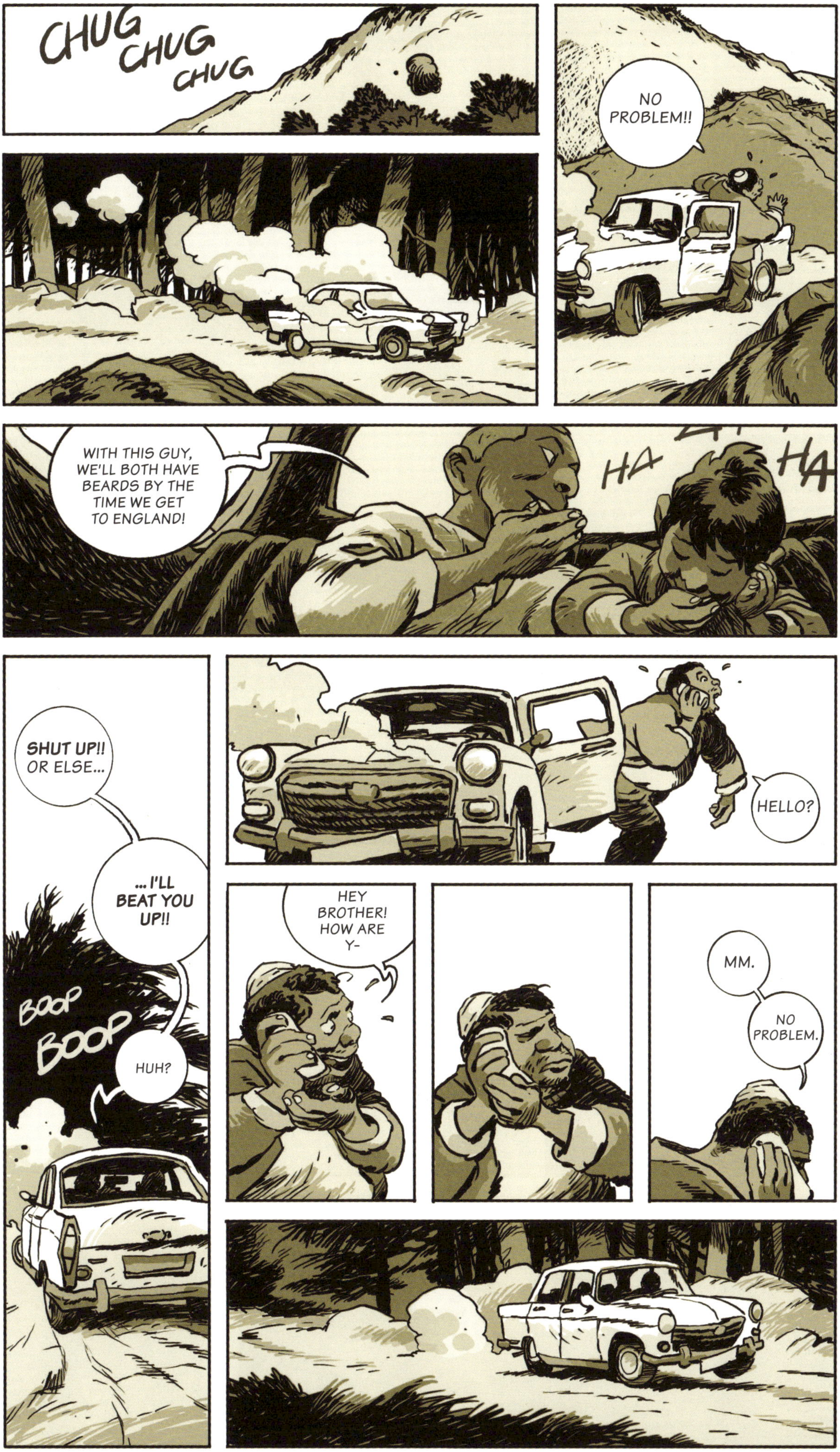
CHUG
CHUG
CHUG
NO PROBLEM!!
WITH THIS GUY, WE'LL BOTH HAVE BEARDS BY THE TIME WE GET TO ENGLAND!
HA
HA
SHUT UP!! OR ELSE...
...I'LL BEAT YOU UP!!
BOOP
BOOP
HUH?
HELLO?
HEY BROTHER! HOW ARE Y-
MM.
NO PROBLEM.

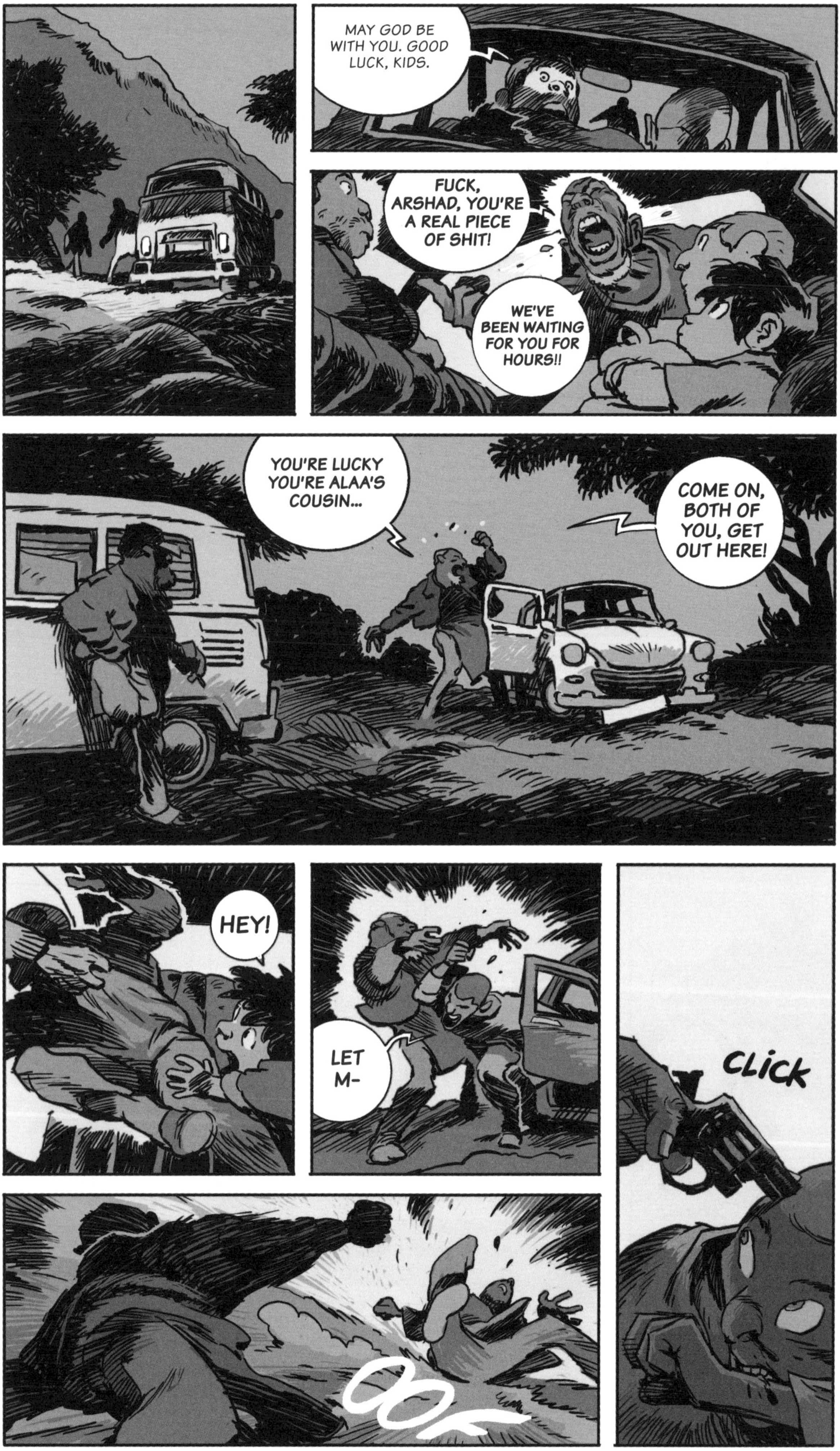
MAY GOD BE WITH YOU. GOOD LUCK, KIDS.
FUCK, ARSHAD, YOU'RE A REAL PIECE OF SHIT!
WE'VE BEEN WAITING FOR YOU FOR HOURS!!
YOU'RE LUCKY YOU'RE ALAA'S COUSIN...
COME ON, BOTH OF YOU, GET OUT HERE!
HEY!
LET M-
CLICK
OOF

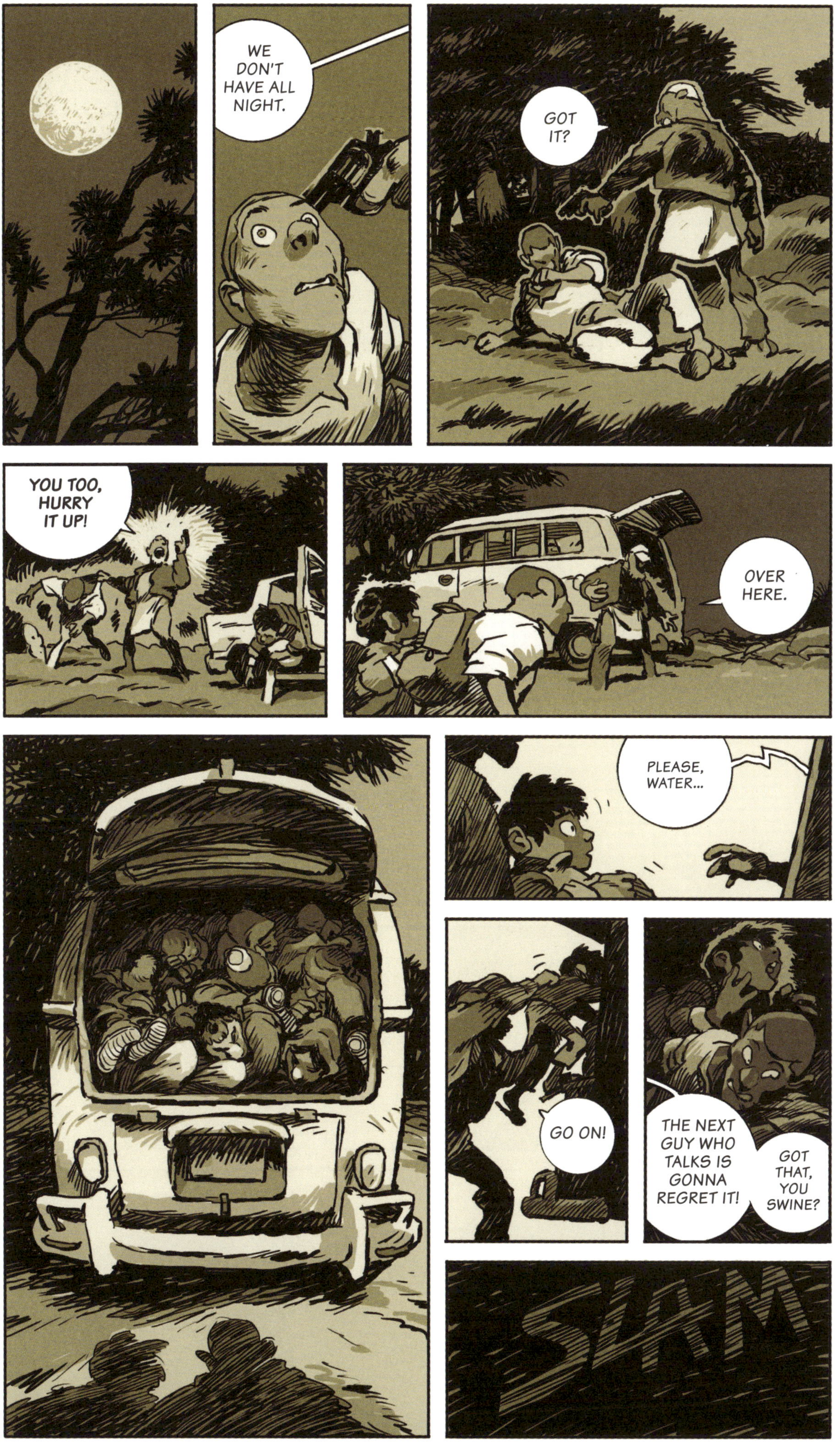
WE DON'T HAVE ALL NIGHT.
GOT IT?
YOU TOO, HURRY IT UP!
OVER HERE.
PLEASE, WATER...
GO ON!
THE NEXT GUY WHO TALKS IS GONNA REGRET IT!
GOT THAT, YOU SWINE?
SLAM

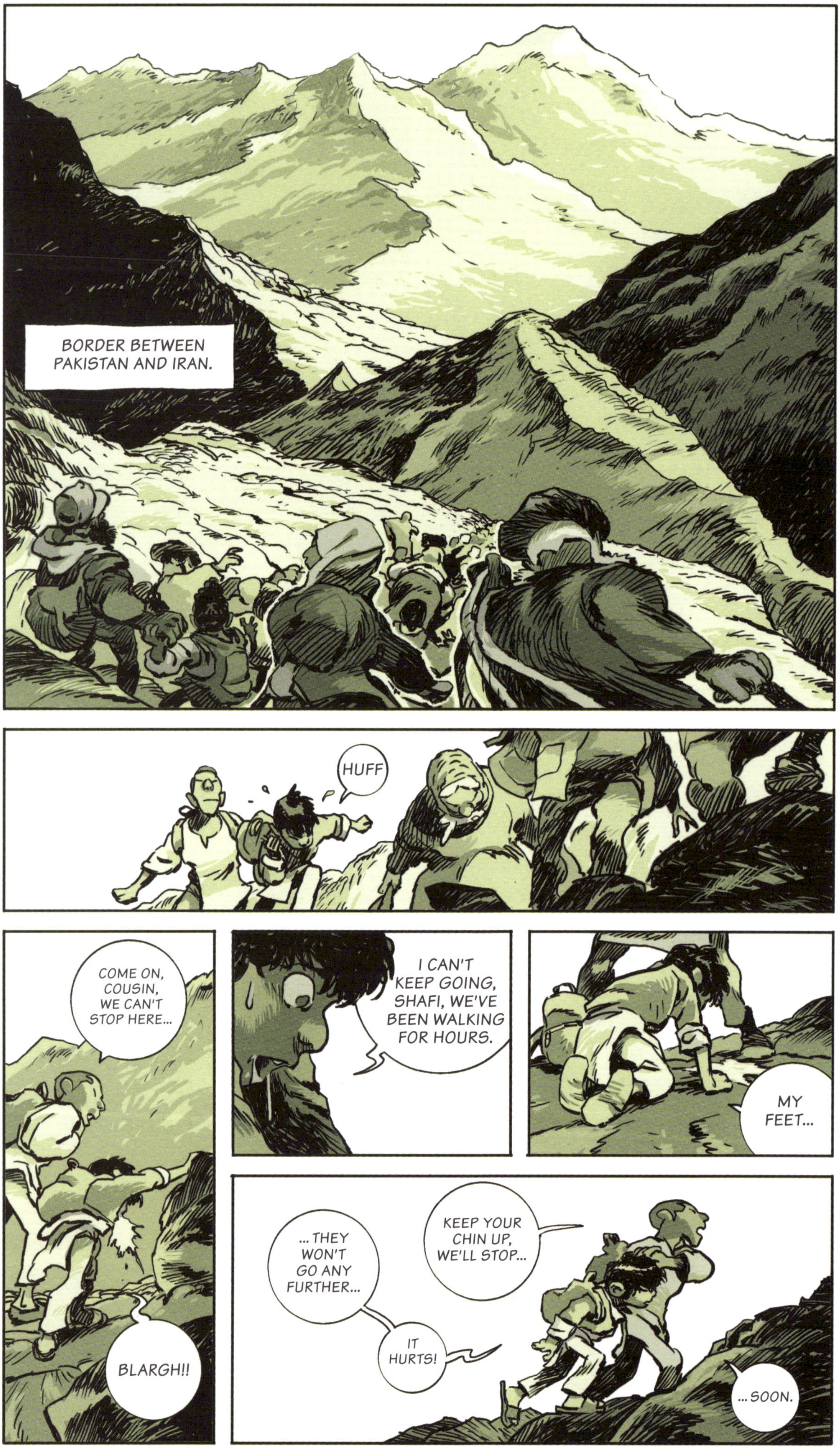

BORDER BETWEEN PAKISTAN AND IRAN.
HUFF
COME ON, COUSIN, WE CAN'T STOP HERE...
BLARGH!!
I CAN'T KEEP GOING, SHAFI, WE'VE BEEN WALKING FOR HOURS.
MY FEET...
...THEY WON'T GO ANY FURTHER...
IT HURTS!
KEEP YOUR CHIN UP, WE'LL STOP...
...SOON.

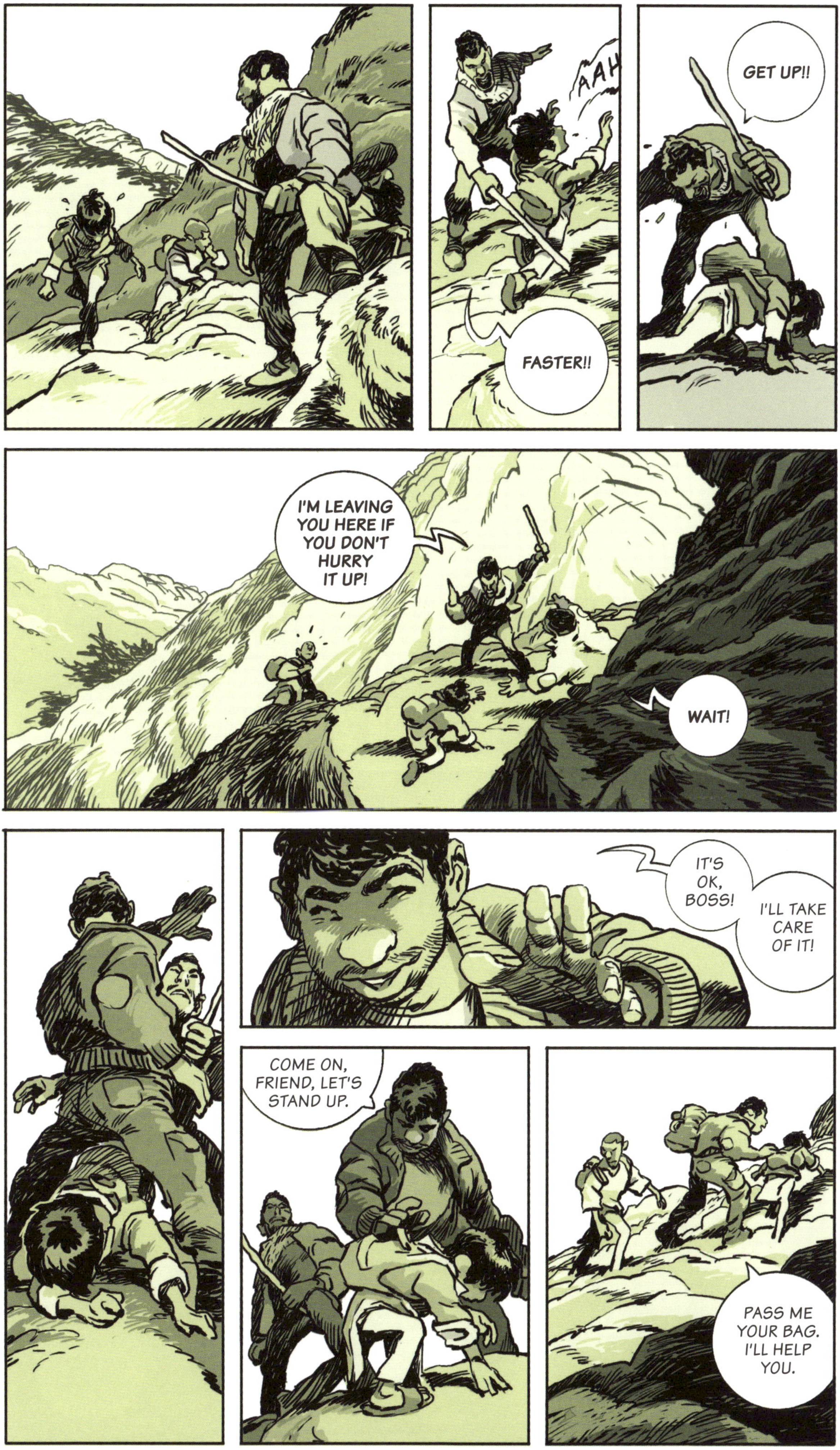
AAH
FASTER!!
GET UP!!
I'M LEAVING YOU HERE IF YOU DON'T HURRY IT UP!
WAIT!
IT'S OK, BOSS!
I'LL TAKE CARE OF IT!
COME ON, FRIEND, LET'S STAND UP.
PASS ME YOUR BAG. I'LL HELP YOU.

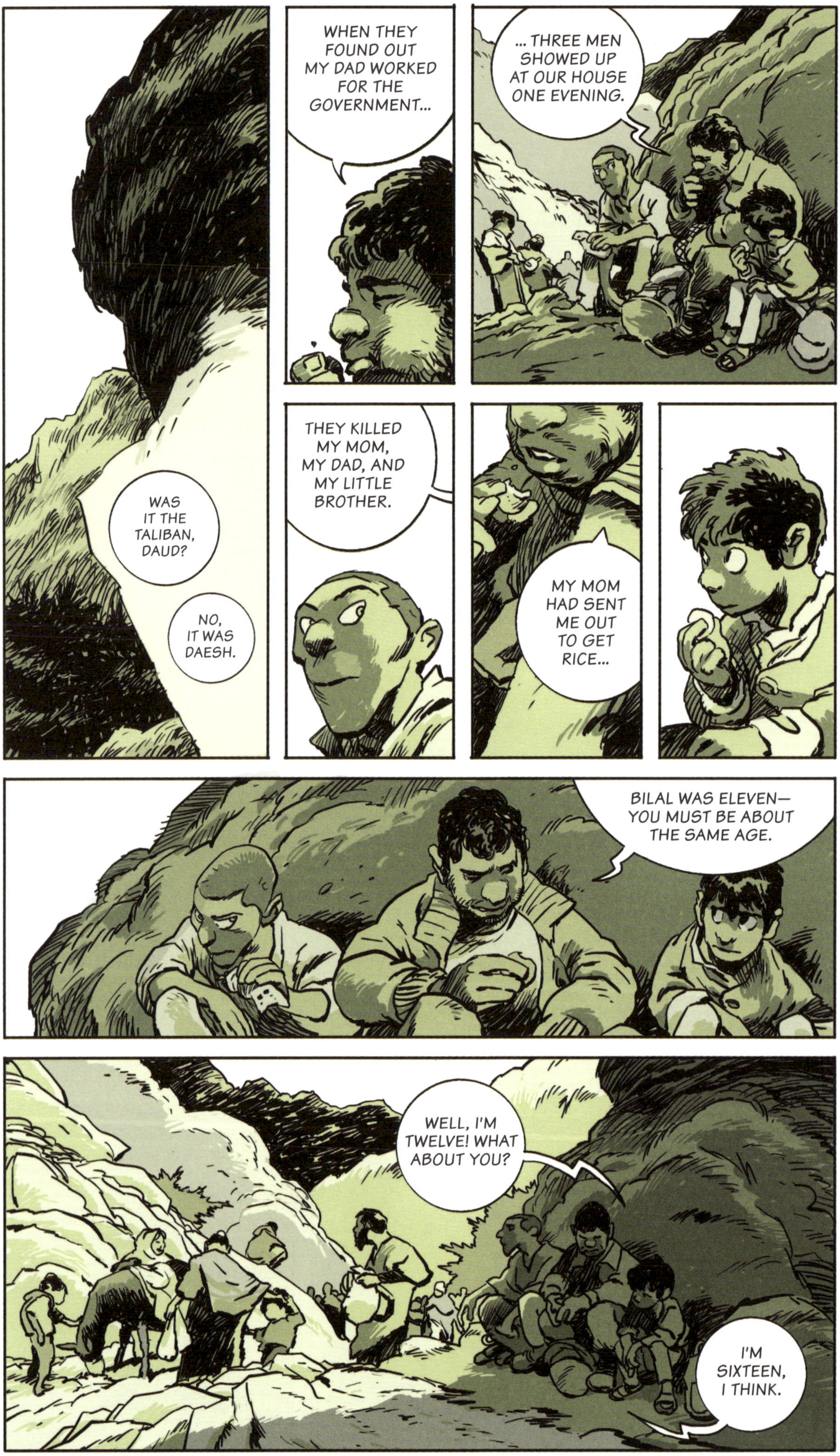
WHEN THEY FOUND OUT MY DAD WORKED FOR THE GOVERNMENT...
... THREE MEN SHOWED UP AT OUR HOUSE ONE EVENING.
WAS IT THE TALIBAN, DAUD?
NO, IT WAS DAESH.
THEY KILLED MY MOM, MY DAD, AND MY LITTLE BROTHER.
MY MOM HAD SENT ME OUT TO GET RICE...
BILAL WAS ELEVEN— YOU MUST BE ABOUT THE SAME AGE.
WELL, I'M TWELVE! WHAT ABOUT YOU?
I'M SIXTEEN, I THINK.

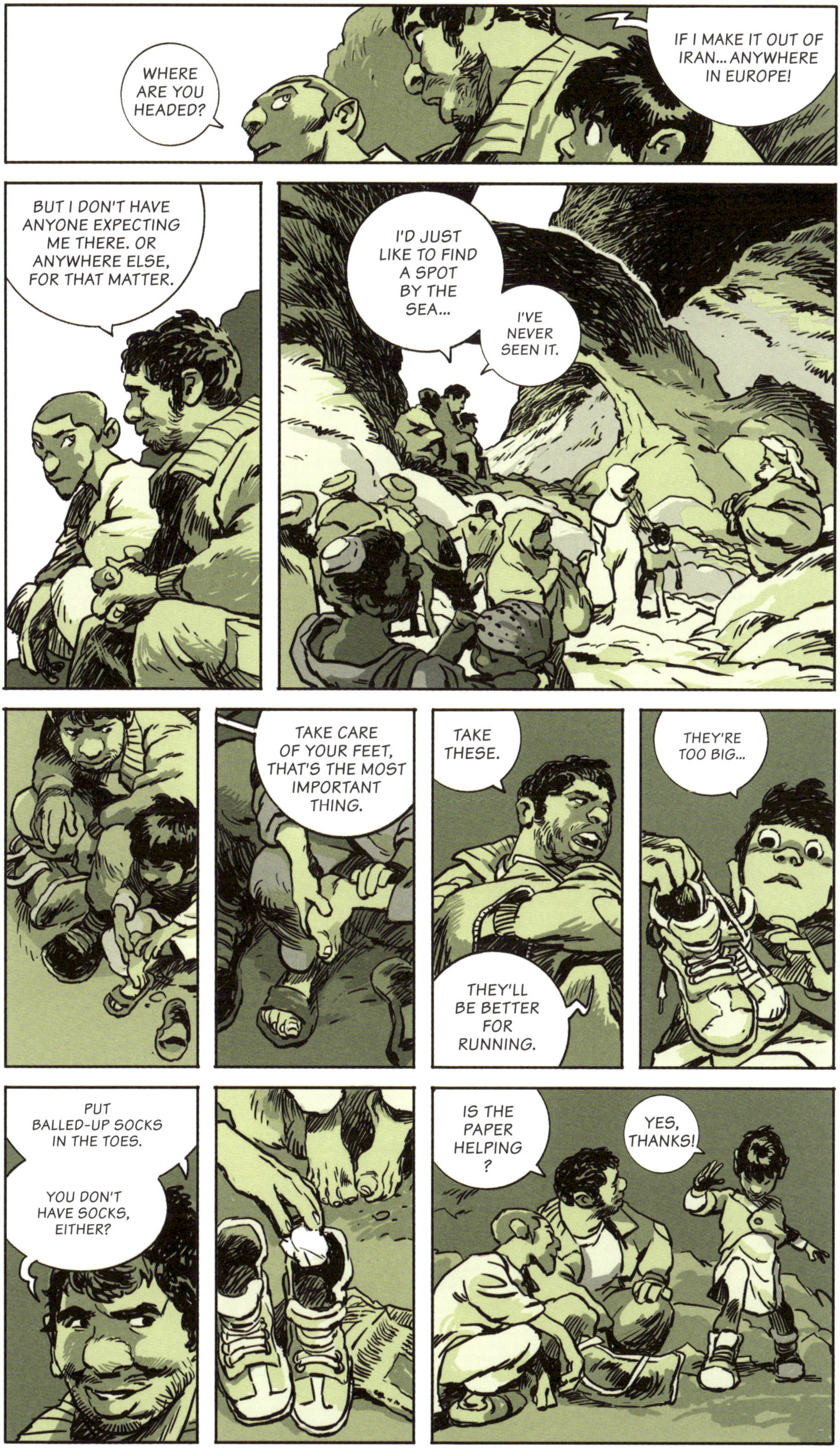
WHERE ARE YOU HEADED?
IF I MAKE IT OUT OF IRAN... ANYWHERE IN EUROPE!
BUT I DON'T HAVE ANYONE EXPECTING ME THERE. OR ANYWHERE ELSE, FOR THAT MATTER.
I'D JUST LIKE TO FIND A SPOT BY THE SEA...
I'VE NEVER SEEN IT.
TAKE CARE OF YOUR FEET, THAT'S THE MOST IMPORTANT THING.
TAKE THESE.
THEY'LL BE BETTER FOR RUNNING.
THEY'RE TOO BIG...
PUT BALLED-UP SOCKS IN THE TOES.
YOU DON'T HAVE SOCKS, EITHER?
IS THE PAPER HELPING ?
YES, THANKS!

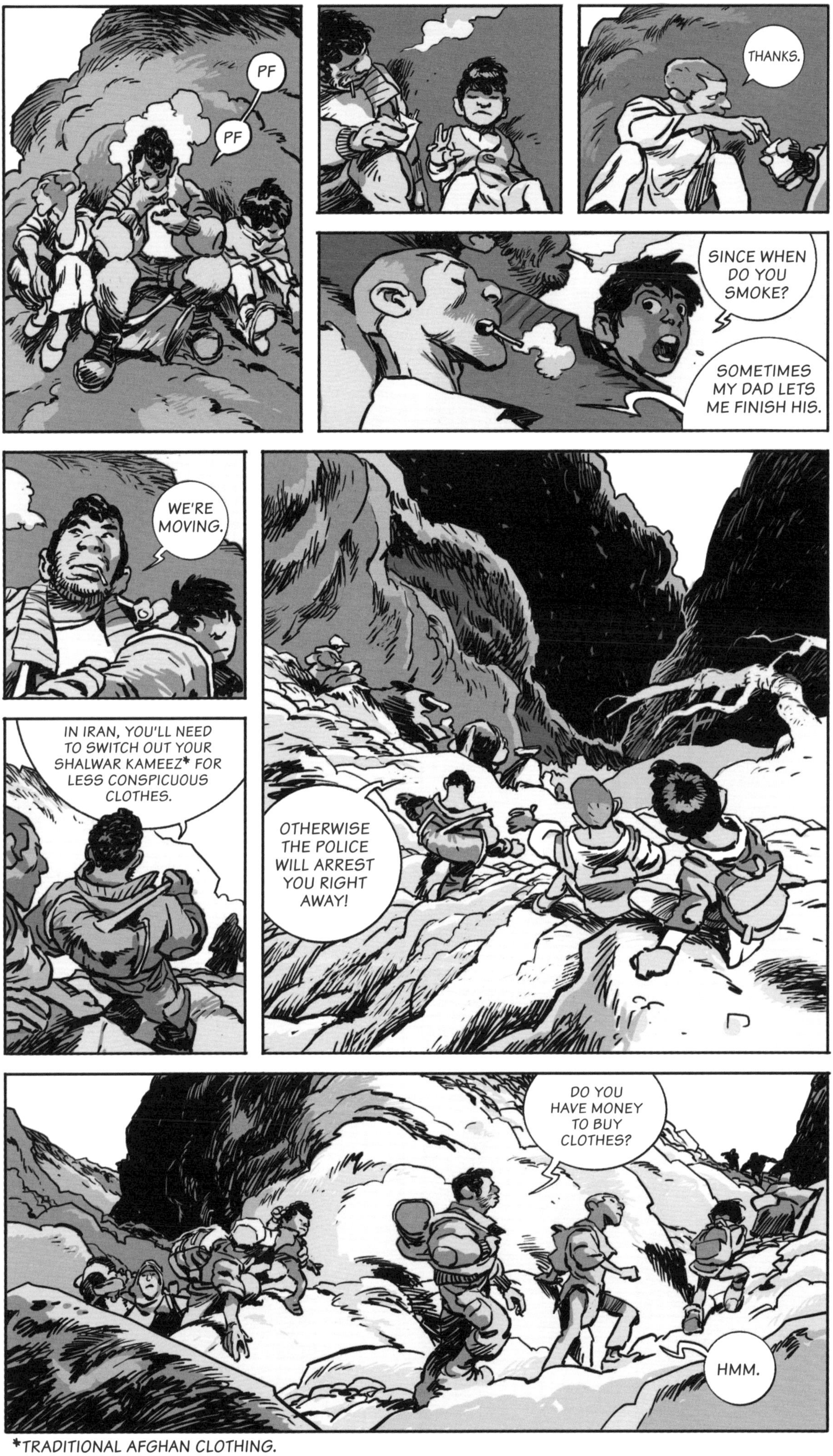
PF
PF
THANKS.
SINCE WHEN DO YOU SMOKE?
SOMETIMES MY DAD LETS ME FINISH HIS.
WE'RE MOVING.
IN IRAN, YOU'LL NEED TO SWITCH OUT YOUR SHALWAR KAMEEZ* FOR LESS CONSPICUOUS CLOTHES.
OTHERWISE THE POLICE WILL ARREST YOU RIGHT AWAY!
DO YOU HAVE MONEY TO BUY CLOTHES?
HMM.

*TRADITIONAL AFGHAN CLOTHING.

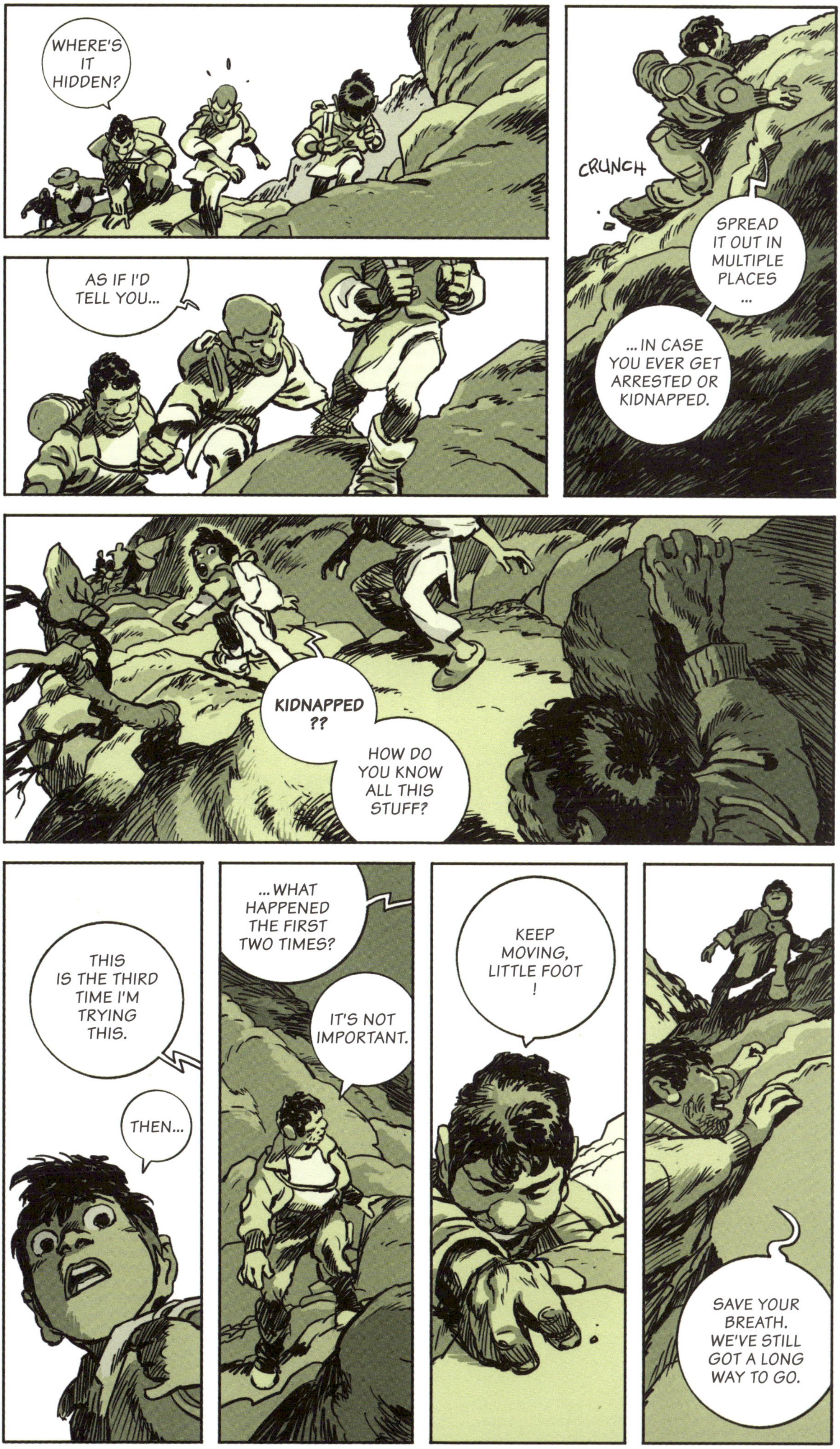
WHERE'S IT HIDDEN?
CRUNCH
AS IF I'D TELL YOU...
SPREAD IT OUT IN MULTIPLE PLACES ...
...IN CASE YOU EVER GET ARRESTED OR KIDNAPPED.
KIDNAPPED ??
HOW DO YOU KNOW ALL THIS STUFF?
THIS IS THE THIRD TIME I'M TRYING THIS.
THEN...
...WHAT HAPPENED THE FIRST TWO TIMES?
IT'S NOT IMPORTANT.
KEEP MOVING, LITTLE FOOT !
SAVE YOUR BREATH. WE'VE STILL GOT A LONG WAY TO GO.

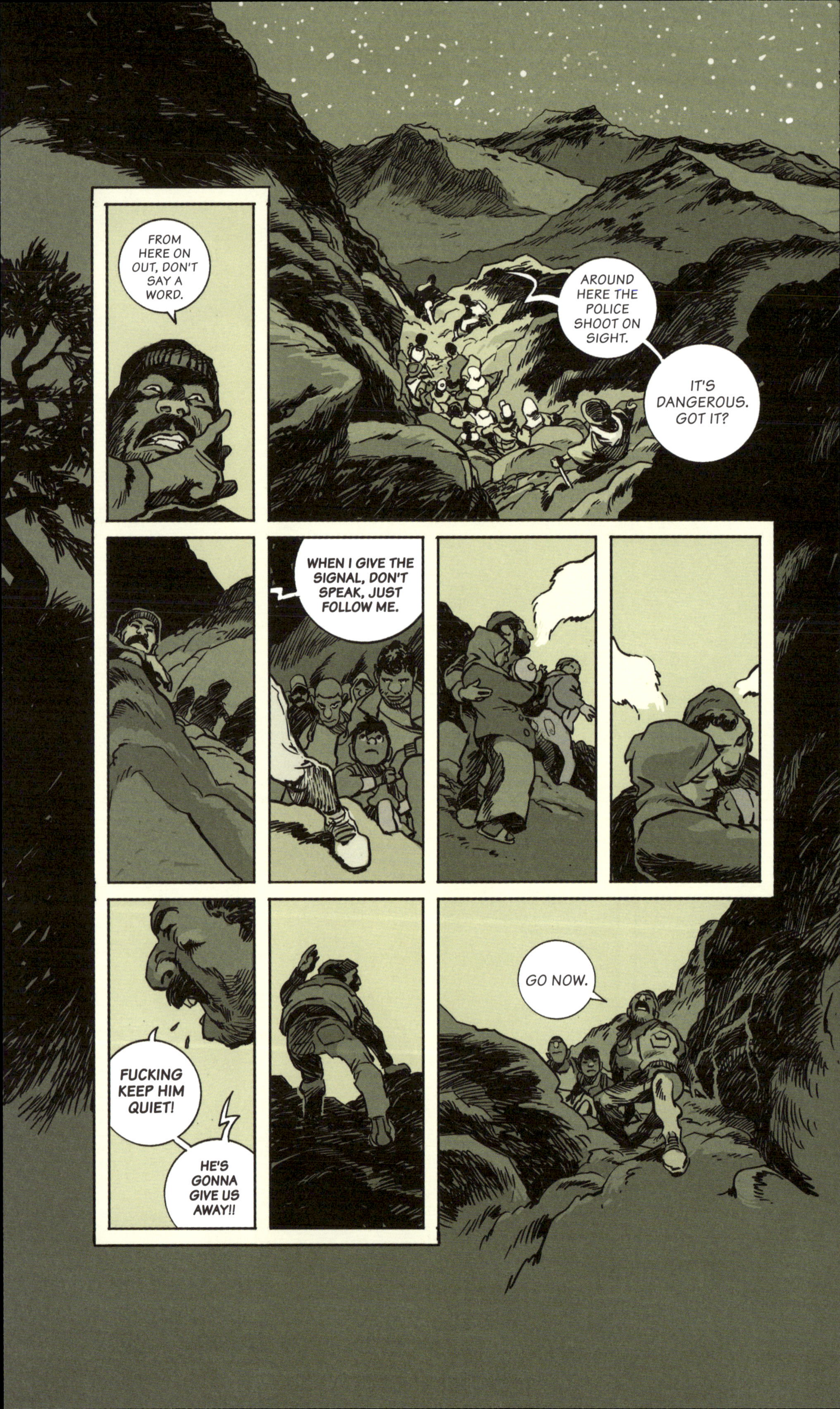
FROM HERE ON OUT, DON'T SAY A WORD.
AROUND HERE THE POLICE SHOOT ON SIGHT.
IT'S DANGEROUS. GOT IT?
WHEN I GIVE THE SIGNAL, DON'T SPEAK, JUST FOLLOW ME.
FUCKING KEEP HIM QUIET!
HE'S GONNA GIVE US AWAY!!
GO NOW.

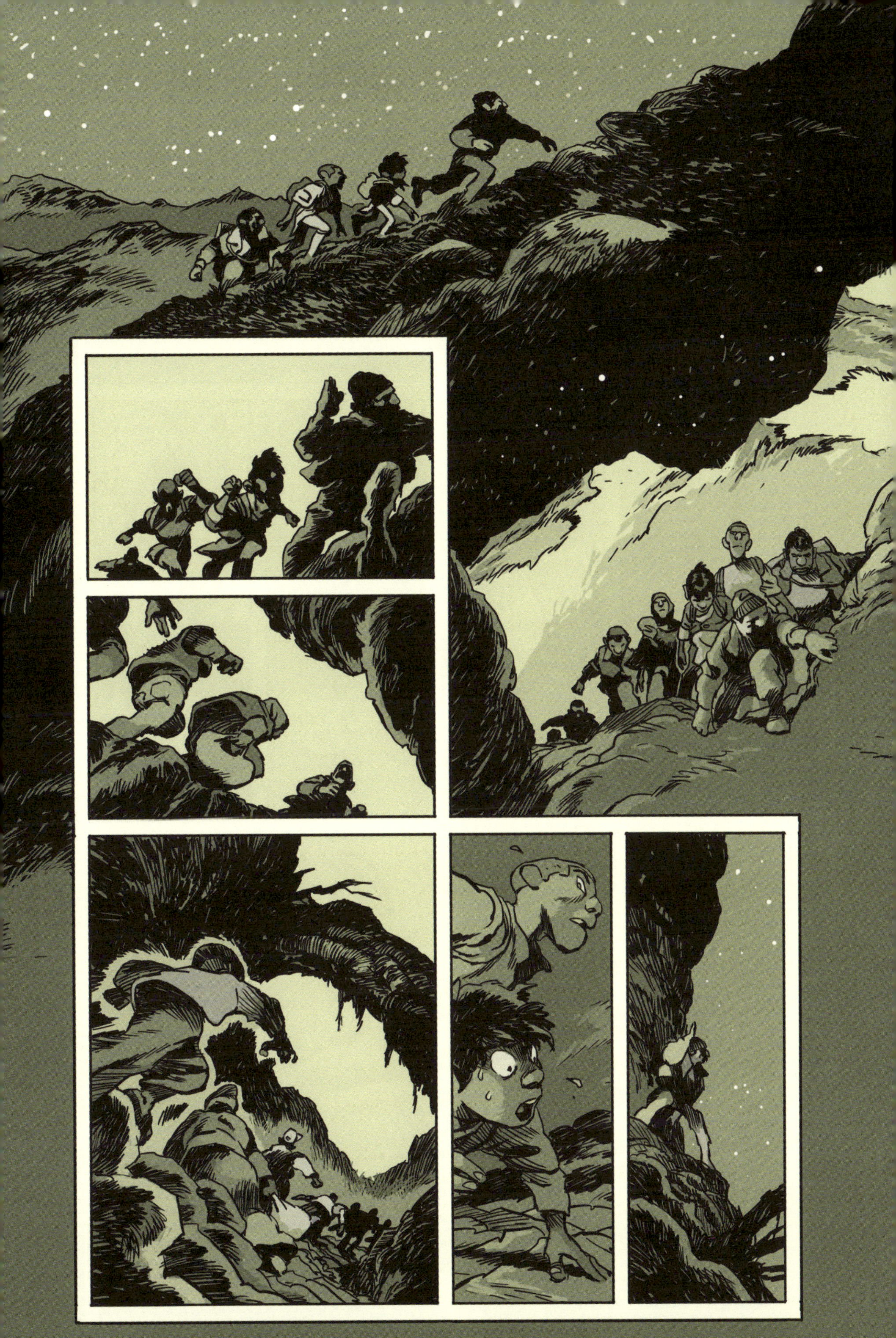

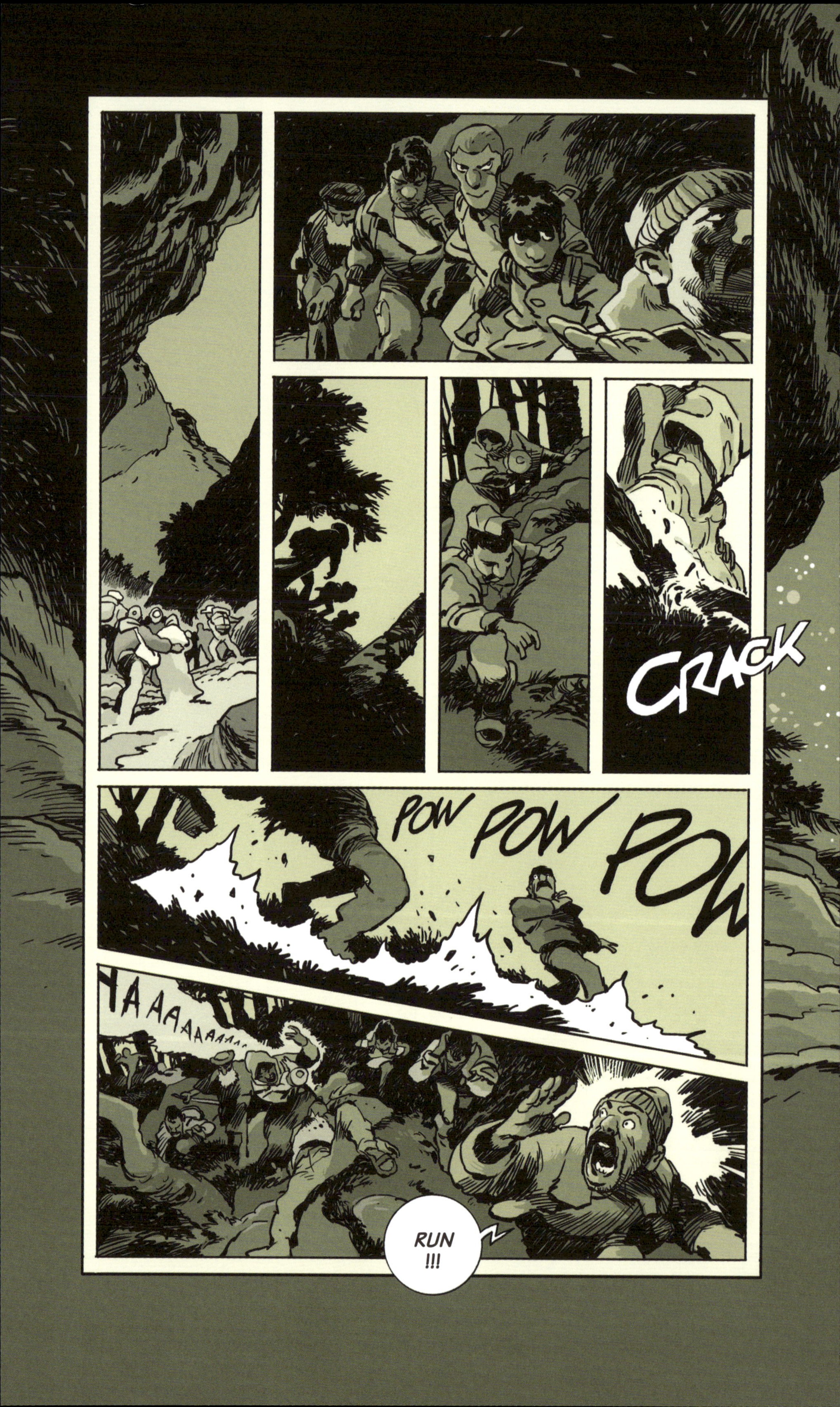
CRACK
POW POW POW
HAAAAAAAA...
RUN !!!

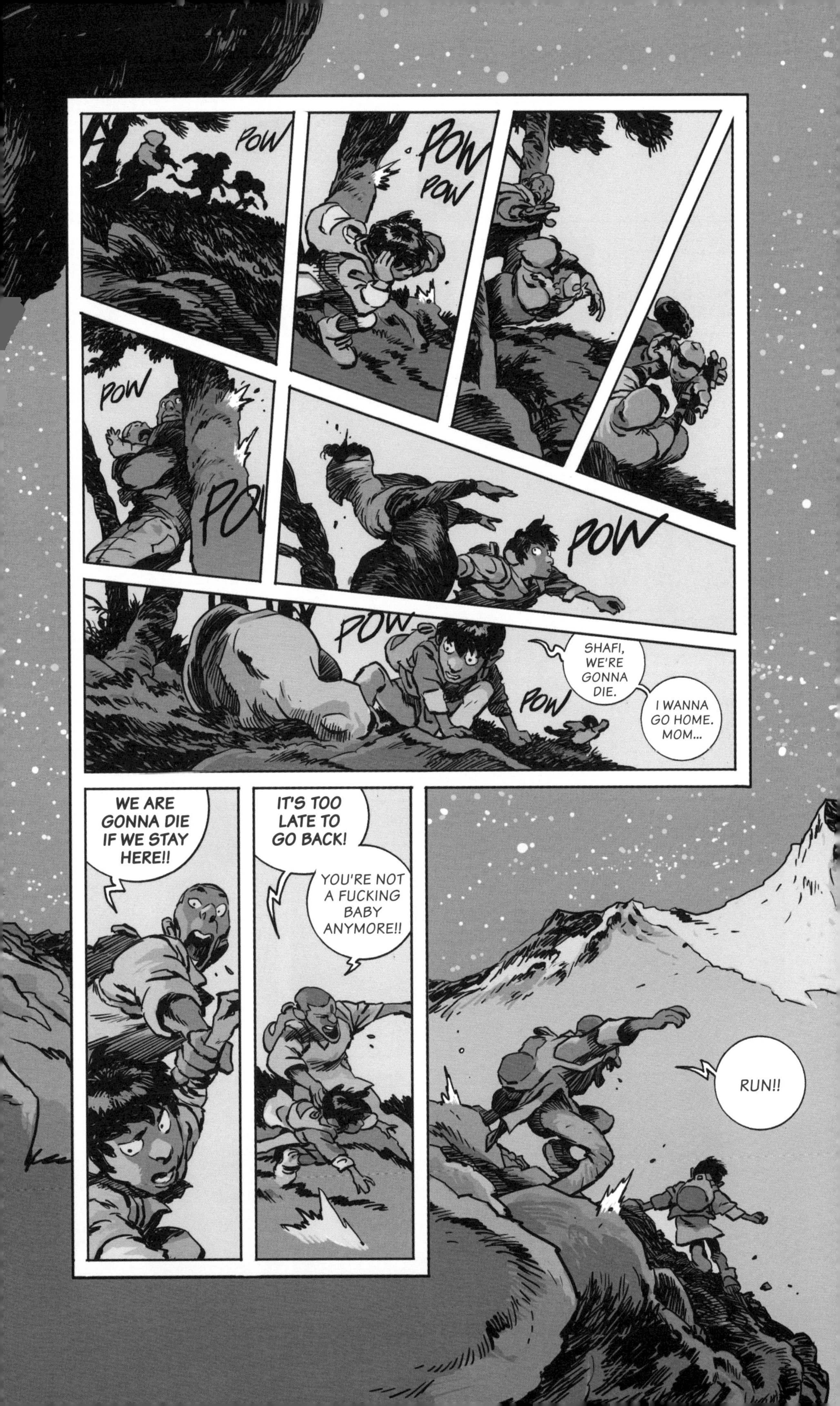
POW
POW
POW
POW
POW
POW
POW
SHAFI, WE'RE GONNA DIE.
POW
I WANNA GO HOME. MOM...
WE ARE GONNA DIE IF WE STAY HERE!!
IT'S TOO LATE TO GO BACK!
YOU'RE NOT A FUCKING BABY ANYMORE!!
RUN!!

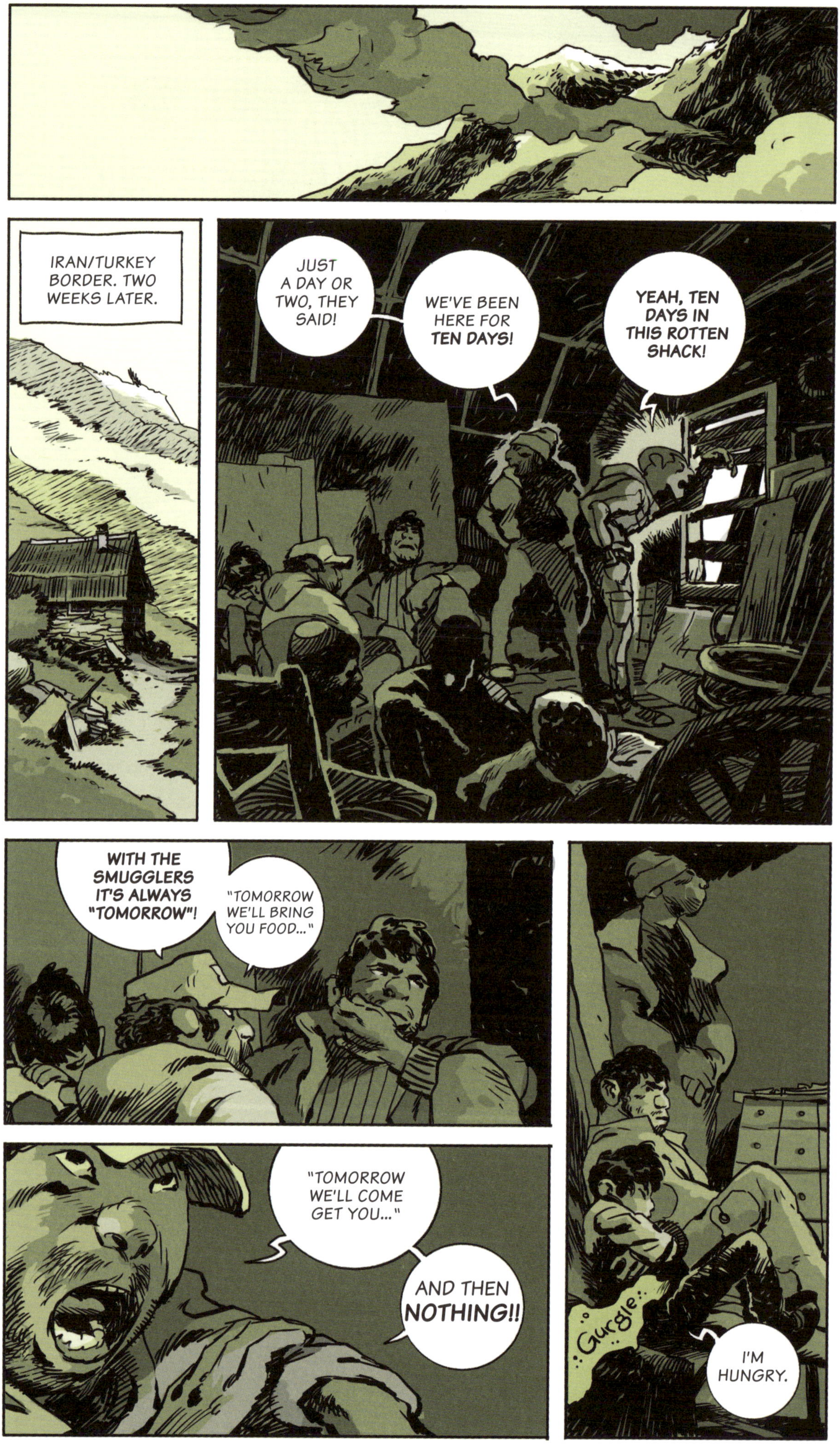
IRAN/TURKEY BORDER. TWO WEEKS LATER.
JUST A DAY OR TWO, THEY SAID!
WE'VE BEEN HERE FOR **TEN DAYS!**
YEAH, TEN DAYS IN THIS ROTTEN SHACK!
WITH THE SMUGGLERS IT'S ALWAYS "TOMORROW"!
"TOMORROW WE'LL BRING YOU FOOD..."
"TOMORROW WE'LL COME GET YOU..."
AND THEN **NOTHING!!**
Gurgle
I'M HUNGRY.

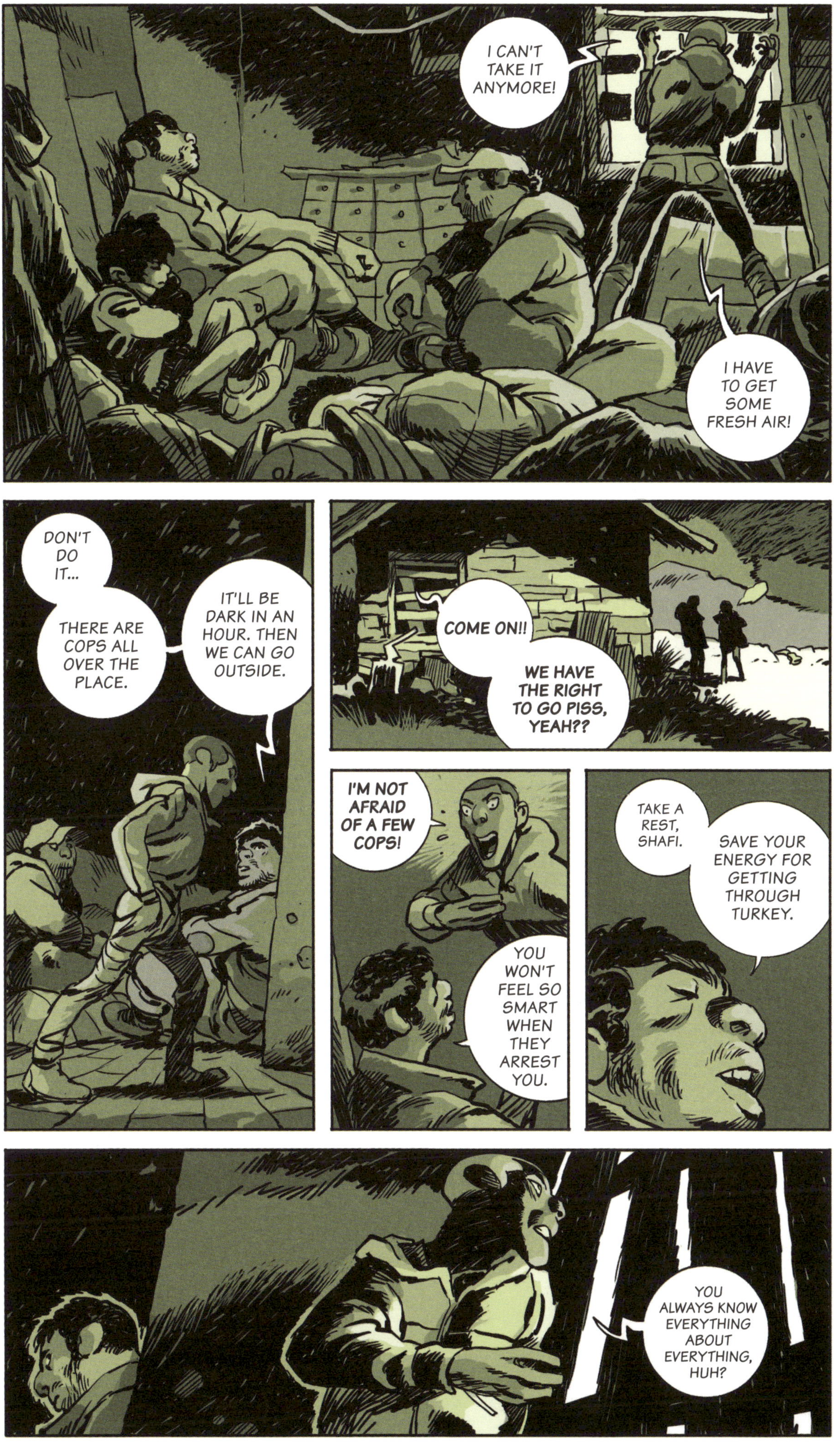
I CAN'T TAKE IT ANYMORE!
I HAVE TO GET SOME FRESH AIR!
DON'T DO IT...
THERE ARE COPS ALL OVER THE PLACE.
IT'LL BE DARK IN AN HOUR. THEN WE CAN GO OUTSIDE.
COME ON!!
WE HAVE THE RIGHT TO GO PISS, YEAH??
I'M NOT AFRAID OF A FEW COPS!
YOU WON'T FEEL SO SMART WHEN THEY ARREST YOU.
TAKE A REST, SHAFI.
SAVE YOUR ENERGY FOR GETTING THROUGH TURKEY.
YOU ALWAYS KNOW EVERYTHING ABOUT EVERYTHING, HUH?

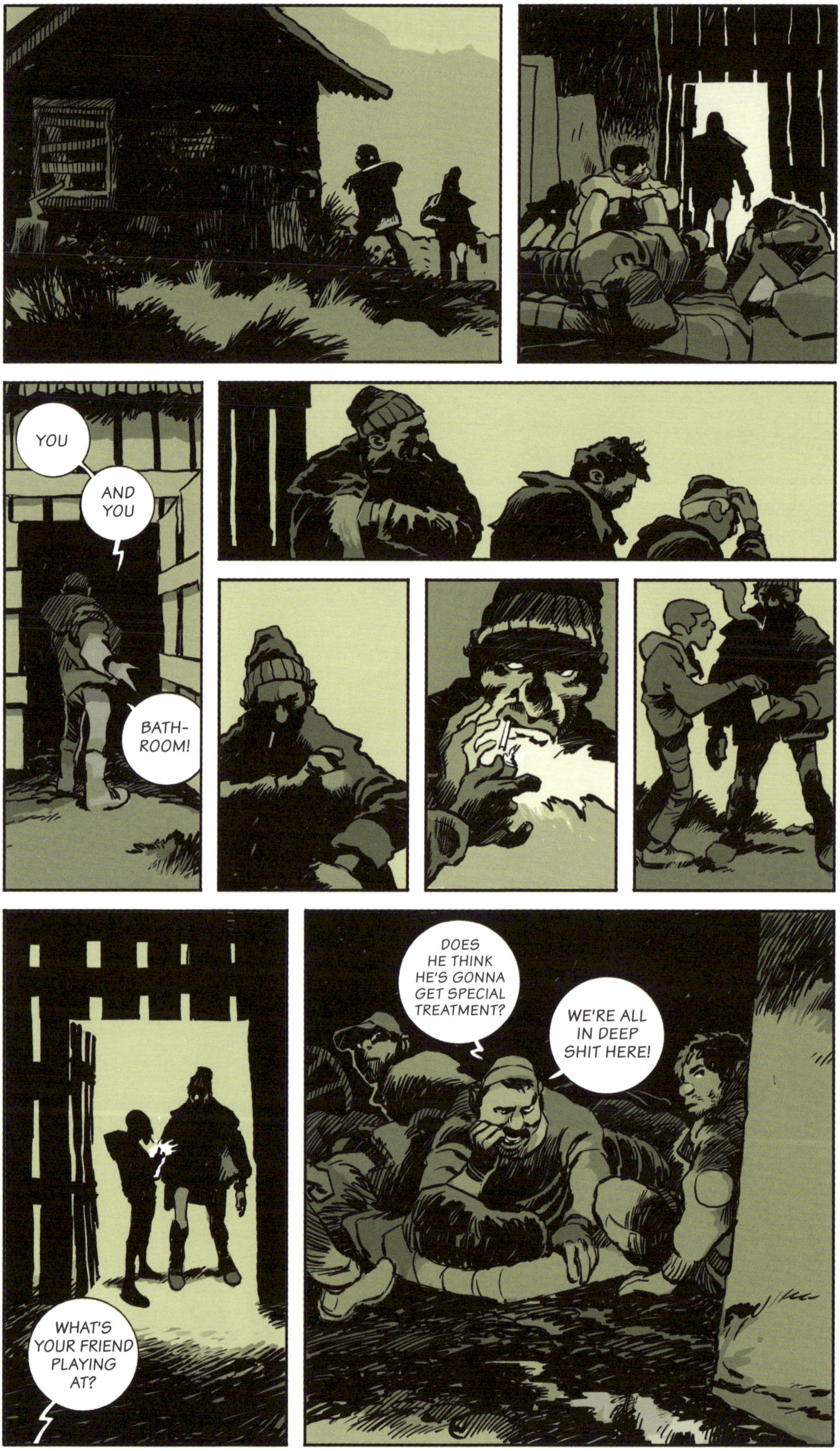
YOU
AND YOU
BATH-ROOM!
DOES HE THINK HE'S GONNA GET SPECIAL TREATMENT?
WE'RE ALL IN DEEP SHIT HERE!
WHAT'S YOUR FRIEND PLAYING AT?

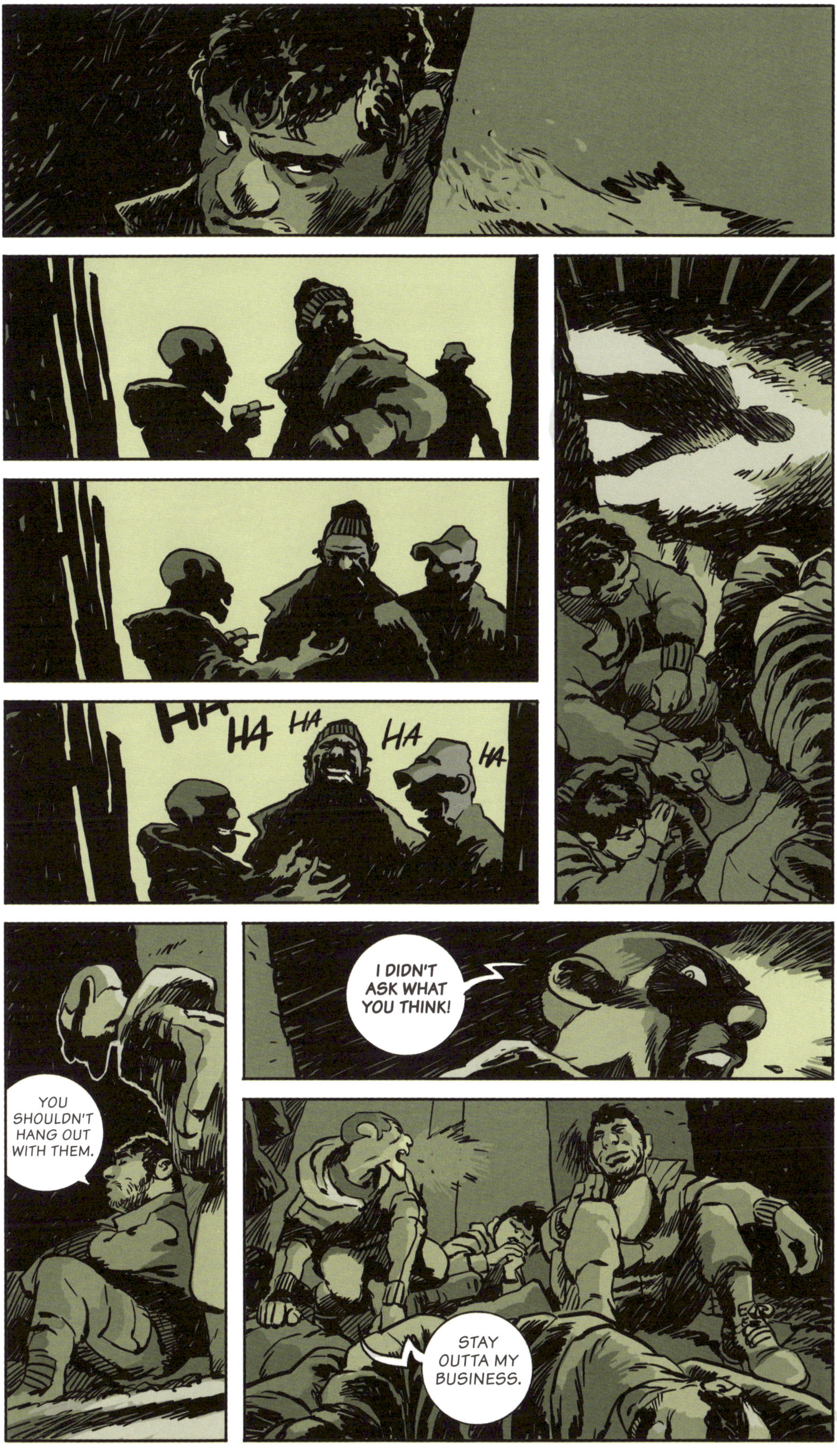
HA
HA
HA
HA
HA
I DIDN'T ASK WHAT YOU THINK!
YOU SHOULDN'T HANG OUT WITH THEM.
STAY OUTTA MY BUSINESS.

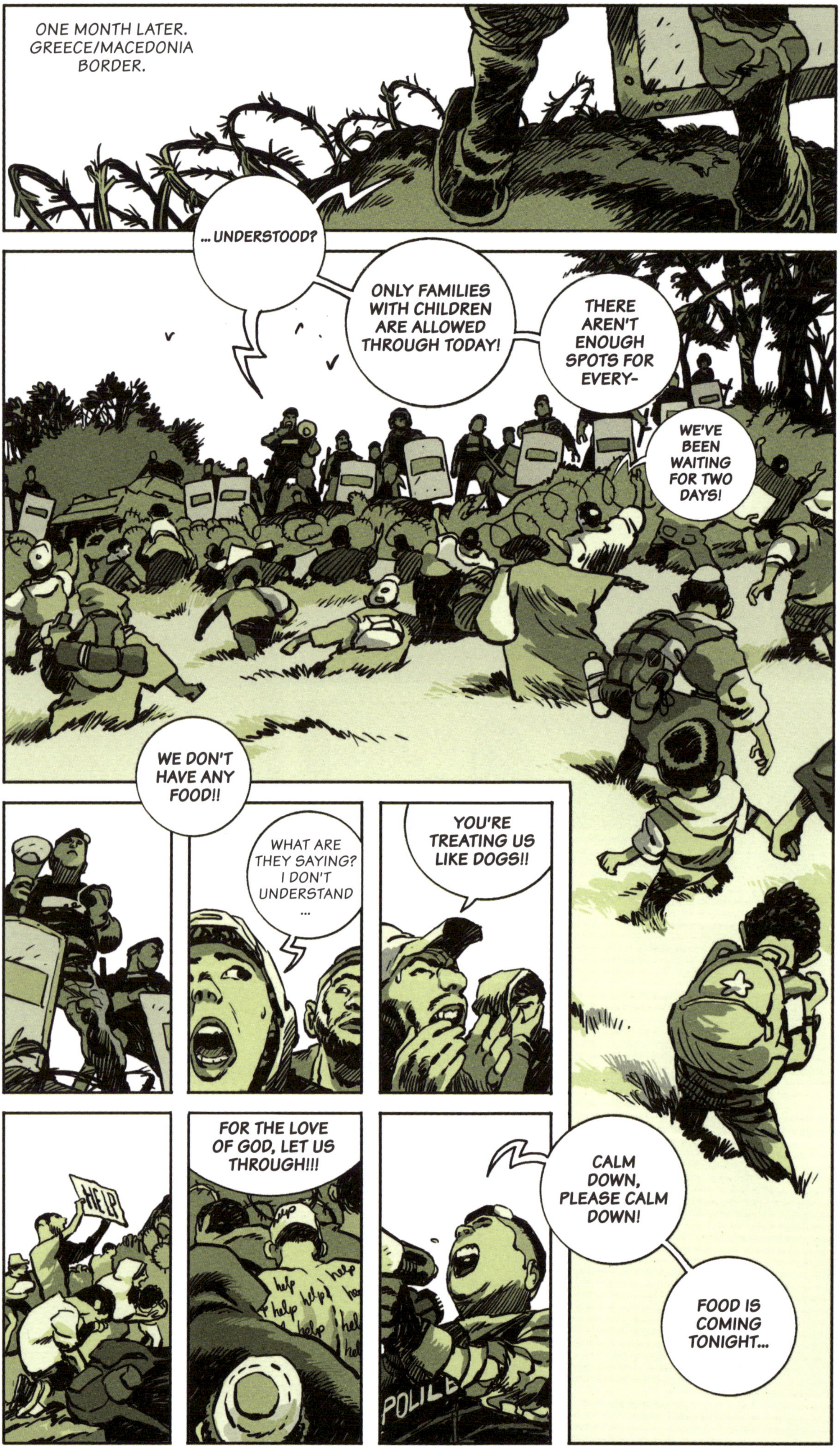
ONE MONTH LATER. GREECE/MACEDONIA BORDER.
...UNDERSTOOD?
ONLY FAMILIES WITH CHILDREN ARE ALLOWED THROUGH TODAY!
THERE AREN'T ENOUGH SPOTS FOR EVERY-
WE'VE BEEN WAITING FOR TWO DAYS!
WE DON'T HAVE ANY FOOD!!
WHAT ARE THEY SAYING? I DON'T UNDERSTAND ...
YOU'RE TREATING US LIKE DOGS!!
HELP
FOR THE LOVE OF GOD, LET US THROUGH!!!
help help help help help help help
CALM DOWN, PLEASE CALM DOWN!
FOOD IS COMING TONIGHT...
POLICE

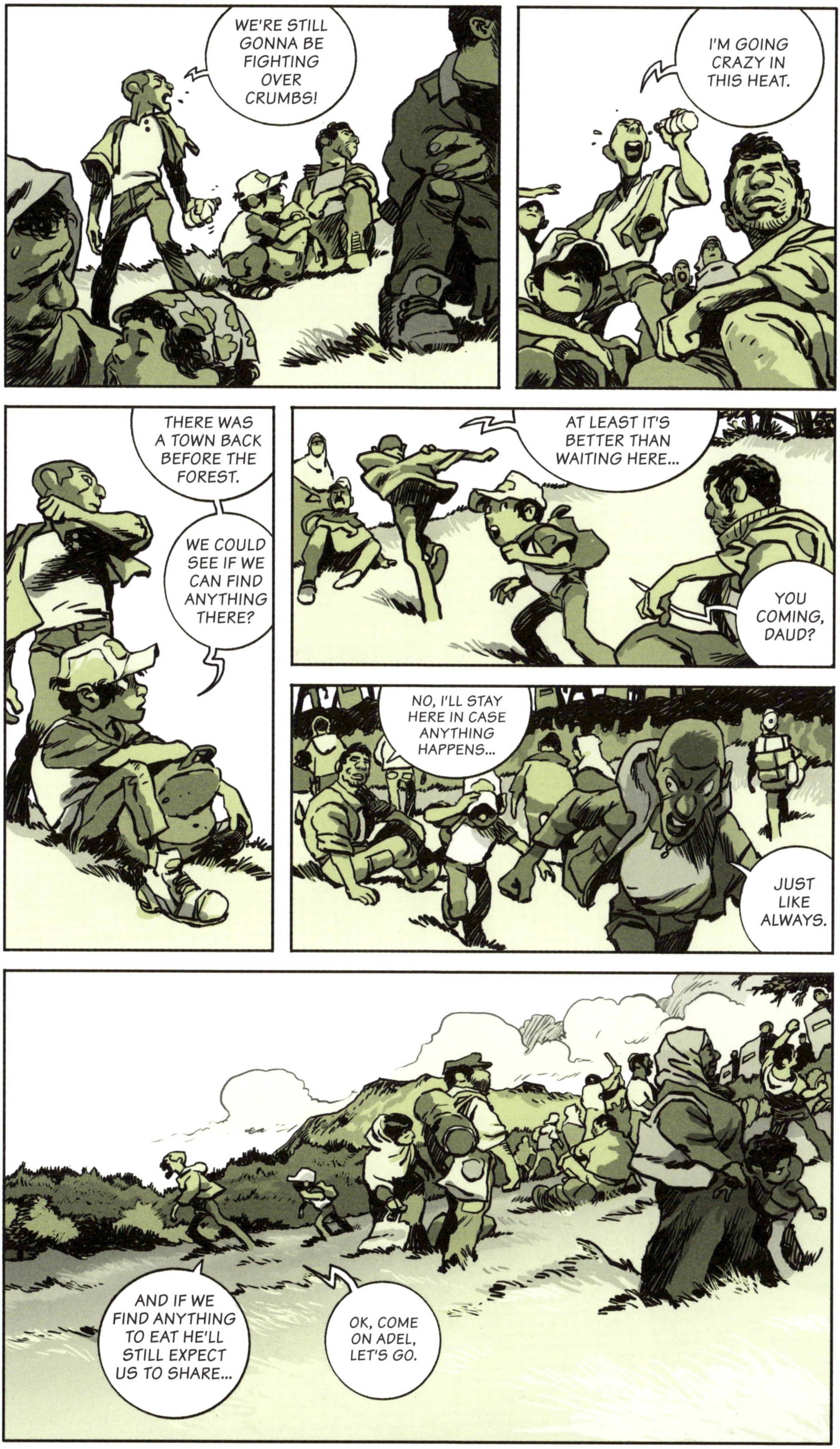
WE'RE STILL GONNA BE FIGHTING OVER CRUMBS!
I'M GOING CRAZY IN THIS HEAT.
THERE WAS A TOWN BACK BEFORE THE FOREST.
WE COULD SEE IF WE CAN FIND ANYTHING THERE?
AT LEAST IT'S BETTER THAN WAITING HERE...
YOU COMING, DAUD?
NO, I'LL STAY HERE IN CASE ANYTHING HAPPENS...
JUST LIKE ALWAYS.
AND IF WE FIND ANYTHING TO EAT HE'LL STILL EXPECT US TO SHARE...
OK, COME ON ADEL, LET'S GO.

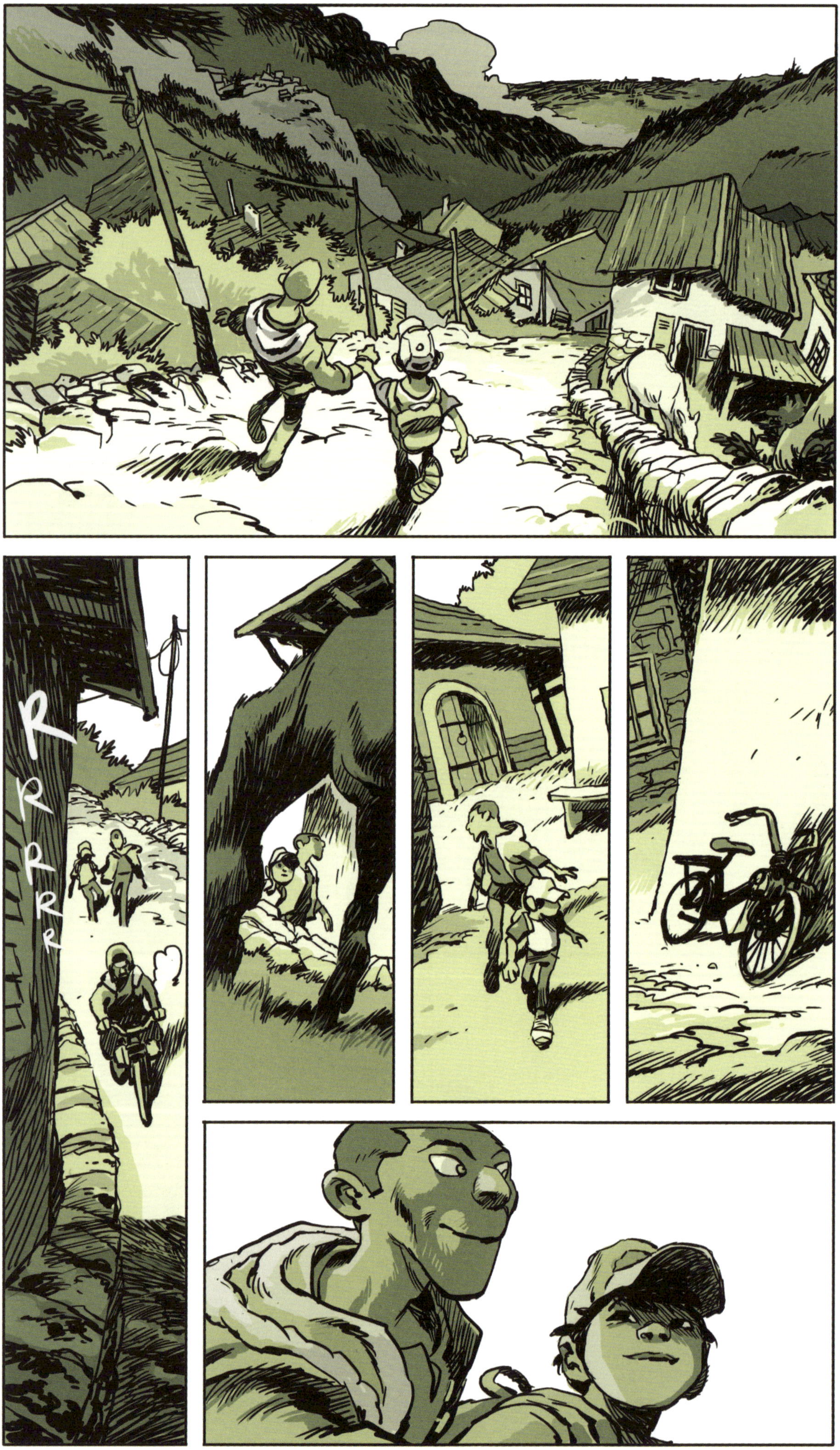
RRRRRR

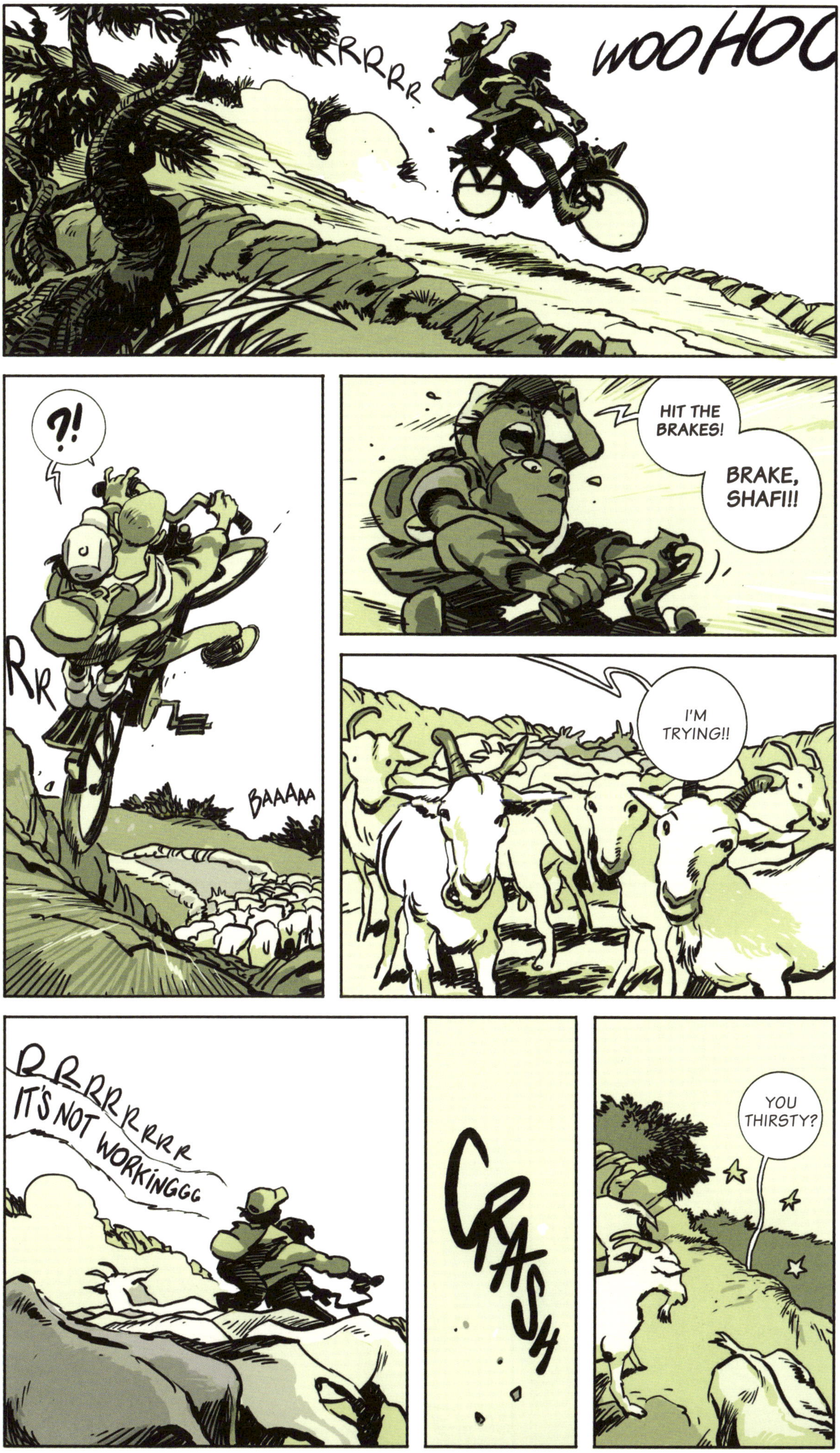
RRRRR
WOOHOO
?!
RR
BAAAAA
HIT THE BRAKES!
BRAKE, SHAFI!!
I'M TRYING!!
RRRRRRRRRR
IT'S NOT WORKINGGG
CRASH
YOU THIRSTY?

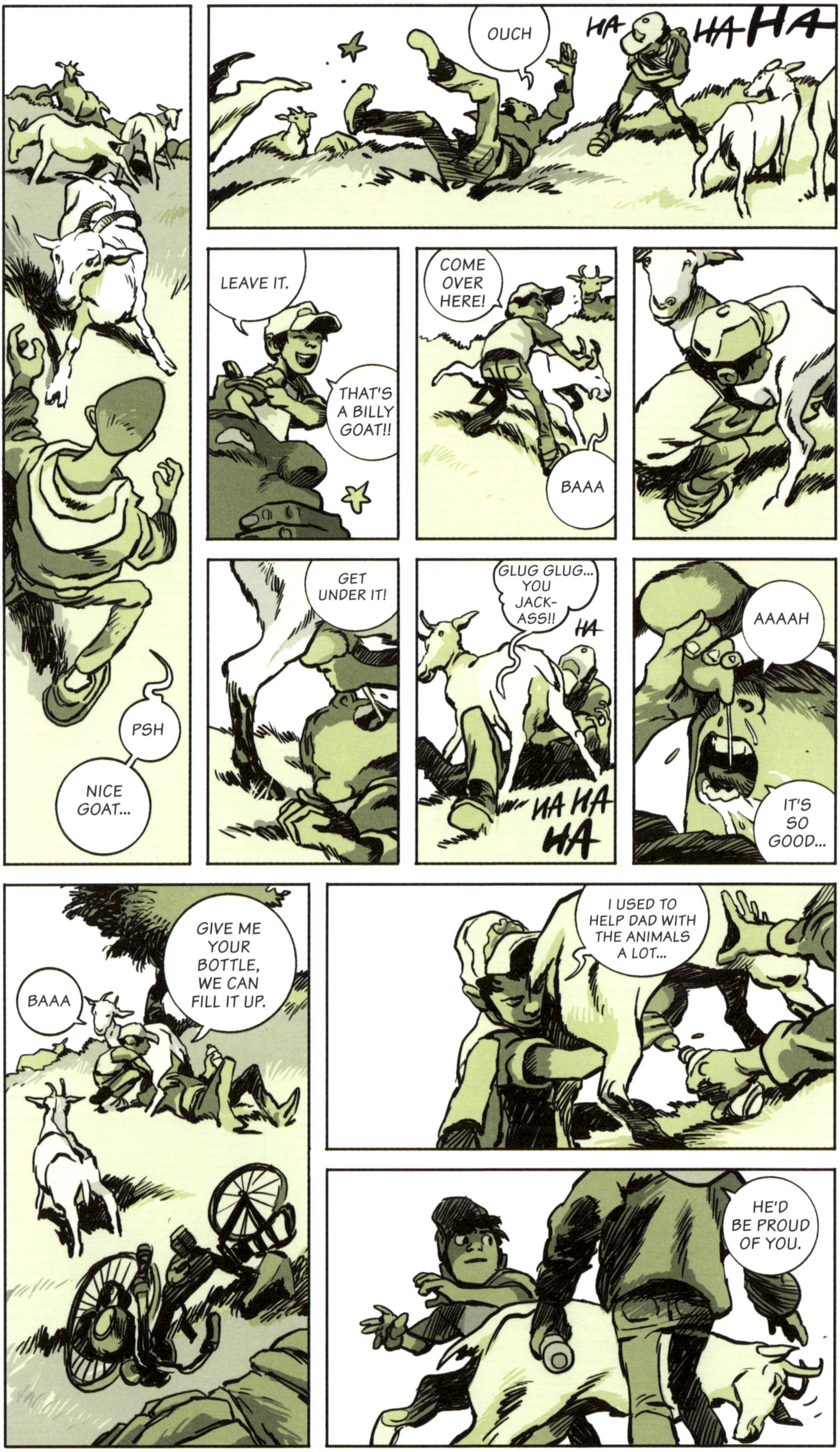
PSH
NICE GOAT...
OUCH
HA HA HA
LEAVE IT.
THAT'S A BILLY GOAT!!
COME OVER HERE!
BAAA
GET UNDER IT!
GLUG GLUG... YOU JACK-ASS!!
HA
HA HA HA
AAAAH
IT'S SO GOOD...
BAAA
GIVE ME YOUR BOTTLE, WE CAN FILL IT UP.
I USED TO HELP DAD WITH THE ANIMALS A LOT...
HE'D BE PROUD OF YOU.

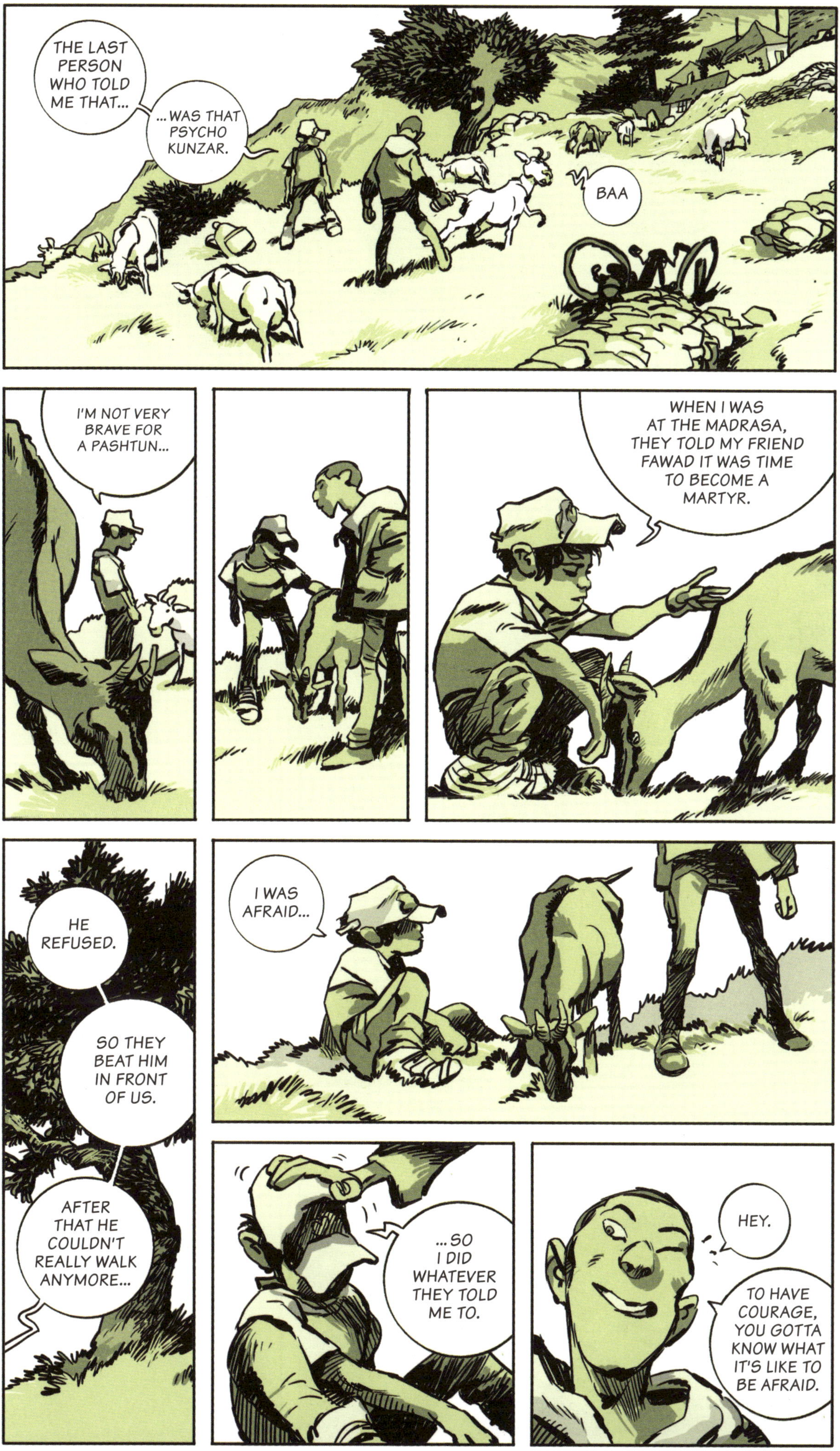
THE LAST PERSON WHO TOLD ME THAT...
...WAS THAT PSYCHO KUNZAR.
BAA
I'M NOT VERY BRAVE FOR A PASHTUN...
WHEN I WAS AT THE MADRASA, THEY TOLD MY FRIEND FAWAD IT WAS TIME TO BECOME A MARTYR.
HE REFUSED.
SO THEY BEAT HIM IN FRONT OF US.
AFTER THAT HE COULDN'T REALLY WALK ANYMORE...
I WAS AFRAID...
...SO I DID WHATEVER THEY TOLD ME TO.
HEY.
TO HAVE COURAGE, YOU GOTTA KNOW WHAT IT'S LIKE TO BE AFRAID.

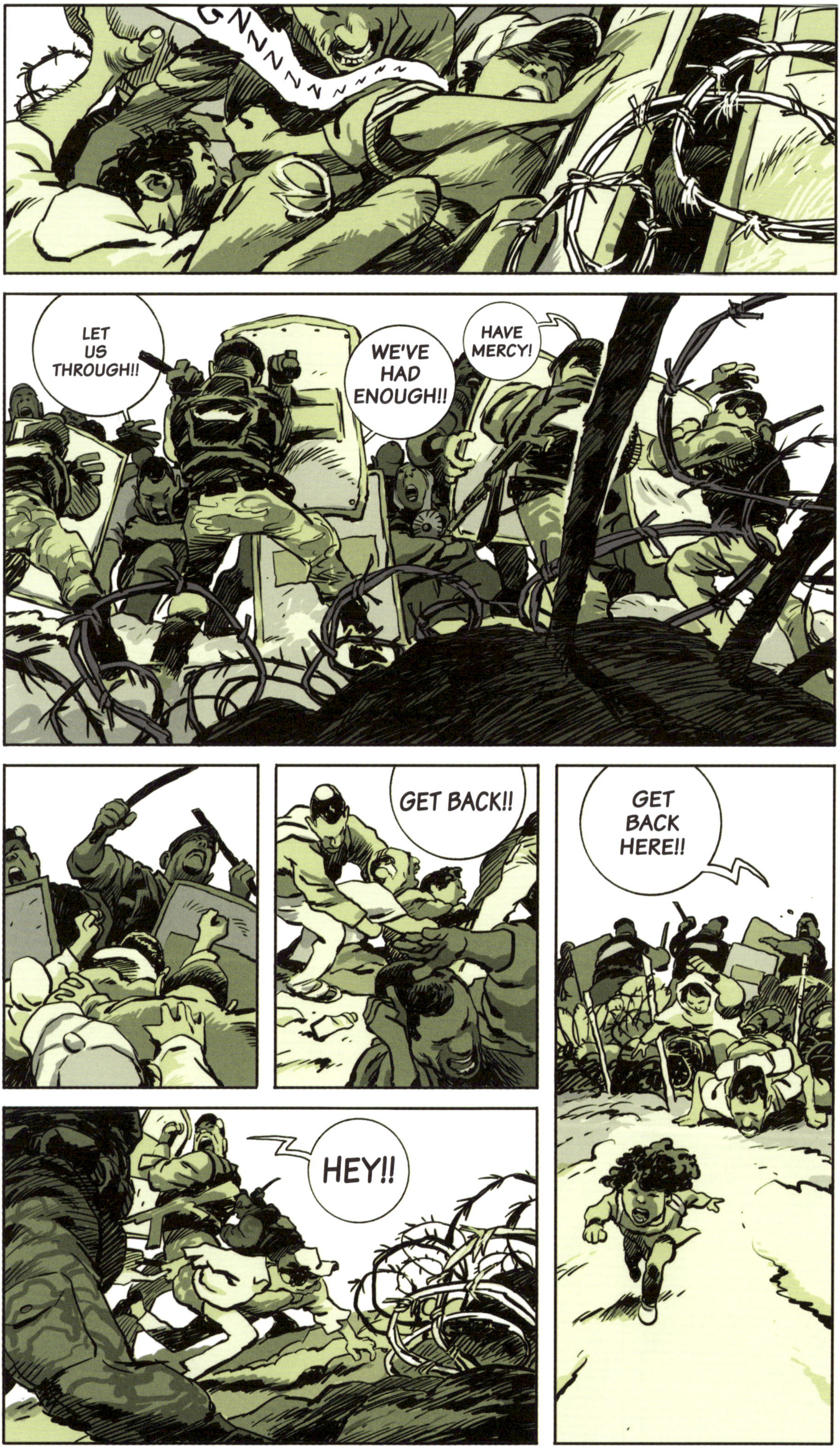
GNNNNNNNNN
LET US THROUGH!!
WE'VE HAD ENOUGH!!
HAVE MERCY!
GET BACK!!
GET BACK HERE!!
HEY!!

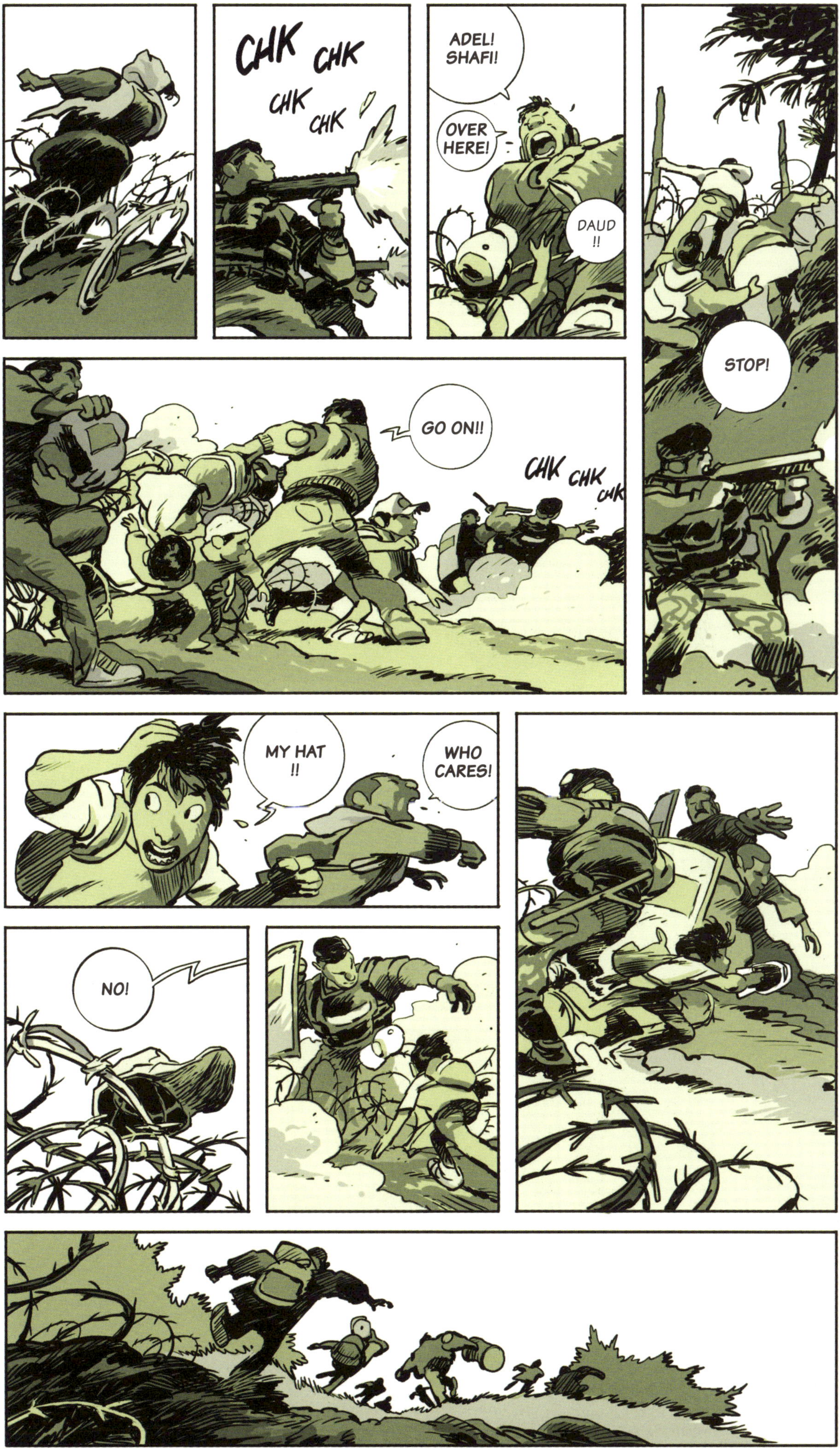
CHK CHK
CHK CHK
ADEL! SHAFI!
OVER HERE!
DAUD !!
STOP!
GO ON!!
CHK CHK CHK
MY HAT !!
WHO CARES!
NO!

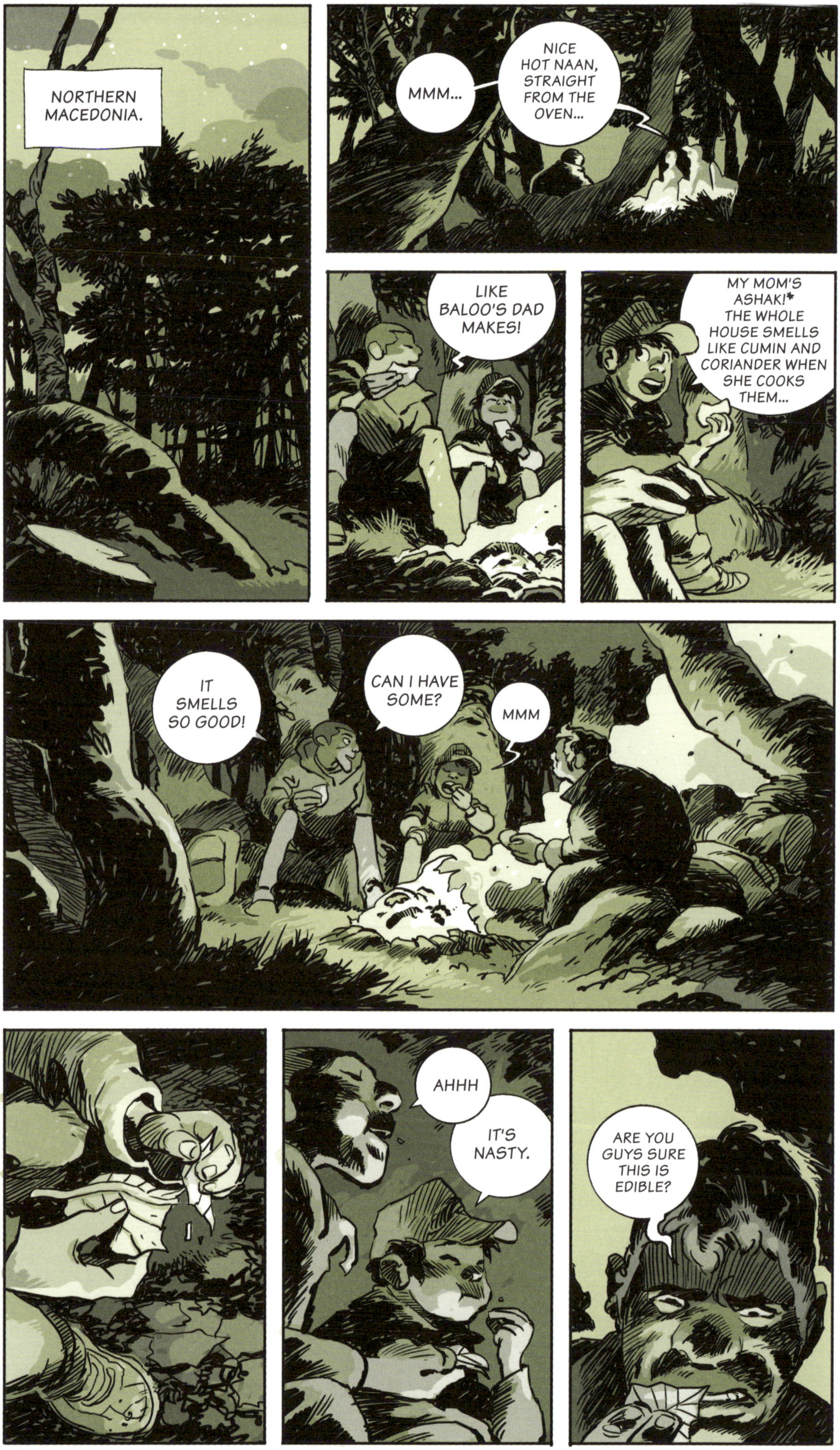
NORTHERN MACEDONIA.
MMM...
NICE HOT NAAN, STRAIGHT FROM THE OVEN...
LIKE BALOO'S DAD MAKES!
MY MOM'S ASHAK!* THE WHOLE HOUSE SMELLS LIKE CUMIN AND CORIANDER WHEN SHE COOKS THEM...
IT SMELLS SO GOOD!
CAN I HAVE SOME?
MMM
AHHH
IT'S NASTY.
ARE YOU GUYS SURE THIS IS EDIBLE?

*A TYPE OF AFGHAN DUMPLING.

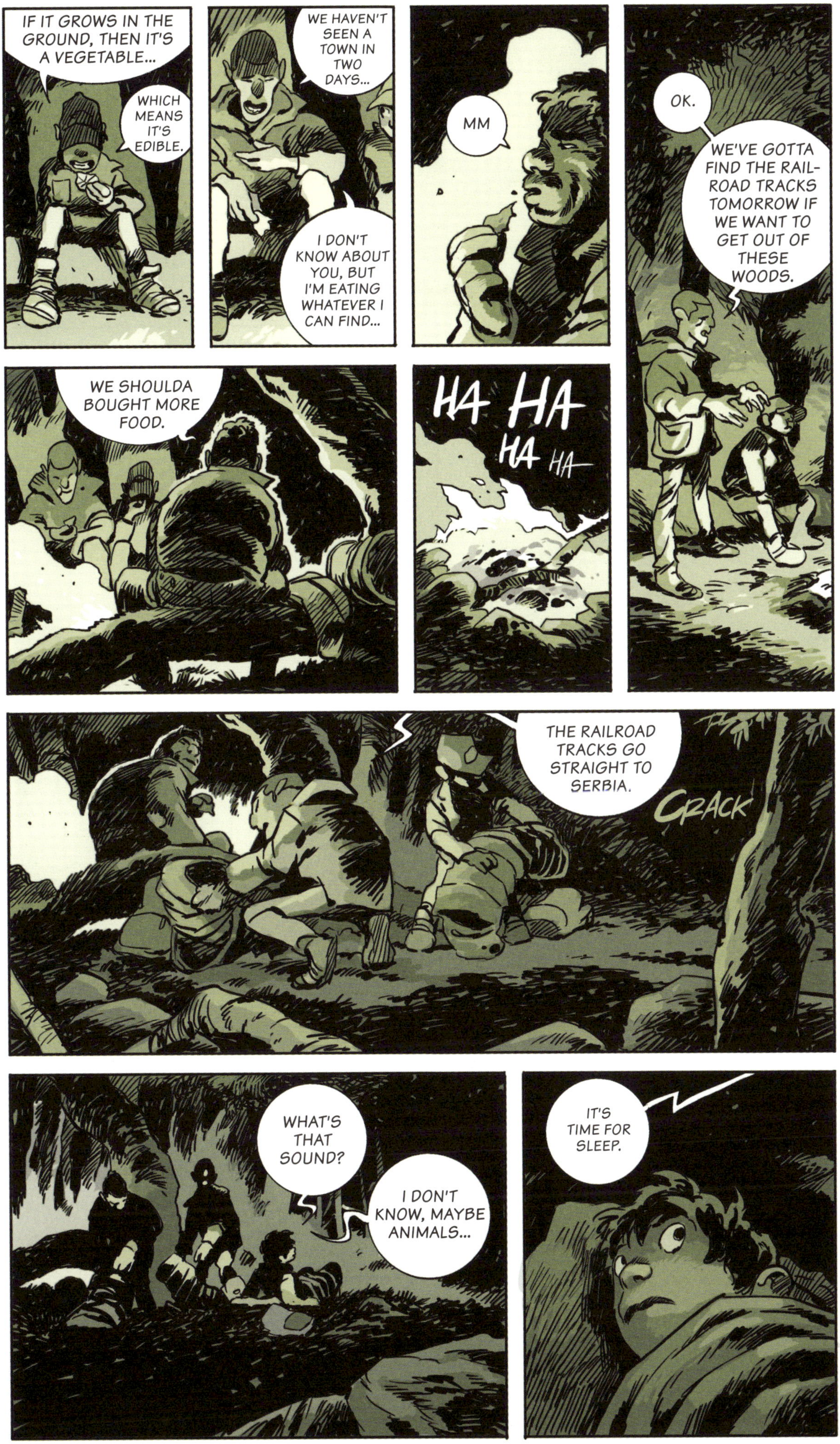
IF IT GROWS IN THE GROUND, THEN IT'S A VEGETABLE...
WHICH MEANS IT'S EDIBLE.
WE HAVEN'T SEEN A TOWN IN TWO DAYS...
I DON'T KNOW ABOUT YOU, BUT I'M EATING WHATEVER I CAN FIND...
MM
OK.
WE'VE GOTTA FIND THE RAIL-ROAD TRACKS TOMORROW IF WE WANT TO GET OUT OF THESE WOODS.
WE SHOULDA BOUGHT MORE FOOD.
HA HA HA HA
THE RAILROAD TRACKS GO STRAIGHT TO SERBIA.
CRACK
WHAT'S THAT SOUND?
I DON'T KNOW, MAYBE ANIMALS...
IT'S TIME FOR SLEEP.

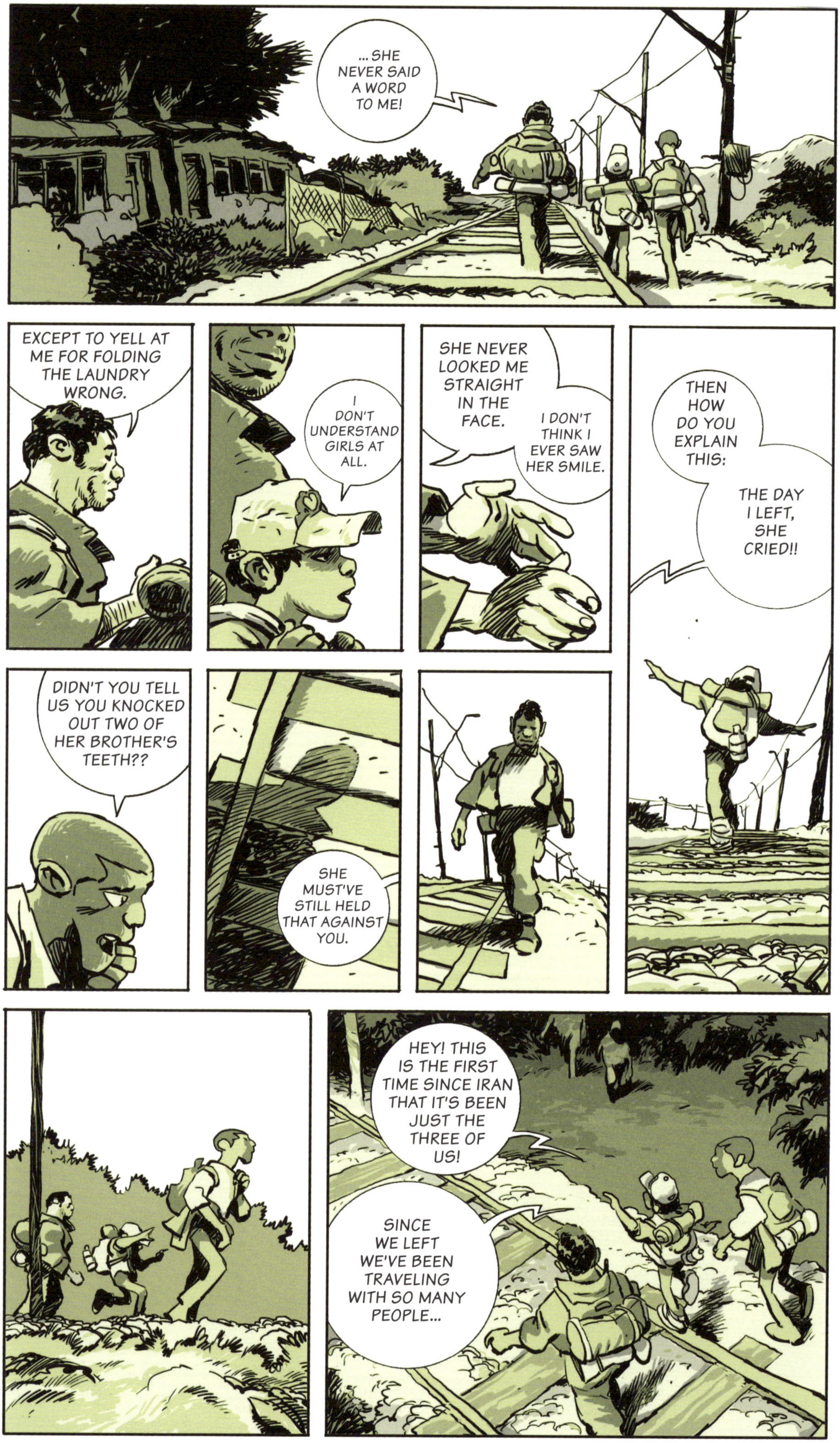
...SHE NEVER SAID A WORD TO ME!
EXCEPT TO YELL AT ME FOR FOLDING THE LAUNDRY WRONG.
I DON'T UNDERSTAND GIRLS AT ALL.
SHE NEVER LOOKED ME STRAIGHT IN THE FACE.
I DON'T THINK I EVER SAW HER SMILE.
THEN HOW DO YOU EXPLAIN THIS:
THE DAY I LEFT, SHE CRIED!!
DIDN'T YOU TELL US YOU KNOCKED OUT TWO OF HER BROTHER'S TEETH??
SHE MUST'VE STILL HELD THAT AGAINST YOU.
HEY! THIS IS THE FIRST TIME SINCE IRAN THAT IT'S BEEN JUST THE THREE OF US!
SINCE WE LEFT WE'VE BEEN TRAVELING WITH SO MANY PEOPLE...

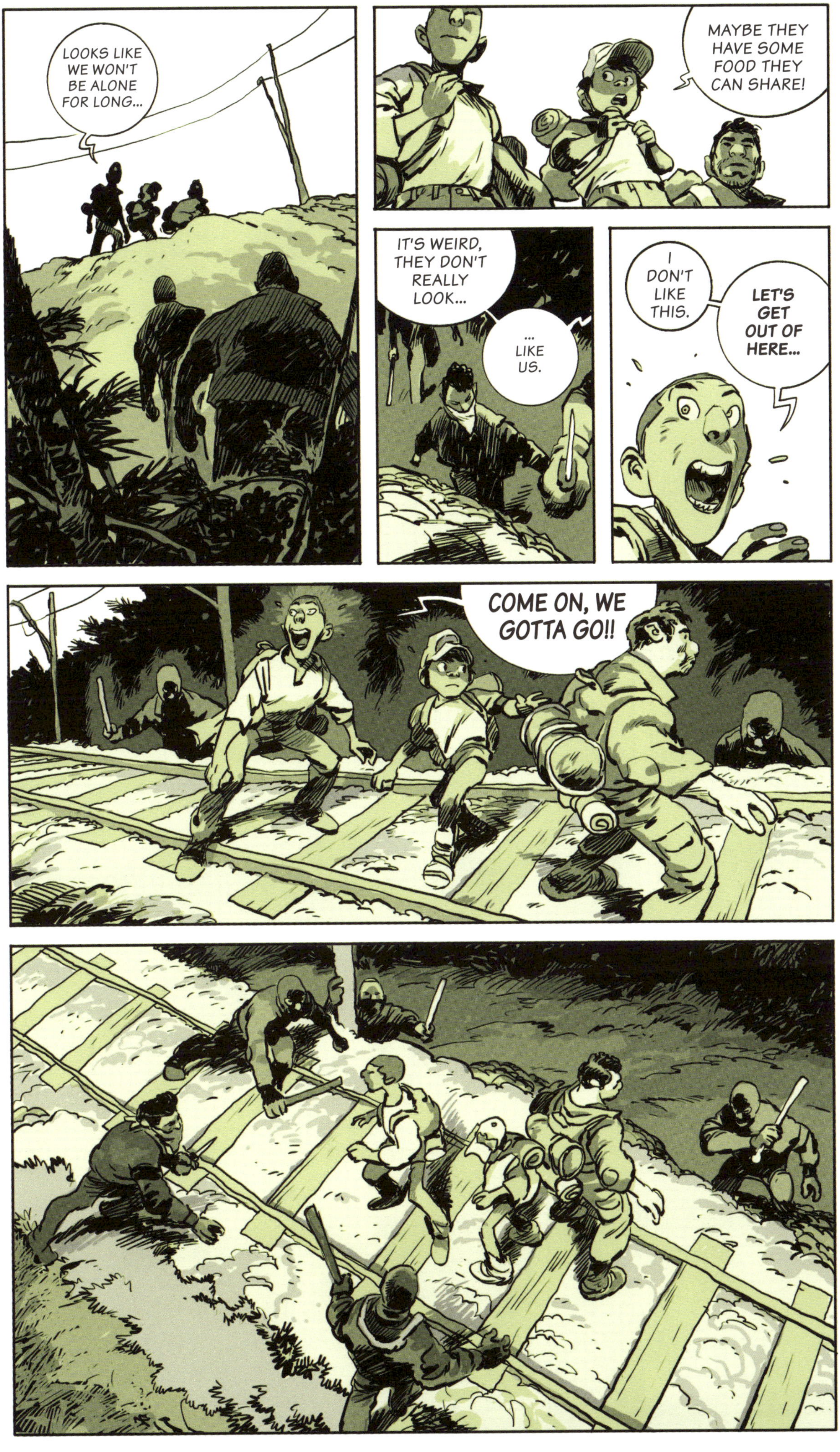
LOOKS LIKE WE WON'T BE ALONE FOR LONG...
MAYBE THEY HAVE SOME FOOD THEY CAN SHARE!
IT'S WEIRD, THEY DON'T REALLY LOOK...
... LIKE US.
I DON'T LIKE THIS.
LET'S GET OUT OF HERE...
COME ON, WE GOTTA GO!!

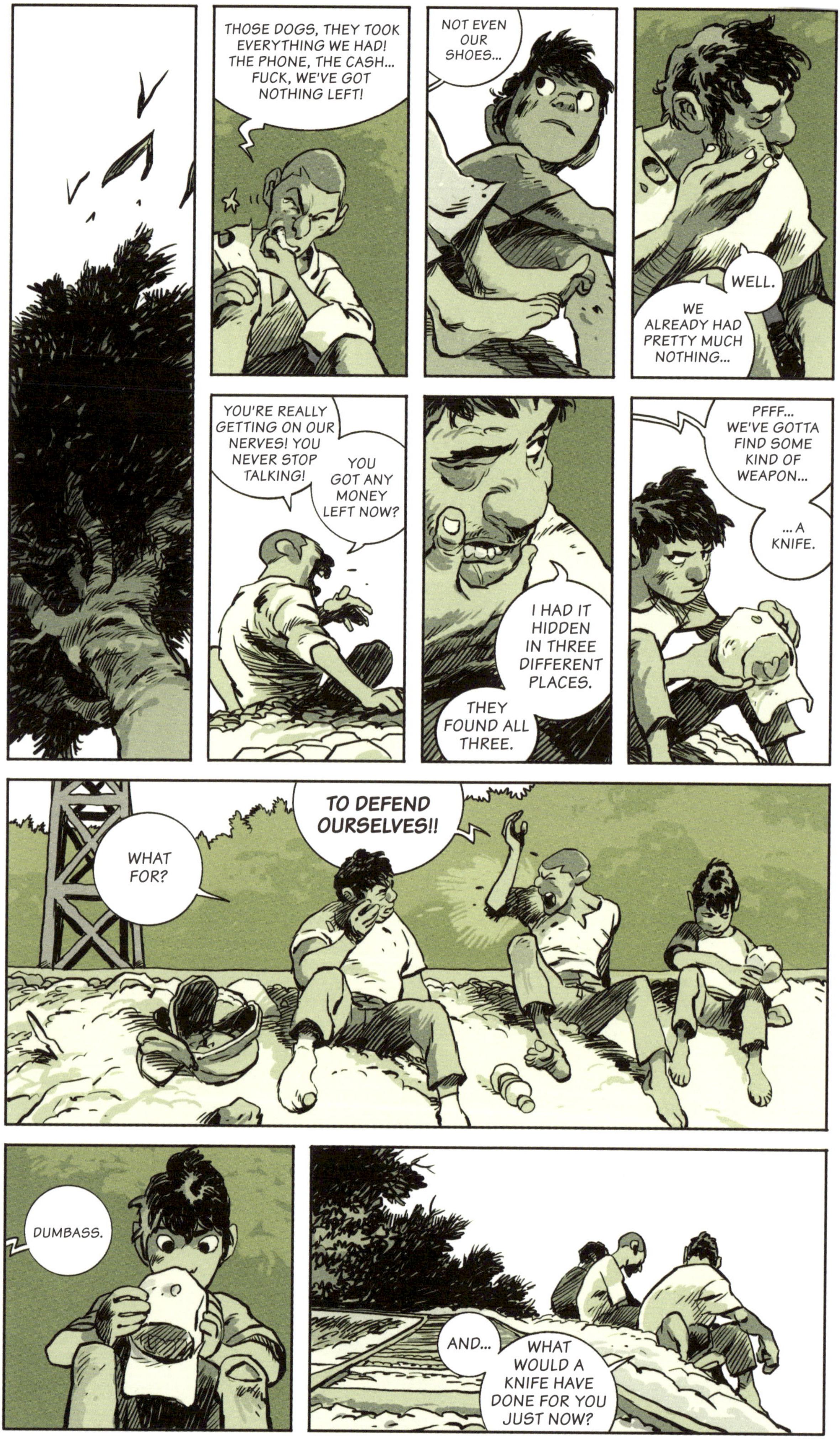
THOSE DOGS, THEY TOOK EVERYTHING WE HAD! THE PHONE, THE CASH... FUCK, WE'VE GOT NOTHING LEFT!
NOT EVEN OUR SHOES...
WELL.
WE ALREADY HAD PRETTY MUCH NOTHING...
YOU'RE REALLY GETTING ON OUR NERVES! YOU NEVER STOP TALKING!
YOU GOT ANY MONEY LEFT NOW?
I HAD IT HIDDEN IN THREE DIFFERENT PLACES.
THEY FOUND ALL THREE.
PFFF... WE'VE GOTTA FIND SOME KIND OF WEAPON...
... A KNIFE.
WHAT FOR?
TO DEFEND OURSELVES!!
DUMBASS.
AND...
WHAT WOULD A KNIFE HAVE DONE FOR YOU JUST NOW?

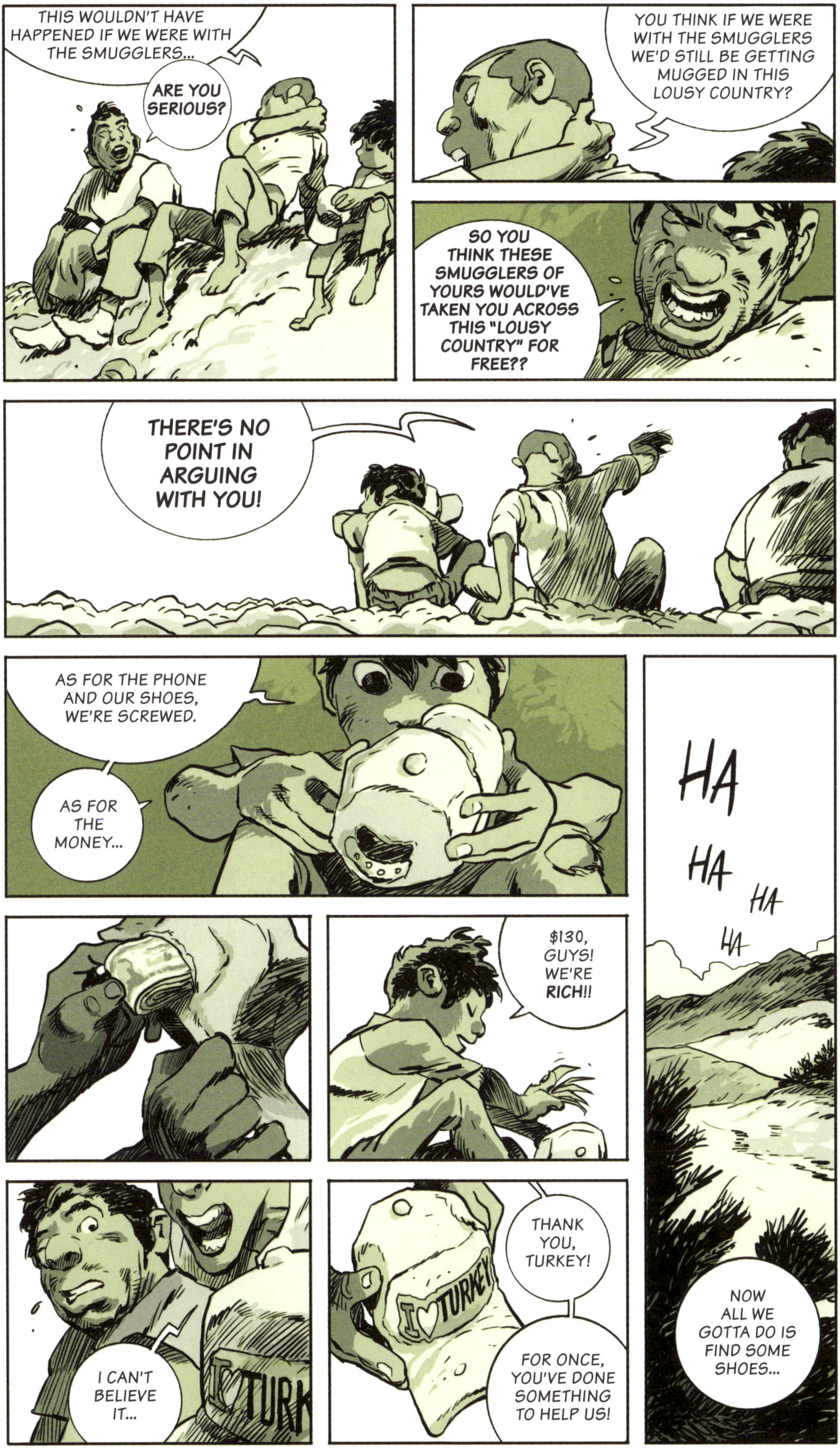
THIS WOULDN'T HAVE HAPPENED IF WE WERE WITH THE SMUGGLERS...
ARE YOU SERIOUS?
YOU THINK IF WE WERE WITH THE SMUGGLERS WE'D STILL BE GETTING MUGGED IN THIS LOUSY COUNTRY?
SO YOU THINK THESE SMUGGLERS OF YOURS WOULD'VE TAKEN YOU ACROSS THIS "LOUSY COUNTRY" FOR FREE??
THERE'S NO POINT IN ARGUING WITH YOU!
AS FOR THE PHONE AND OUR SHOES, WE'RE SCREWED.
AS FOR THE MONEY...
$130, GUYS! WE'RE RICH!!
HA
HA
HA
HA
I CAN'T BELIEVE IT...
I ♥ TURK
I ♥ TURKEY
THANK YOU, TURKEY!
FOR ONCE, YOU'VE DONE SOMETHING TO HELP US!
NOW ALL WE GOTTA DO IS FIND SOME SHOES...

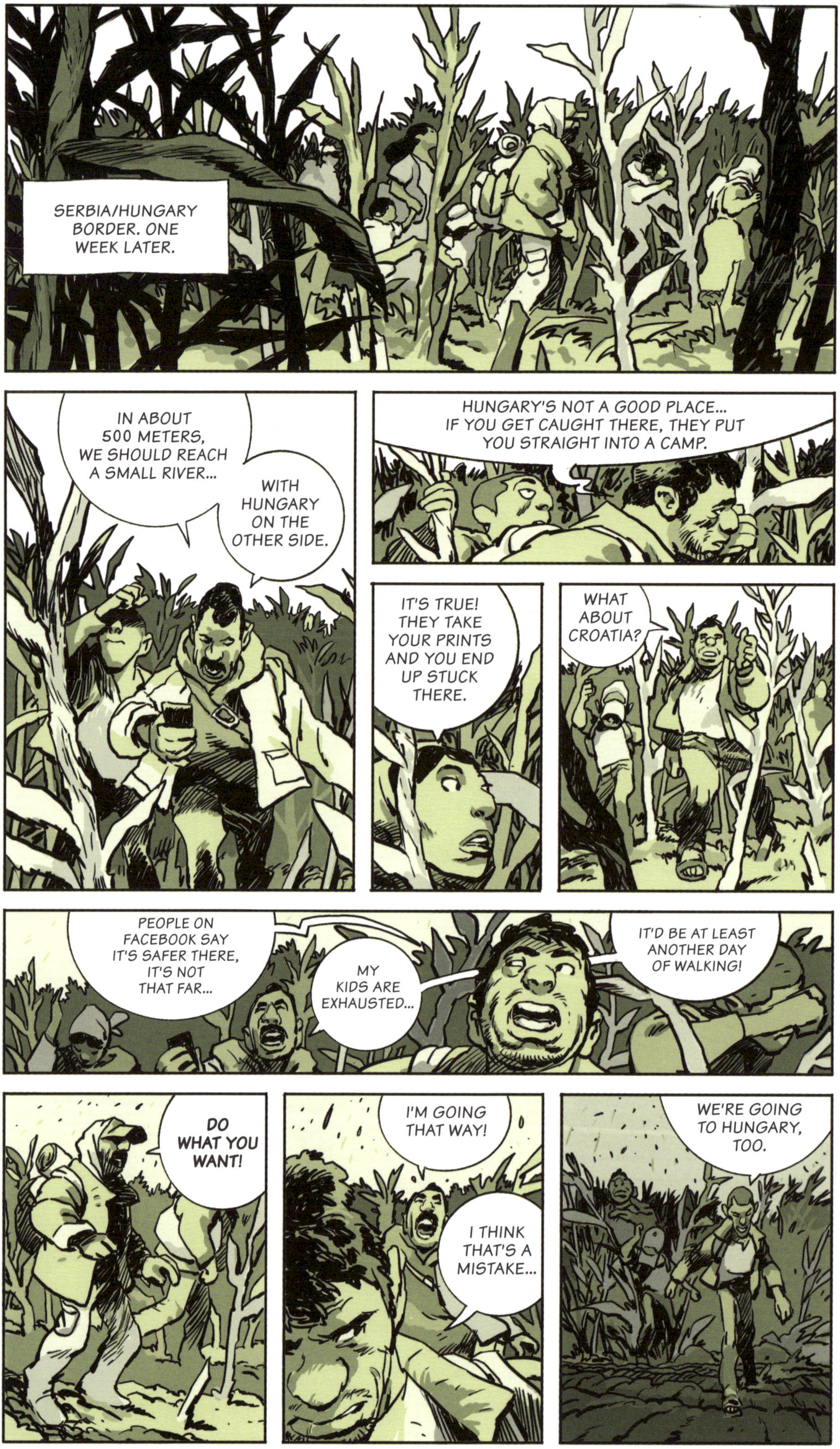
SERBIA/HUNGARY BORDER. ONE WEEK LATER.
IN ABOUT 500 METERS, WE SHOULD REACH A SMALL RIVER...
WITH HUNGARY ON THE OTHER SIDE.
HUNGARY'S NOT A GOOD PLACE... IF YOU GET CAUGHT THERE, THEY PUT YOU STRAIGHT INTO A CAMP.
IT'S TRUE! THEY TAKE YOUR PRINTS AND YOU END UP STUCK THERE.
WHAT ABOUT CROATIA?
PEOPLE ON FACEBOOK SAY IT'S SAFER THERE, IT'S NOT THAT FAR...
MY KIDS ARE EXHAUSTED...
IT'D BE AT LEAST ANOTHER DAY OF WALKING!
DO WHAT YOU WANT!
I'M GOING THAT WAY!
I THINK THAT'S A MISTAKE...
WE'RE GOING TO HUNGARY, TOO.

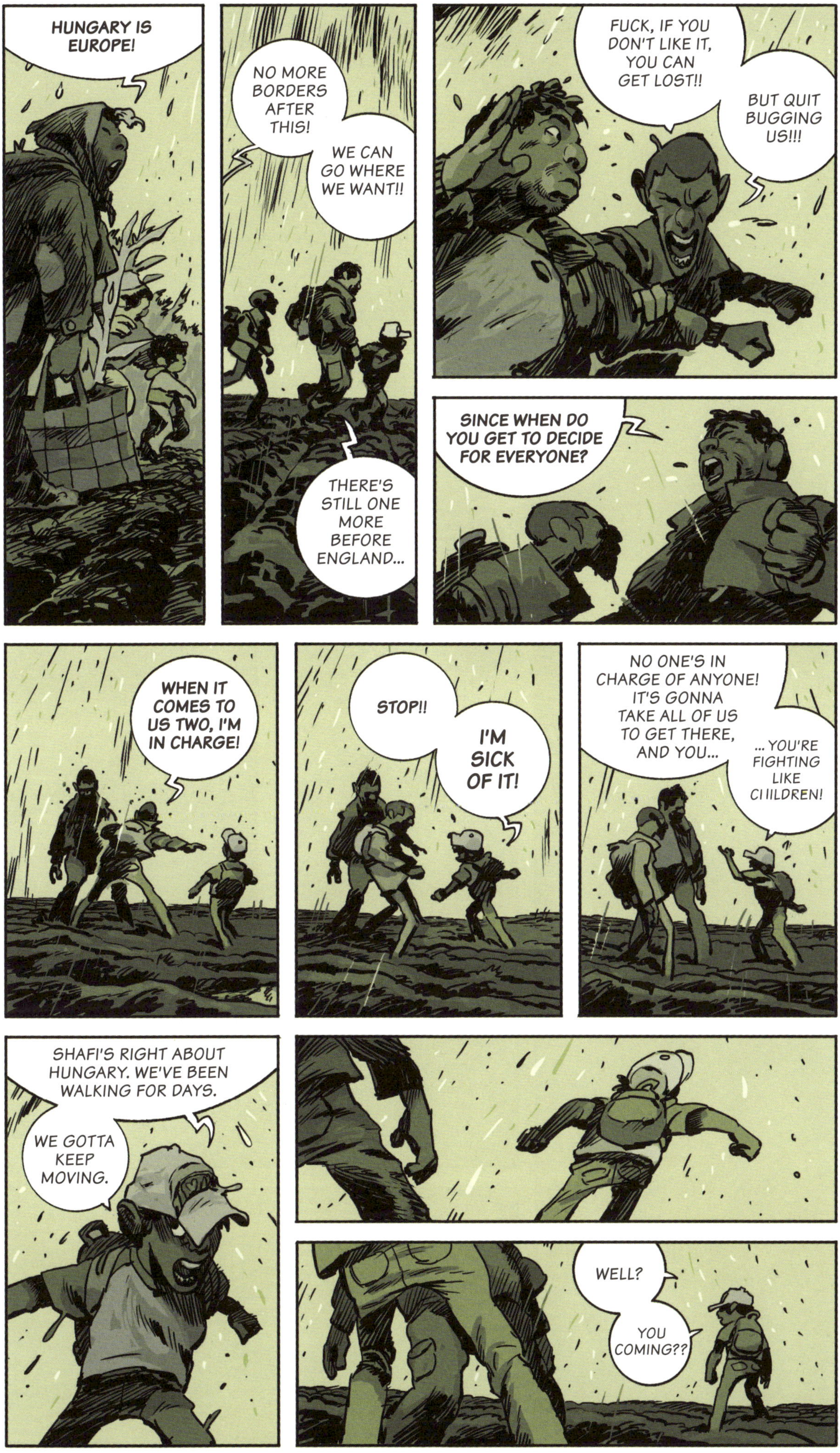
HUNGARY IS EUROPE!
NO MORE BORDERS AFTER THIS!
WE CAN GO WHERE WE WANT!!
THERE'S STILL ONE MORE BEFORE ENGLAND...
FUCK, IF YOU DON'T LIKE IT, YOU CAN GET LOST!!
BUT QUIT BUGGING US!!!
SINCE WHEN DO YOU GET TO DECIDE FOR EVERYONE?
WHEN IT COMES TO US TWO, I'M IN CHARGE!
STOP!!
I'M SICK OF IT!
NO ONE'S IN CHARGE OF ANYONE! IT'S GONNA TAKE ALL OF US TO GET THERE, AND YOU...
...YOU'RE FIGHTING LIKE CHILDREN!
SHAFI'S RIGHT ABOUT HUNGARY. WE'VE BEEN WALKING FOR DAYS.
WE GOTTA KEEP MOVING.
WELL?
YOU COMING??

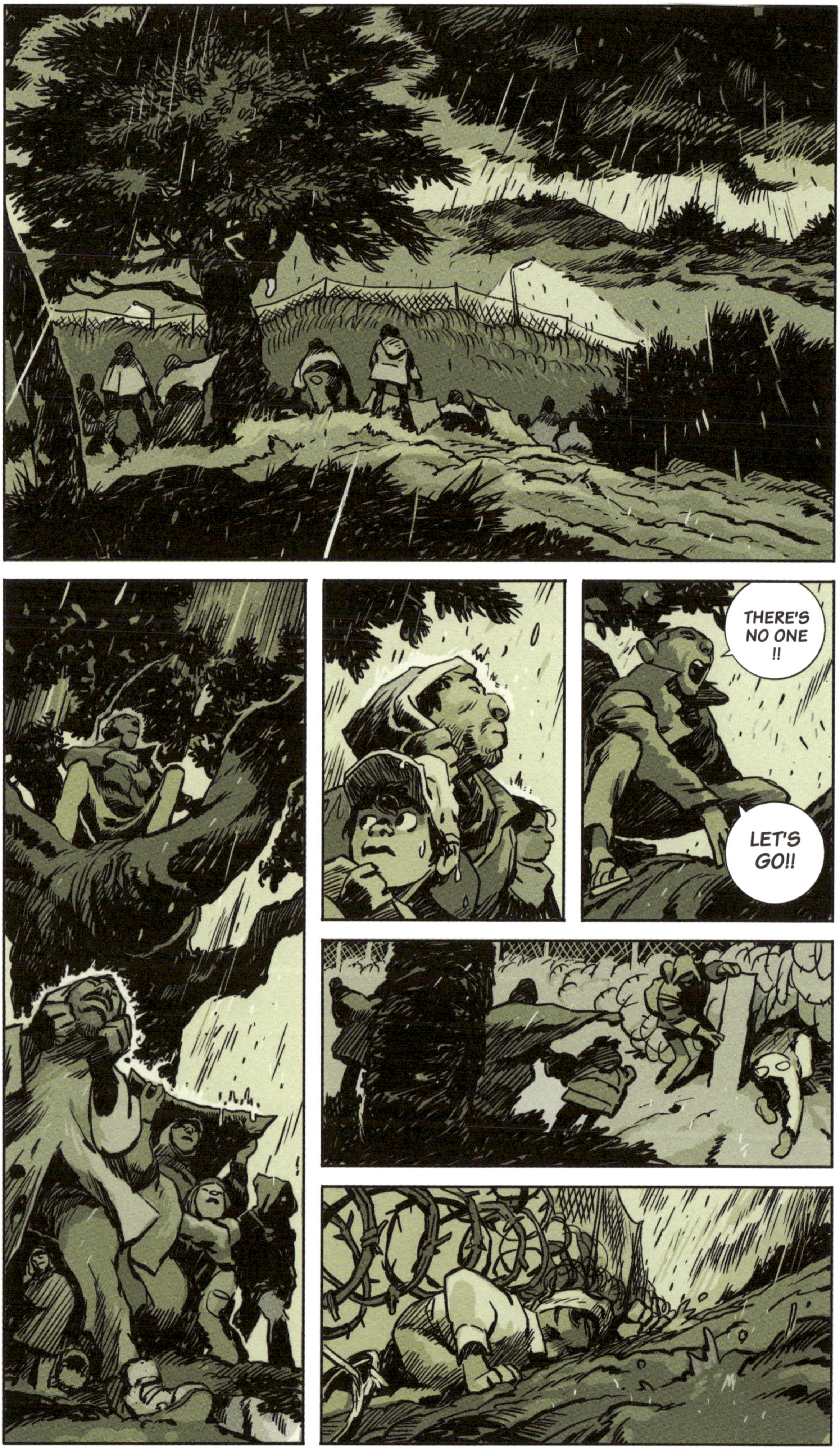
THERE'S NO ONE !!
LET'S GO!!

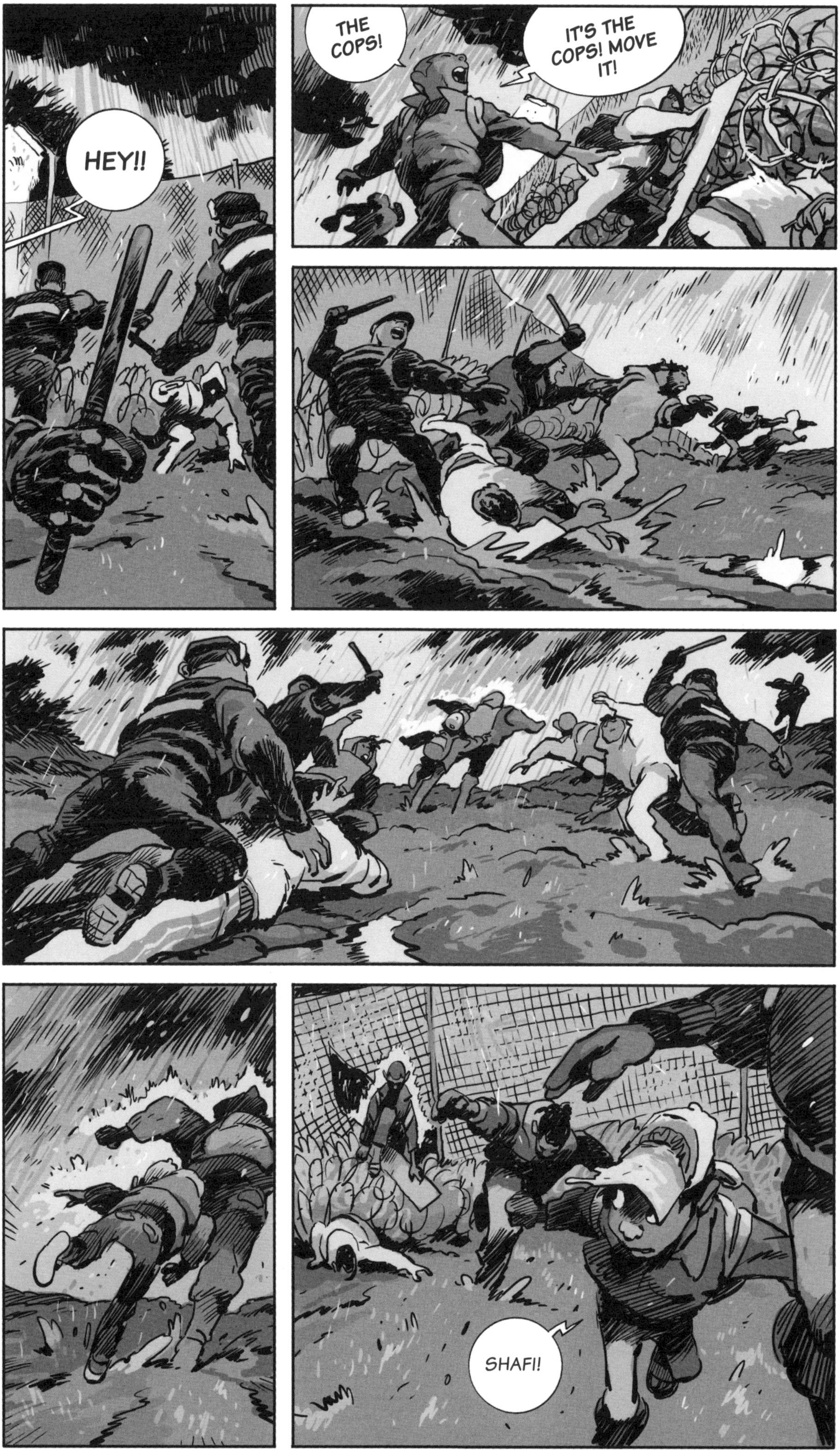
HEY!!
THE COPS!
IT'S THE COPS! MOVE IT!
SHAFI!

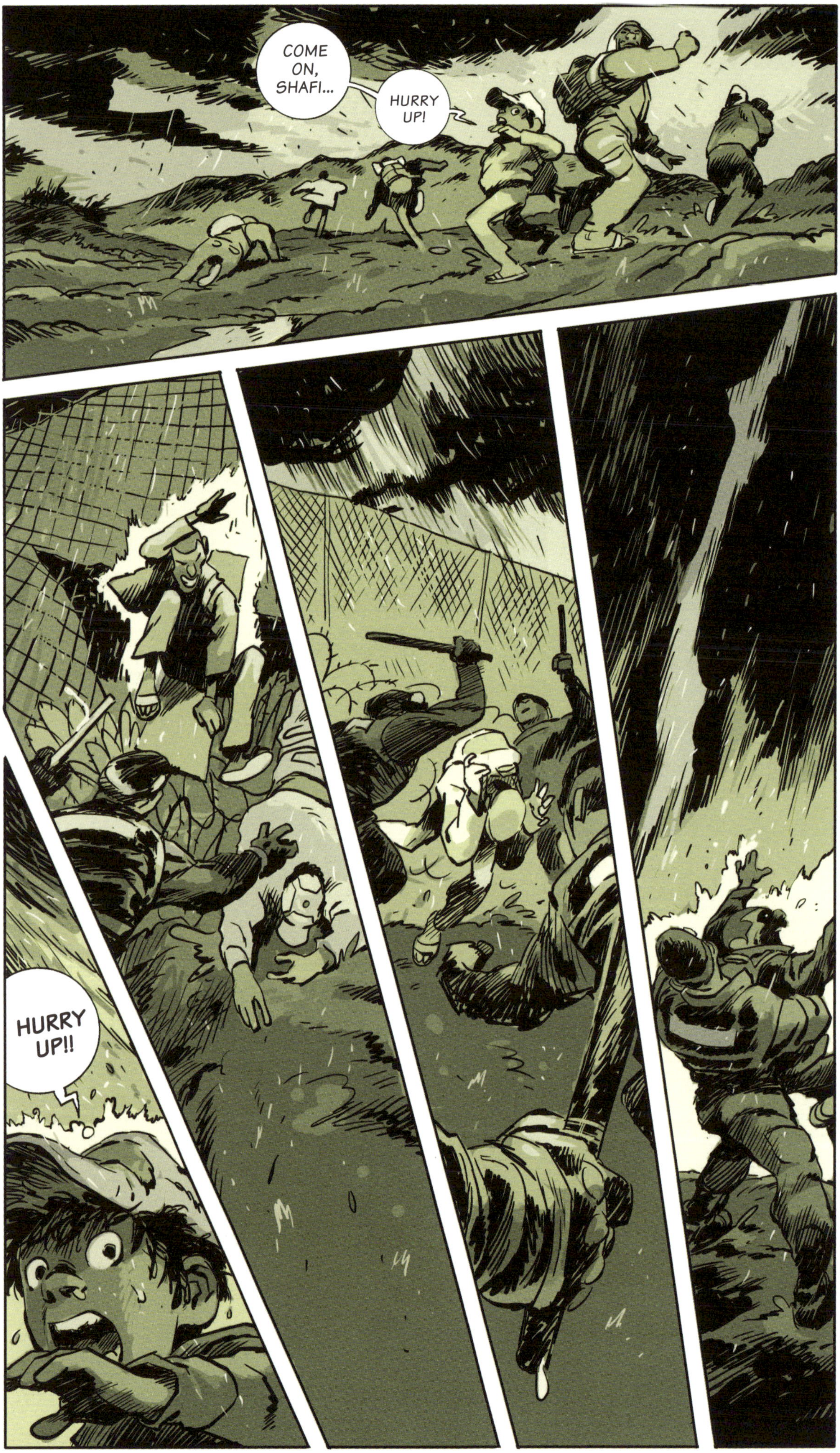
COME ON, SHAFI...
HURRY UP!
HURRY UP!!

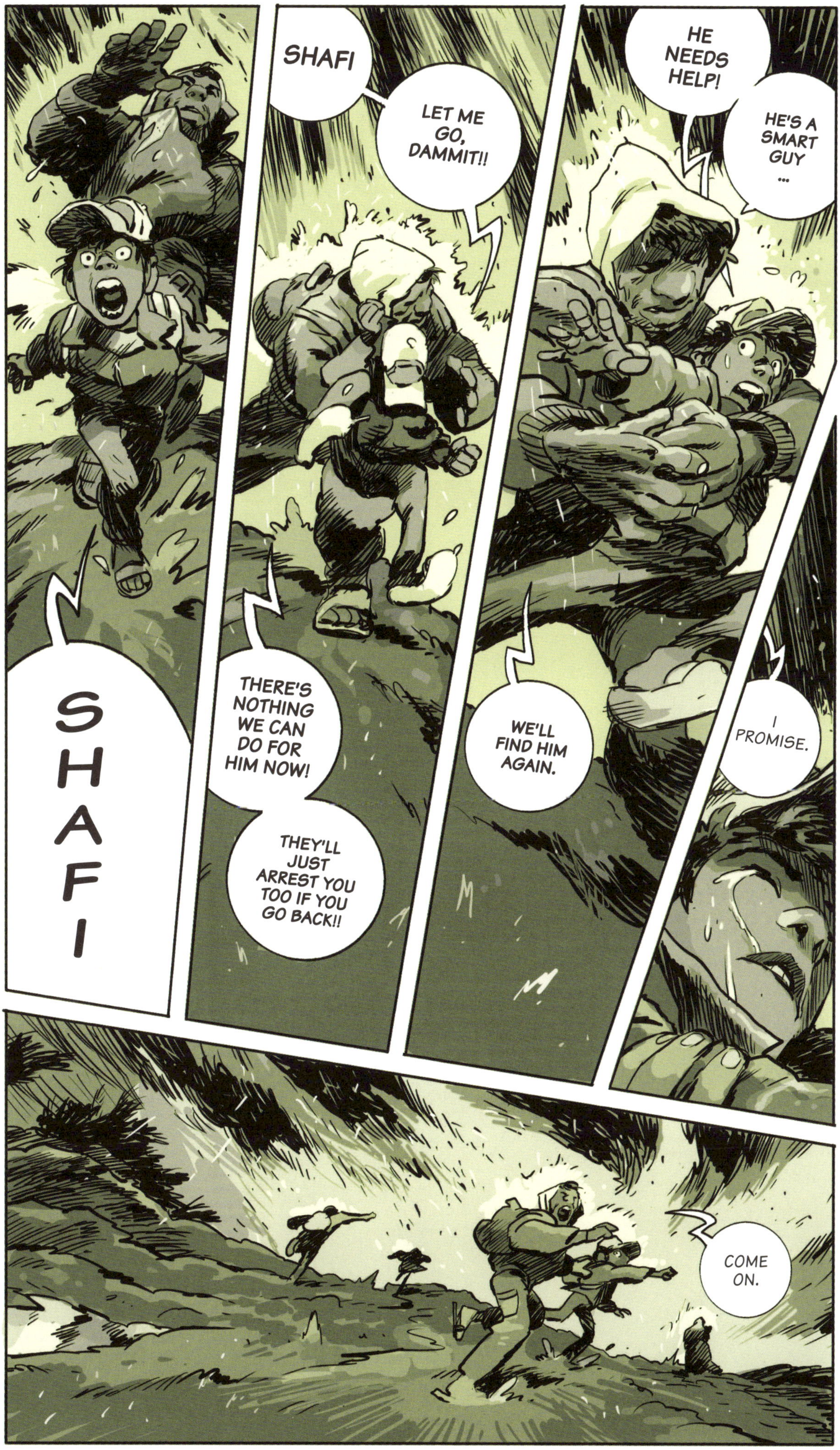
SHAFI
SHAFI
LET ME GO, DAMMIT!!
THERE'S NOTHING WE CAN DO FOR HIM NOW!
THEY'LL JUST ARREST YOU TOO IF YOU GO BACK!!
HE NEEDS HELP!
HE'S A SMART GUY ...
WE'LL FIND HIM AGAIN.
I PROMISE.
COME ON.

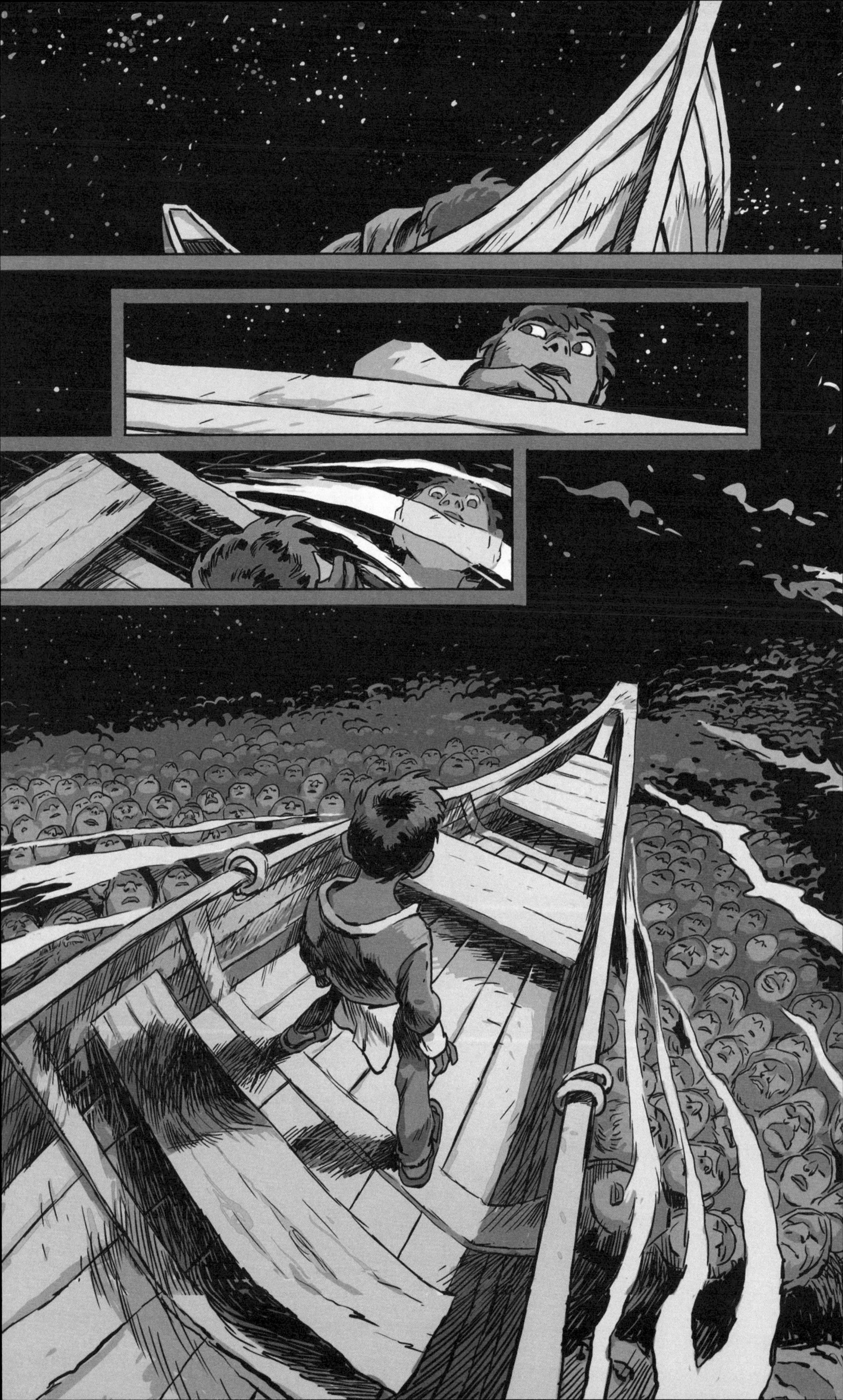

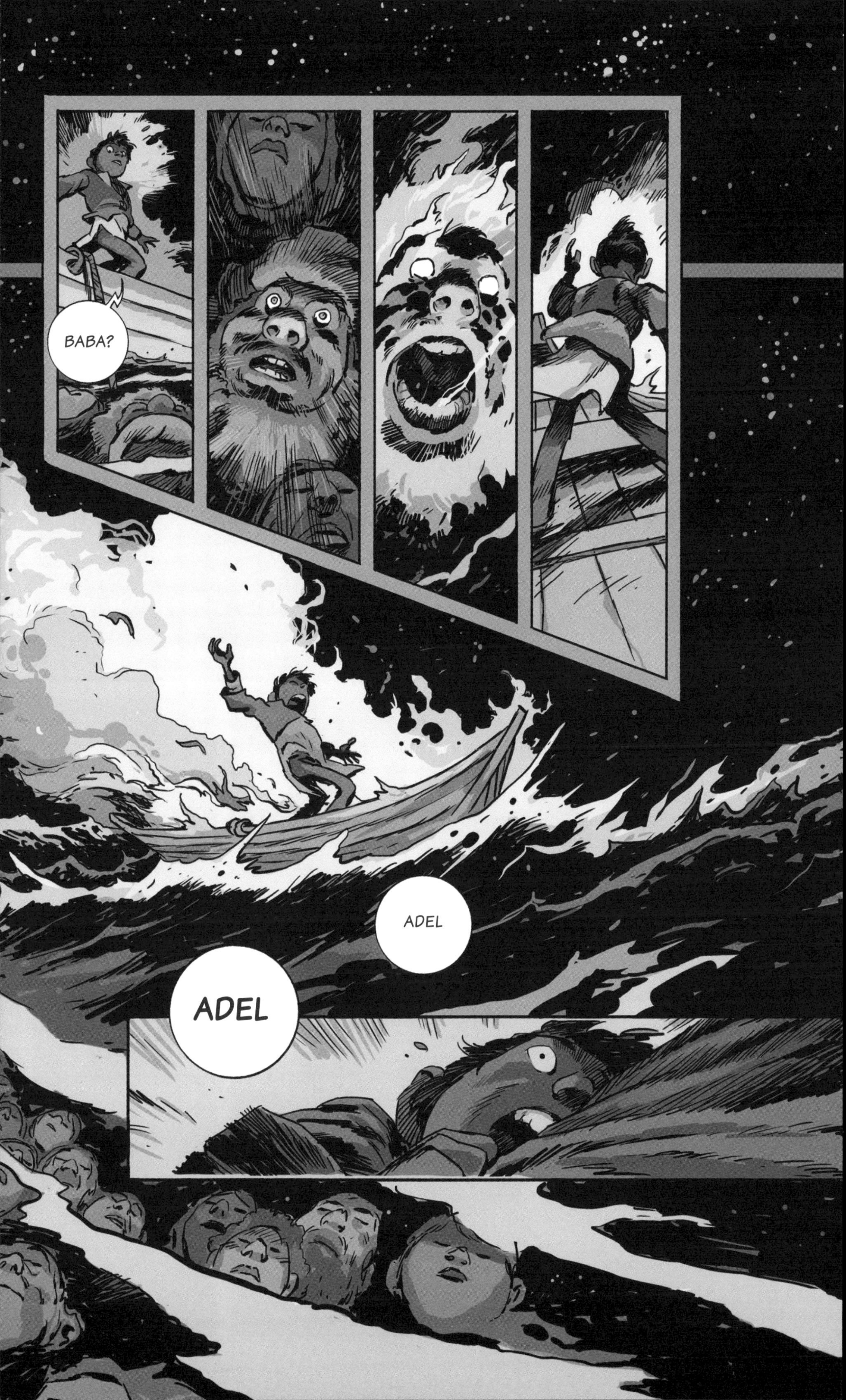
BABA?
ADEL
ADEL

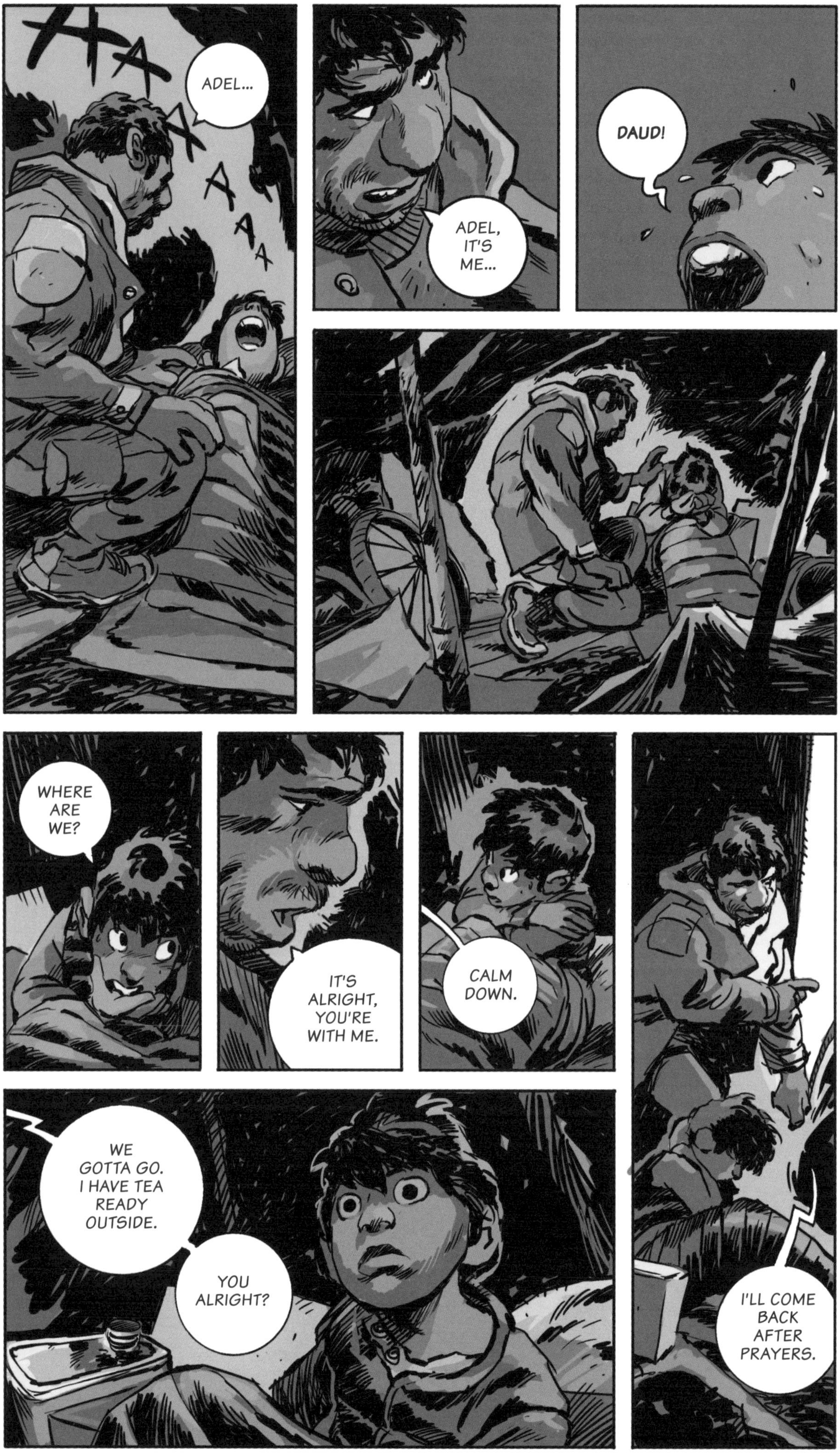
AAAAAAA
ADEL...
ADEL, IT'S ME...
DAUD!
WHERE ARE WE?
IT'S ALRIGHT, YOU'RE WITH ME.
CALM DOWN.
I'LL COME BACK AFTER PRAYERS.
WE GOTTA GO. I HAVE TEA READY OUTSIDE.
YOU ALRIGHT?

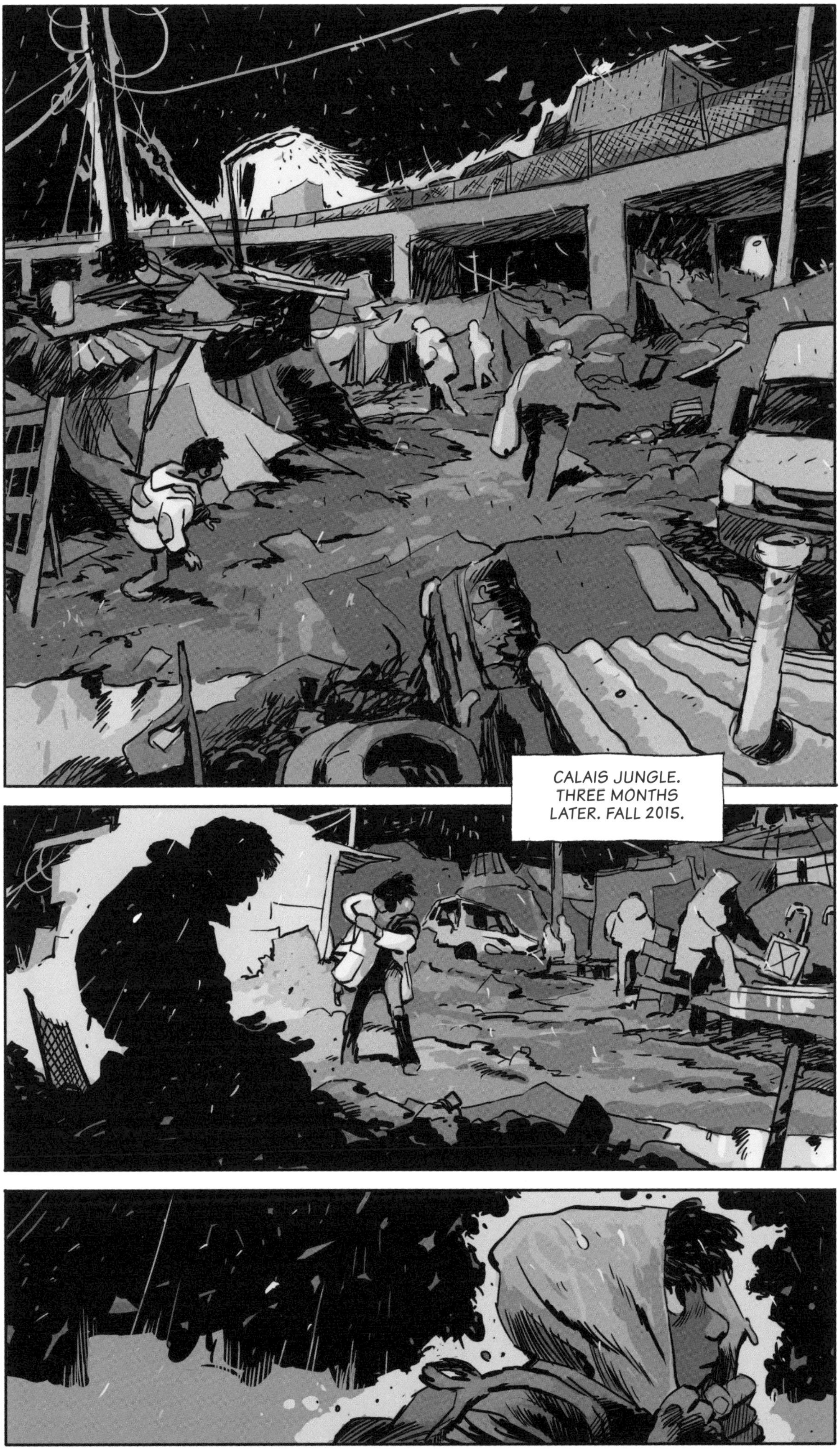
CALAIS JUNGLE.
THREE MONTHS
LATER. FALL 2015.

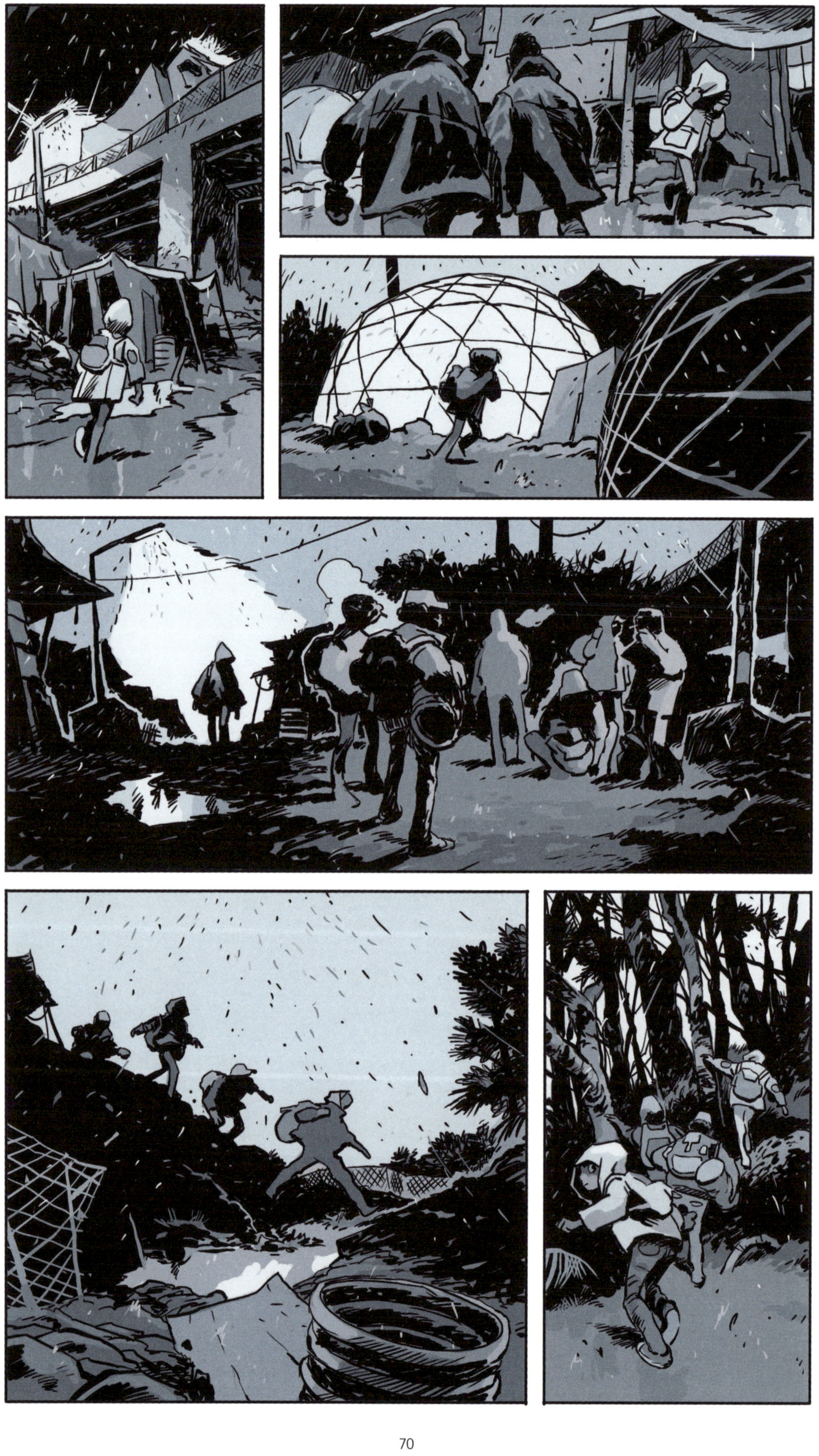

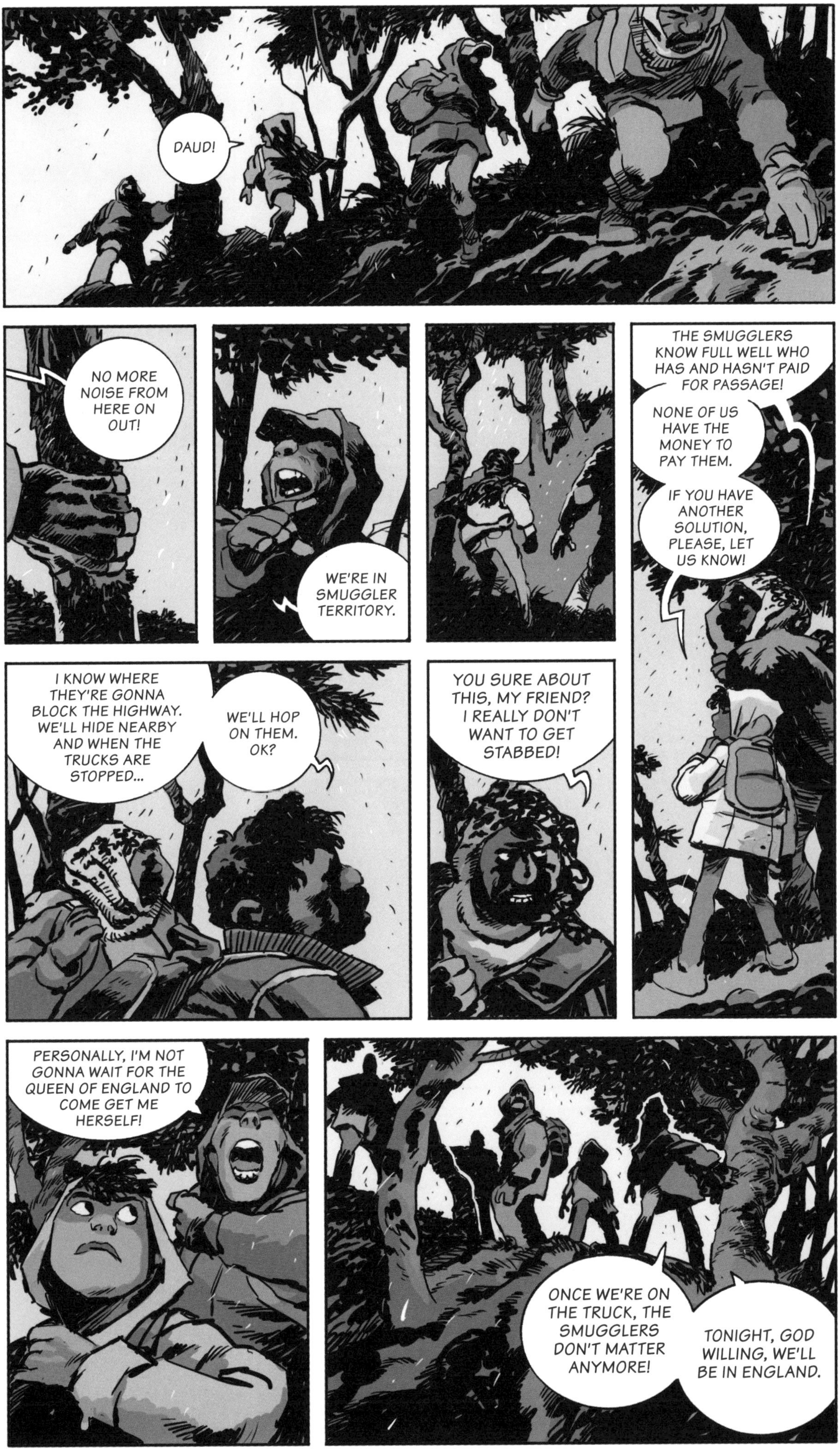
DAUD!
NO MORE NOISE FROM HERE ON OUT!
WE'RE IN SMUGGLER TERRITORY.
THE SMUGGLERS KNOW FULL WELL WHO HAS AND HASN'T PAID FOR PASSAGE!
NONE OF US HAVE THE MONEY TO PAY THEM.
IF YOU HAVE ANOTHER SOLUTION, PLEASE, LET US KNOW!
I KNOW WHERE THEY'RE GONNA BLOCK THE HIGHWAY. WE'LL HIDE NEARBY AND WHEN THE TRUCKS ARE STOPPED...
WE'LL HOP ON THEM. OK?
YOU SURE ABOUT THIS, MY FRIEND? I REALLY DON'T WANT TO GET STABBED!
PERSONALLY, I'M NOT GONNA WAIT FOR THE QUEEN OF ENGLAND TO COME GET ME HERSELF!
ONCE WE'RE ON THE TRUCK, THE SMUGGLERS DON'T MATTER ANYMORE!
TONIGHT, GOD WILLING, WE'LL BE IN ENGLAND.

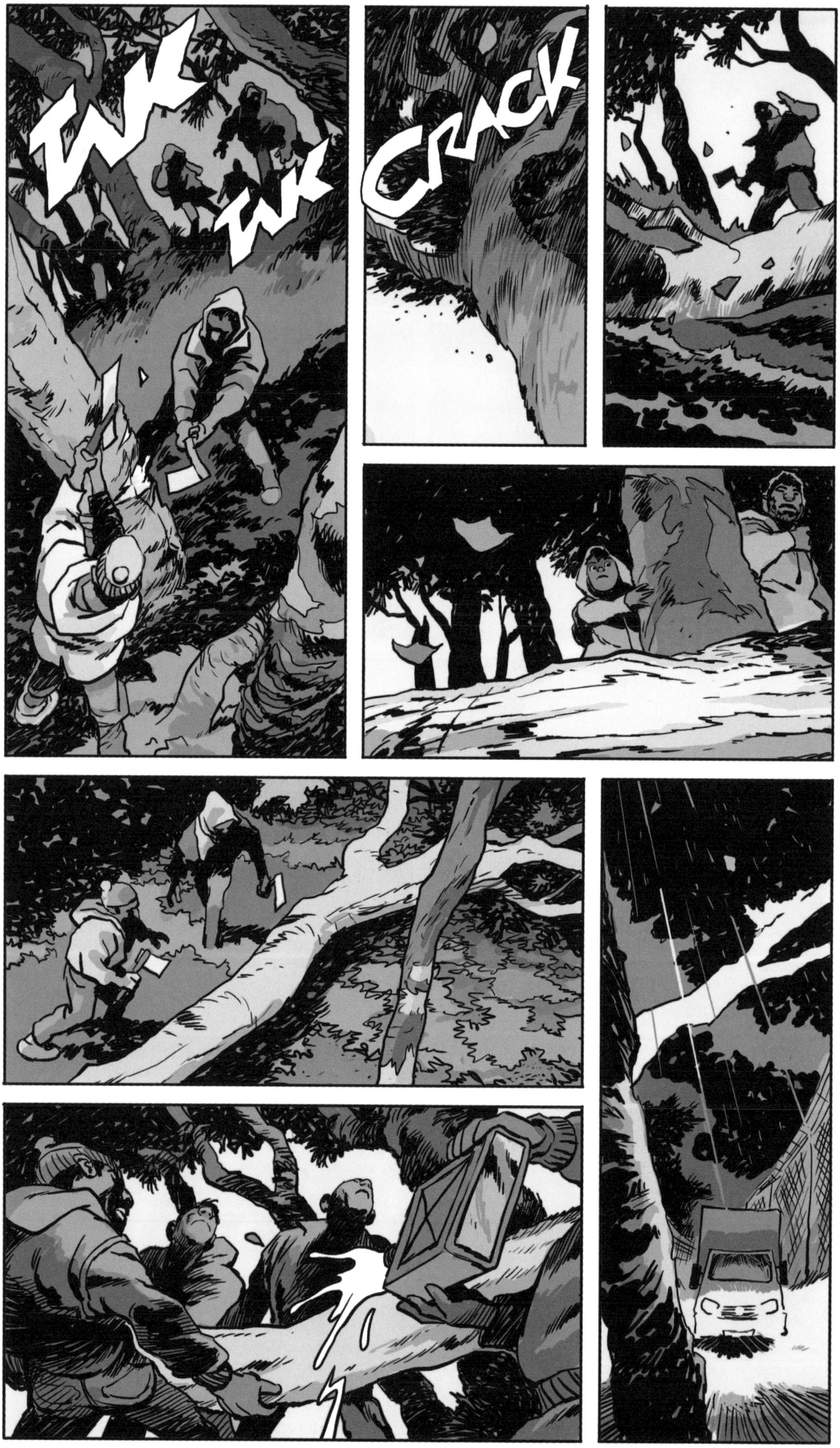
TAK
TAK
CRACK

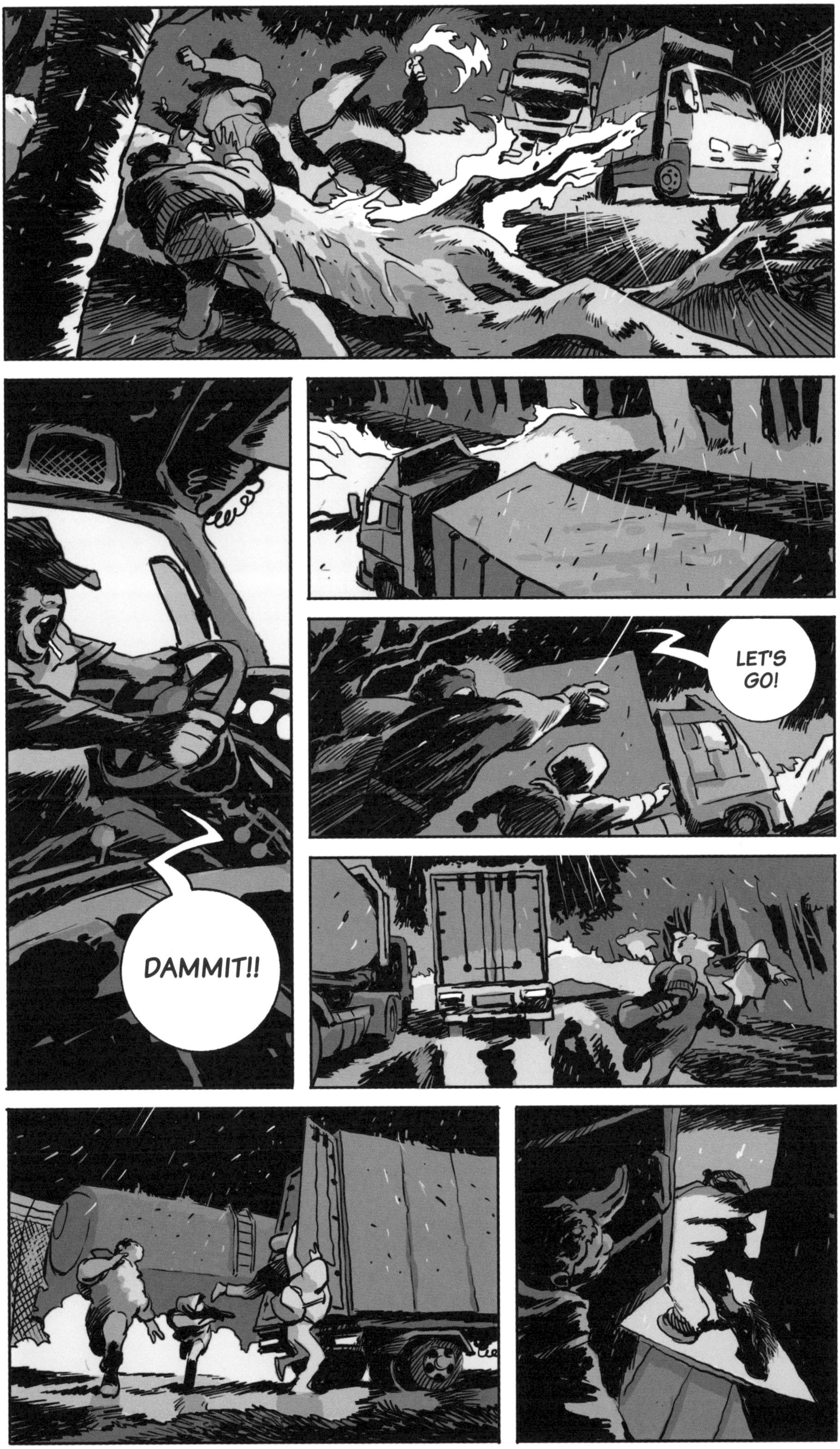
DAMMIT!!
LET'S GO!

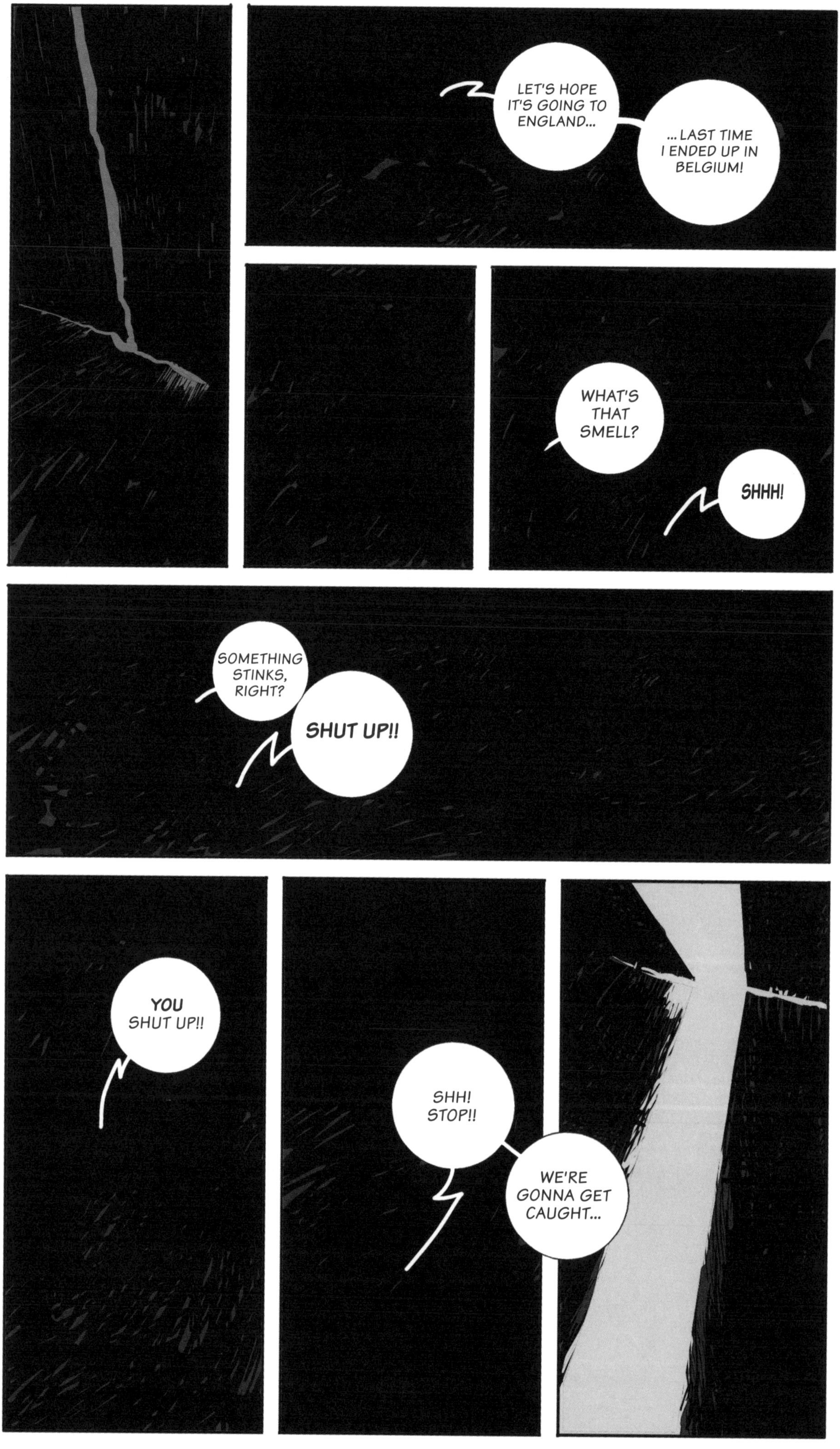

LET'S HOPE IT'S GOING TO ENGLAND...
...LAST TIME I ENDED UP IN BELGIUM!
WHAT'S THAT SMELL?
SHHH!
SOMETHING STINKS, RIGHT?
SHUT UP!!
YOU SHUT UP!!
SHH! STOP!!
WE'RE GONNA GET CAUGHT...

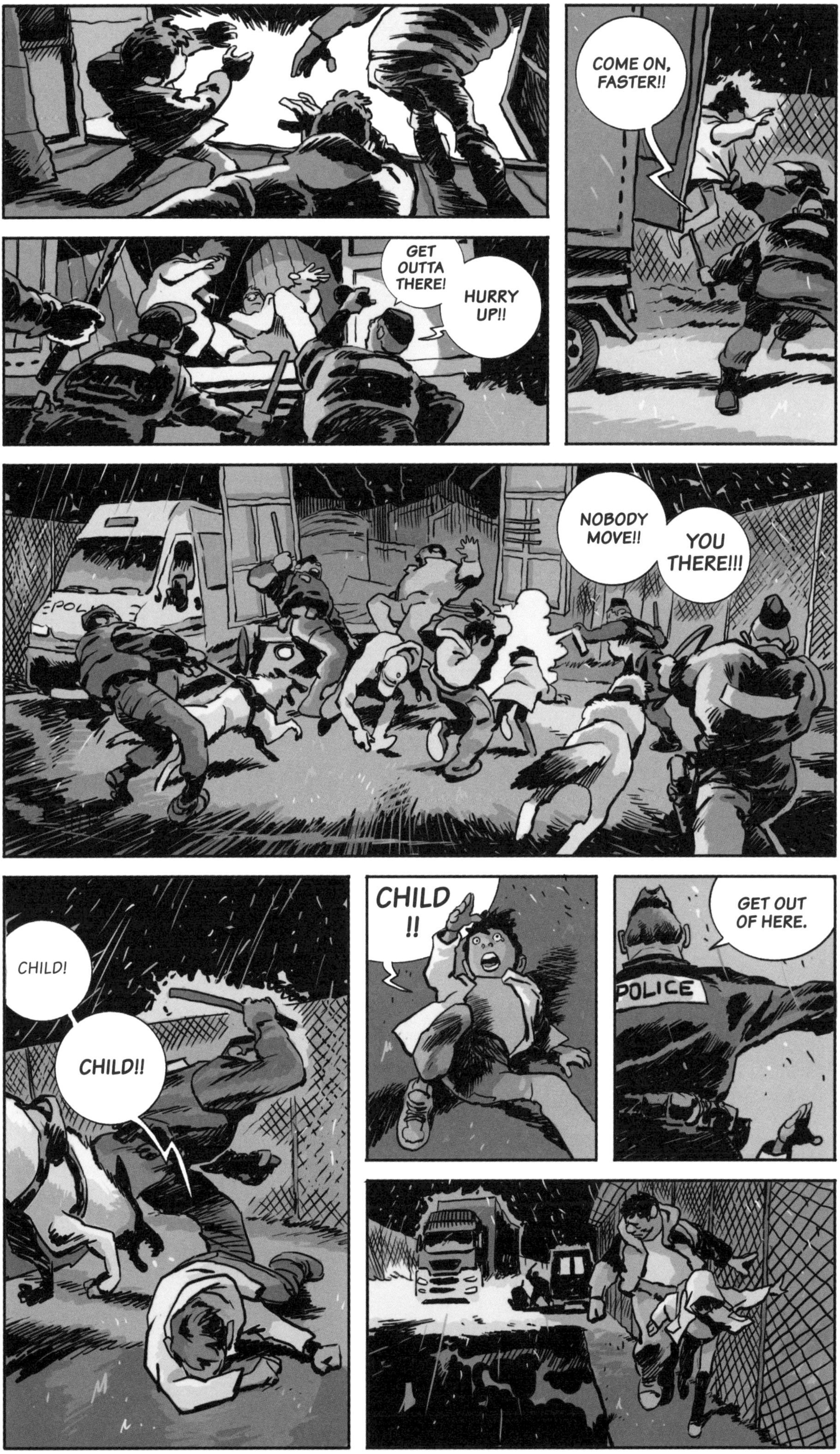
COME ON, FASTER!!
GET OUTTA THERE!
HURRY UP!!
NOBODY MOVE!!
YOU THERE!!!
POLI
CHILD!
CHILD!!
CHILD !!
GET OUT OF HERE.
POLICE

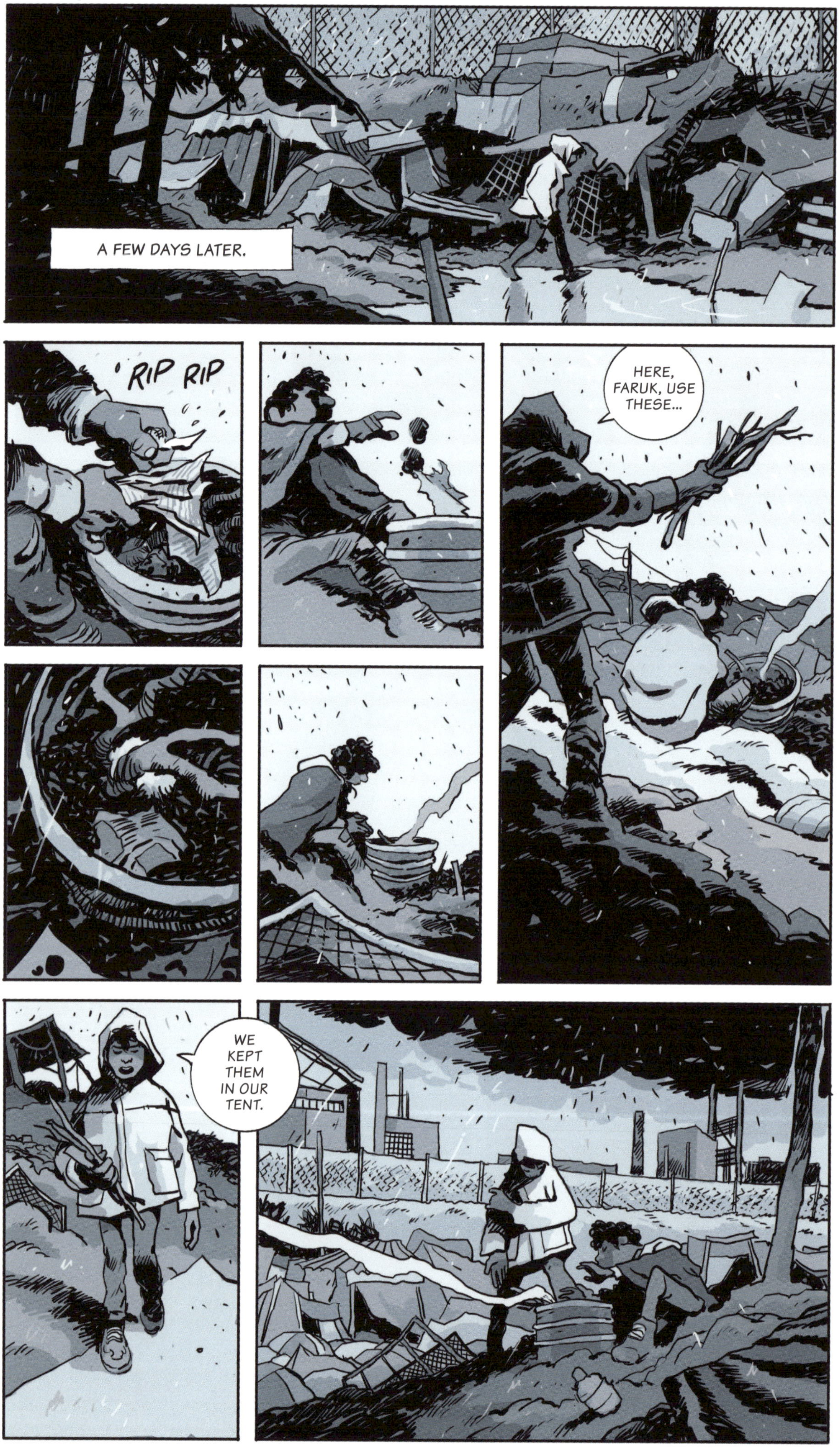
A FEW DAYS LATER.
RIP RIP
HERE, FARUK, USE THESE...
WE KEPT THEM IN OUR TENT.

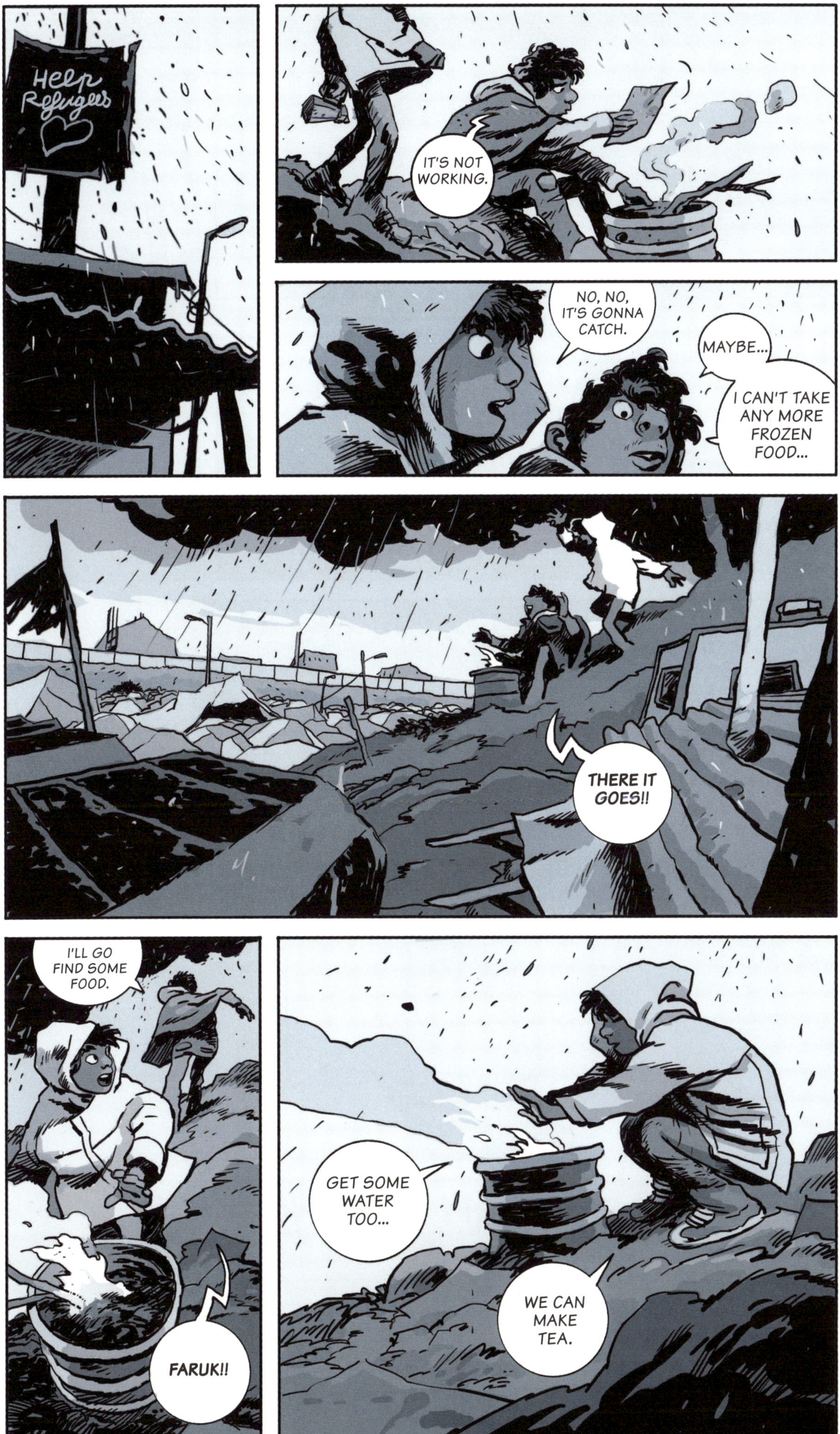
Help Refugees
IT'S NOT WORKING.
NO, NO, IT'S GONNA CATCH.
MAYBE...
I CAN'T TAKE ANY MORE FROZEN FOOD...
THERE IT GOES!!
I'LL GO FIND SOME FOOD.
FARUK!!
GET SOME WATER TOO...
WE CAN MAKE TEA.

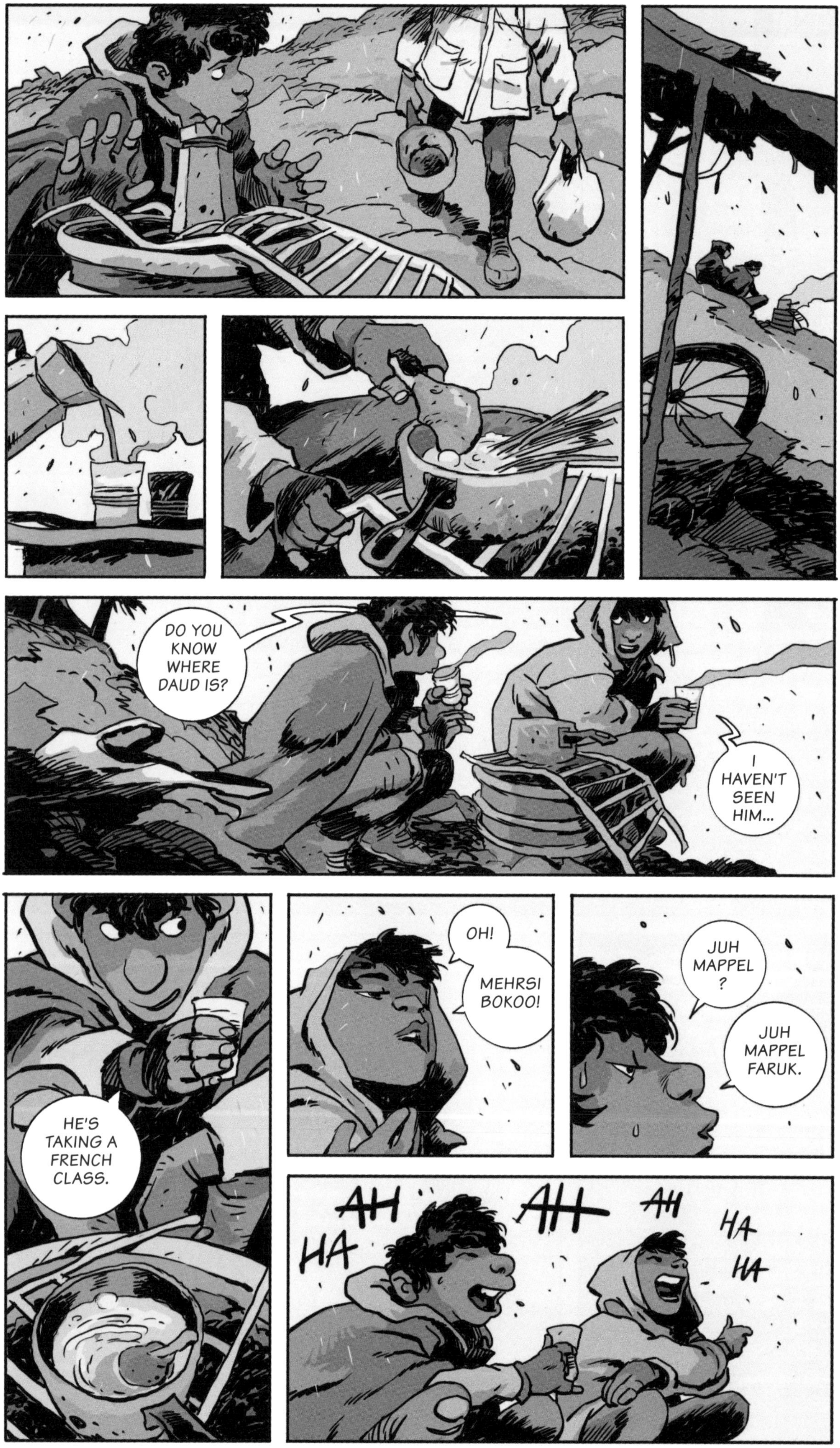
DO YOU KNOW WHERE DAUD IS?
I HAVEN'T SEEN HIM...
HE'S TAKING A FRENCH CLASS.
OH!
MEHRSI BOKOO!
JUH MAPPEL ?
JUH MAPPEL FARUK.
AH HA AH AH HA HA

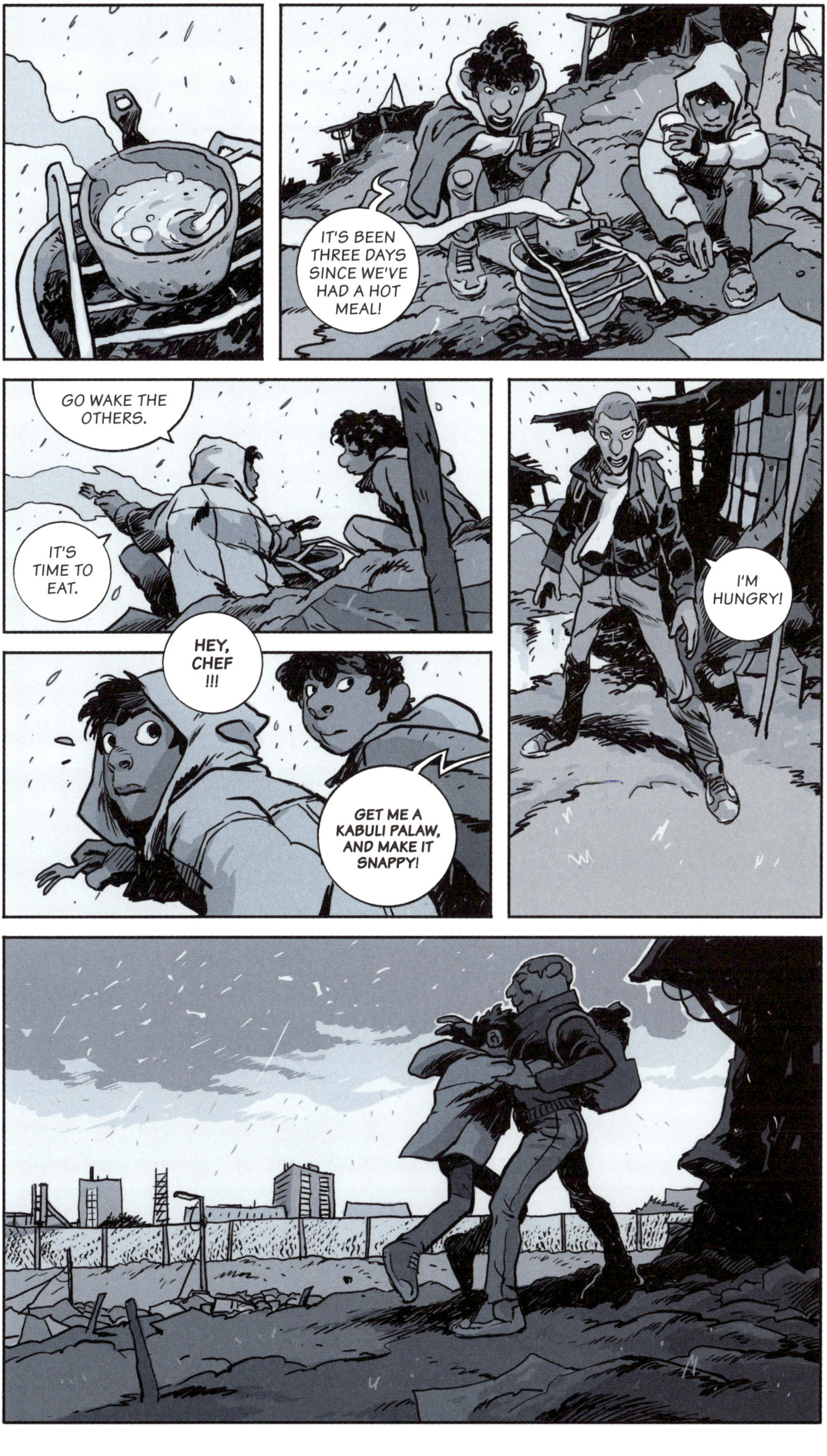
IT'S BEEN THREE DAYS SINCE WE'VE HAD A HOT MEAL!
GO WAKE THE OTHERS.
IT'S TIME TO EAT.
I'M HUNGRY!
HEY, CHEF !!!
GET ME A KABULI PALAW, AND MAKE IT SNAPPY!

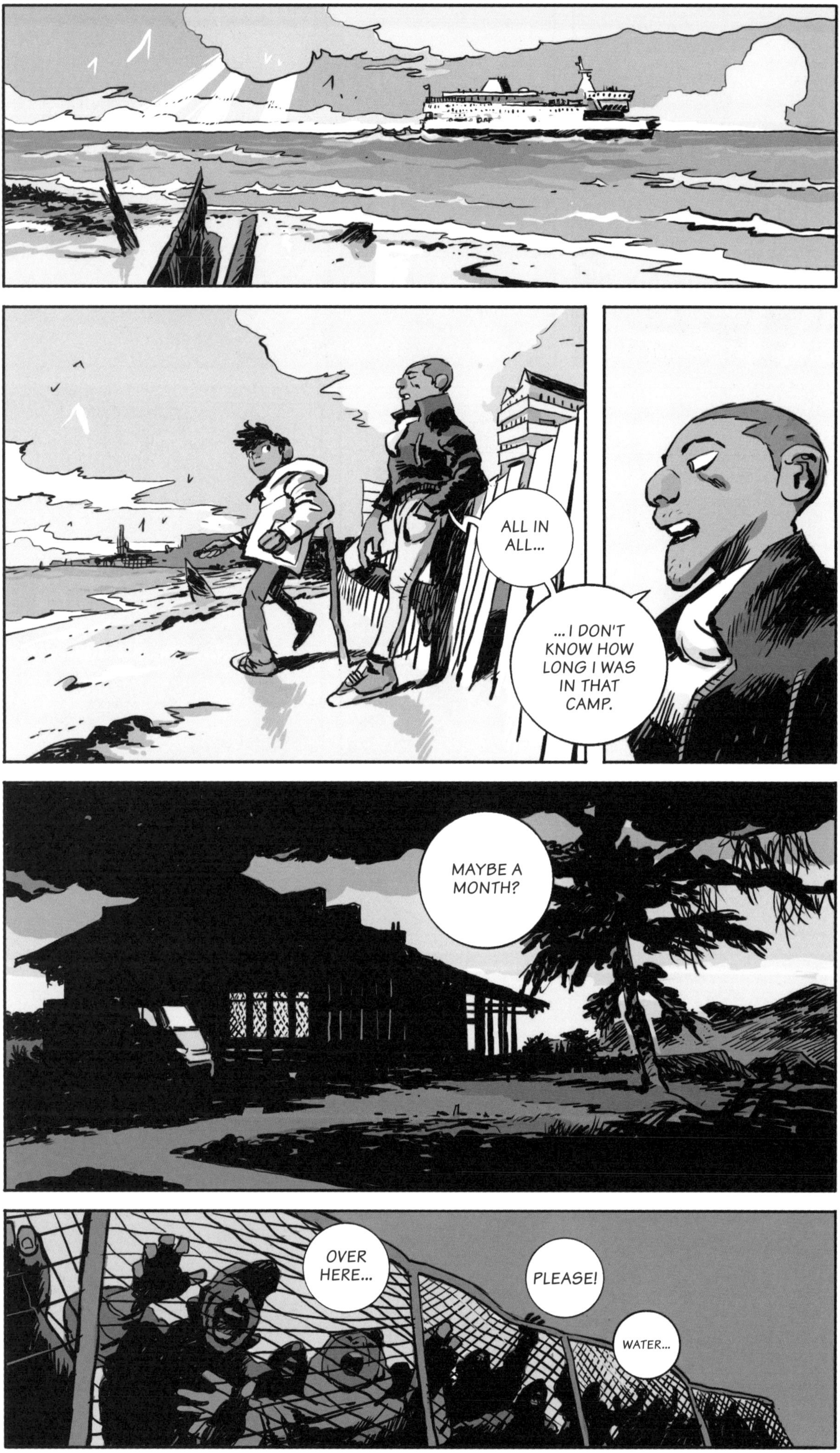
ALL IN ALL...
...I DON'T KNOW HOW LONG I WAS IN THAT CAMP.
MAYBE A MONTH?
OVER HERE...
PLEASE!
WATER...

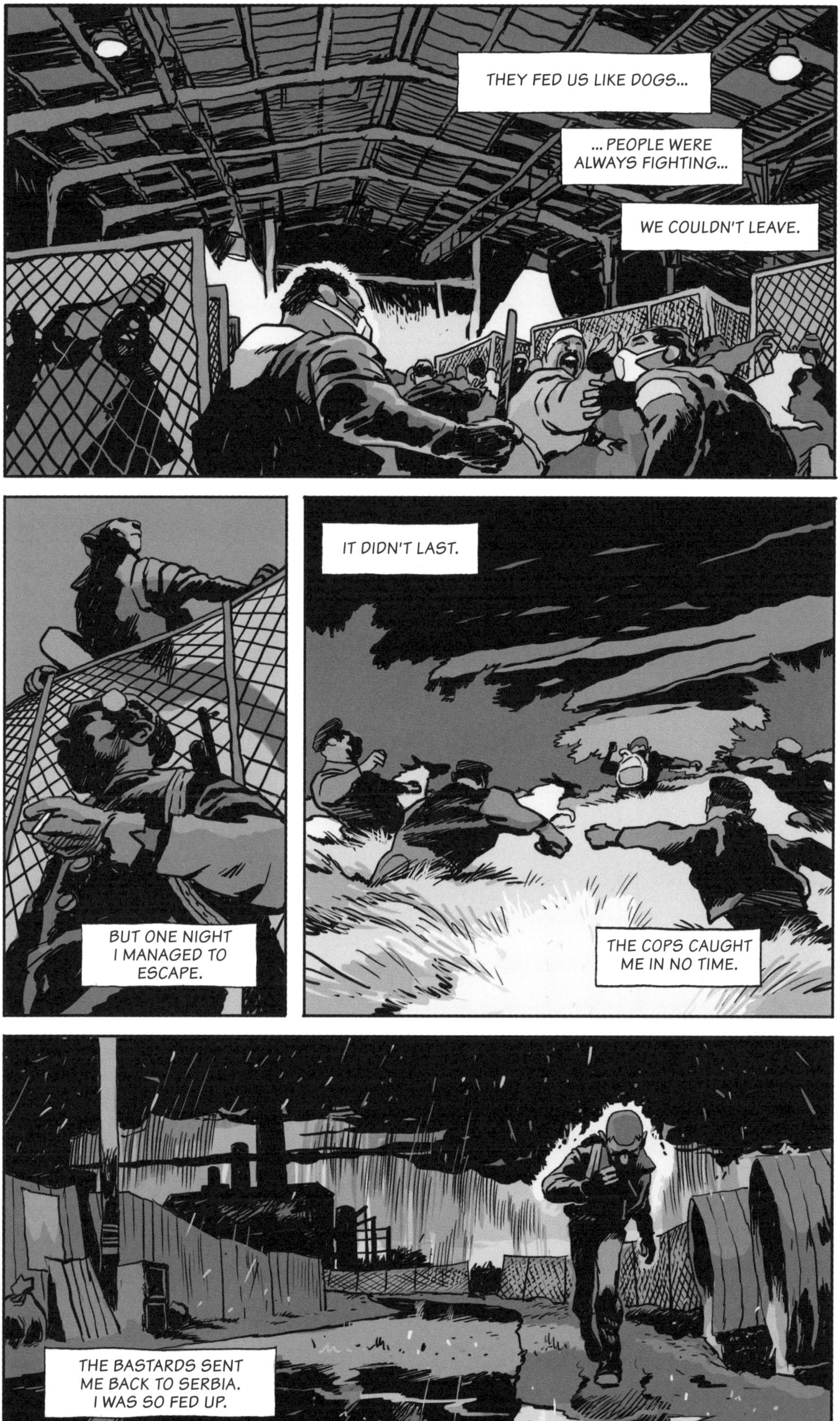
THEY FED US LIKE DOGS...
...PEOPLE WERE ALWAYS FIGHTING...
WE COULDN'T LEAVE.
BUT ONE NIGHT I MANAGED TO ESCAPE.
IT DIDN'T LAST.
THE COPS CAUGHT ME IN NO TIME.
THE BASTARDS SENT ME BACK TO SERBIA. I WAS SO FED UP.

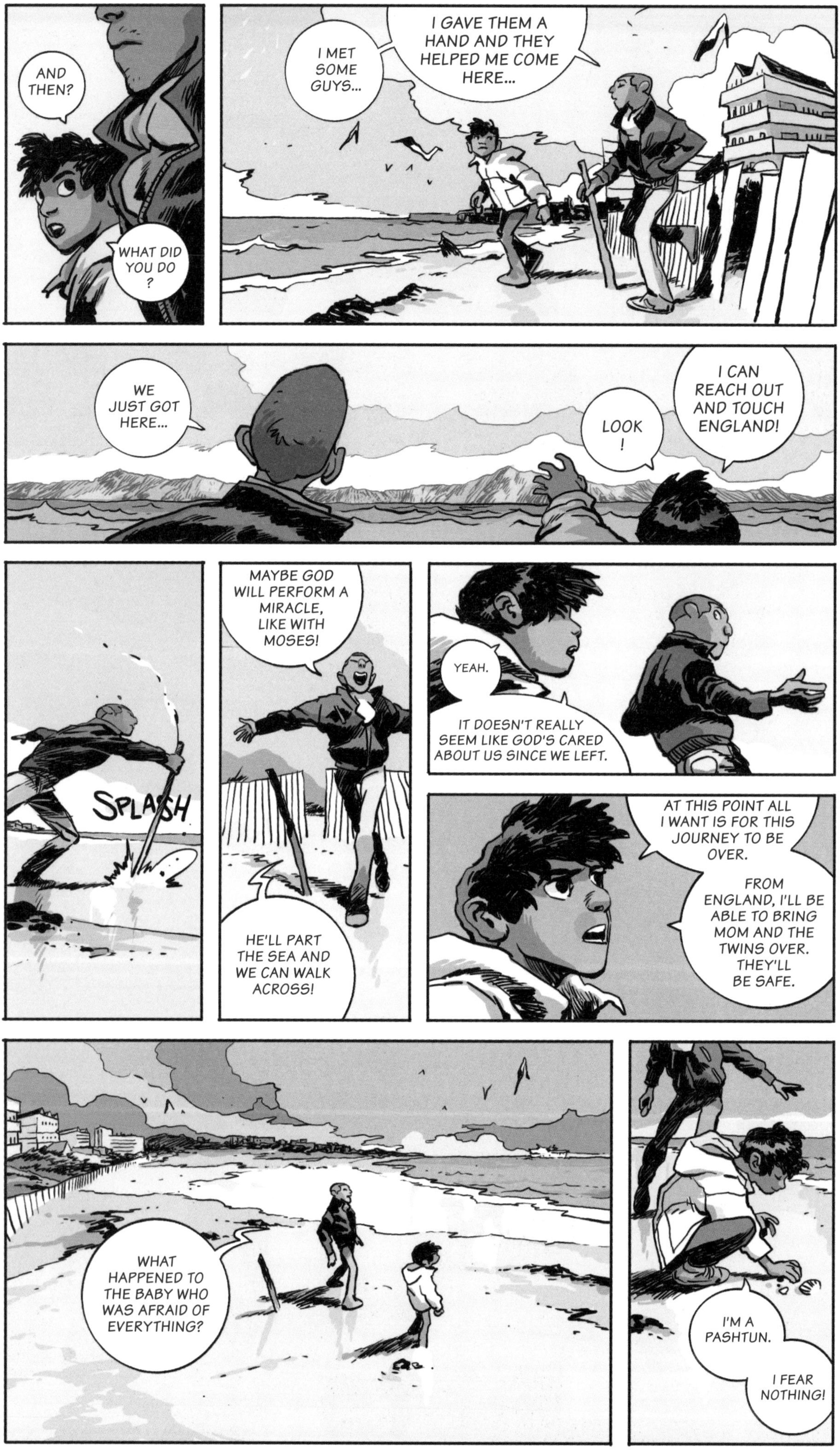
AND THEN?
WHAT DID YOU DO ?
I MET SOME GUYS...
I GAVE THEM A HAND AND THEY HELPED ME COME HERE...
WE JUST GOT HERE...
LOOK !
I CAN REACH OUT AND TOUCH ENGLAND!
SPLASH
MAYBE GOD WILL PERFORM A MIRACLE, LIKE WITH MOSES!
HE'LL PART THE SEA AND WE CAN WALK ACROSS!
YEAH.
IT DOESN'T REALLY SEEM LIKE GOD'S CARED ABOUT US SINCE WE LEFT.
AT THIS POINT ALL I WANT IS FOR THIS JOURNEY TO BE OVER.
FROM ENGLAND, I'LL BE ABLE TO BRING MOM AND THE TWINS OVER. THEY'LL BE SAFE.
WHAT HAPPENED TO THE BABY WHO WAS AFRAID OF EVERYTHING?
I'M A PASHTUN.
I FEAR NOTHING!

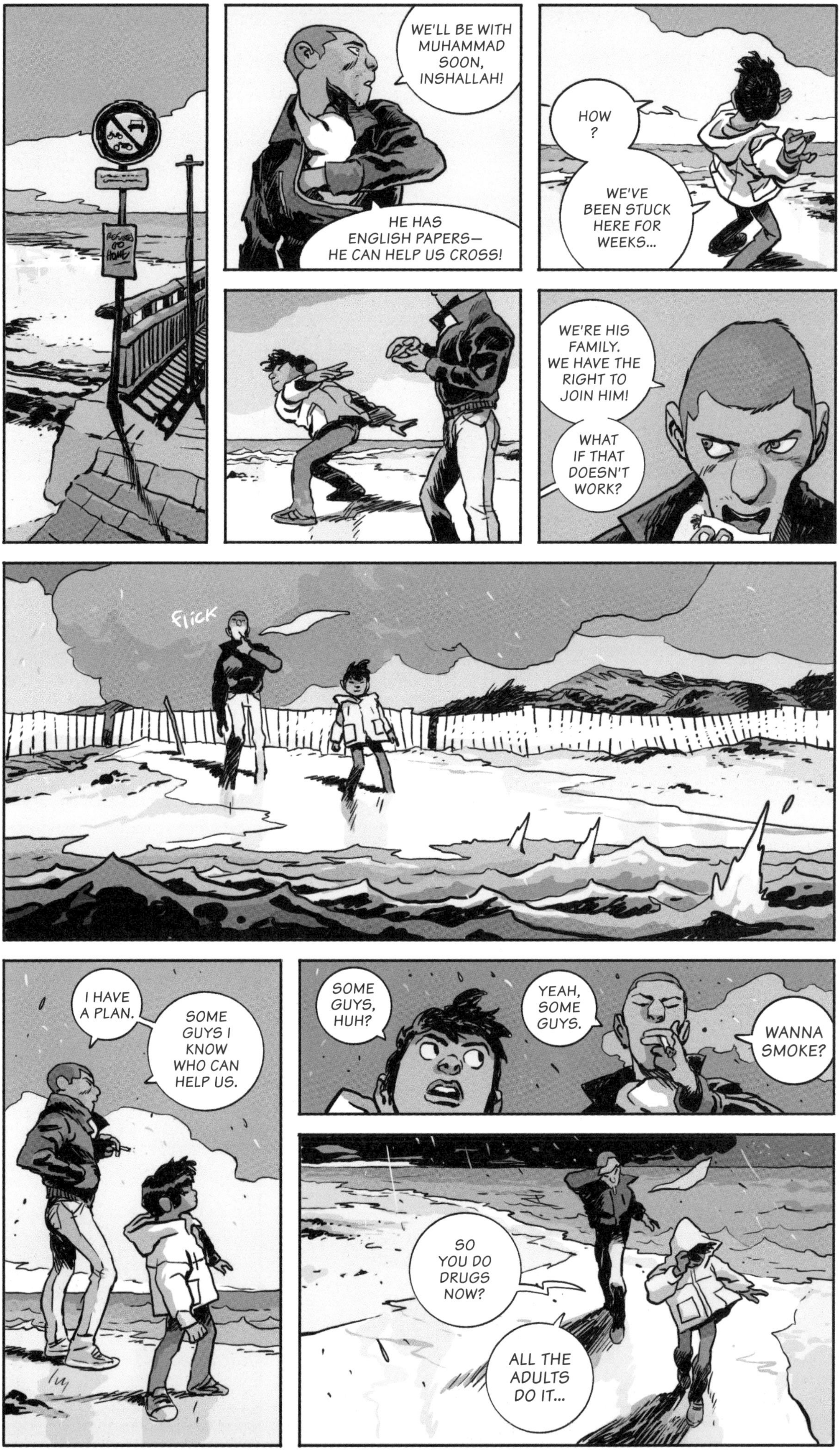
WE'LL BE WITH MUHAMMAD SOON, INSHALLAH!
HE HAS ENGLISH PAPERS— HE CAN HELP US CROSS!
HOW ?
WE'VE BEEN STUCK HERE FOR WEEKS...
WE'RE HIS FAMILY. WE HAVE THE RIGHT TO JOIN HIM!
WHAT IF THAT DOESN'T WORK?
FLICK
I HAVE A PLAN.
SOME GUYS I KNOW WHO CAN HELP US.
SOME GUYS, HUH?
YEAH, SOME GUYS.
WANNA SMOKE?
SO YOU DO DRUGS NOW?
ALL THE ADULTS DO IT...

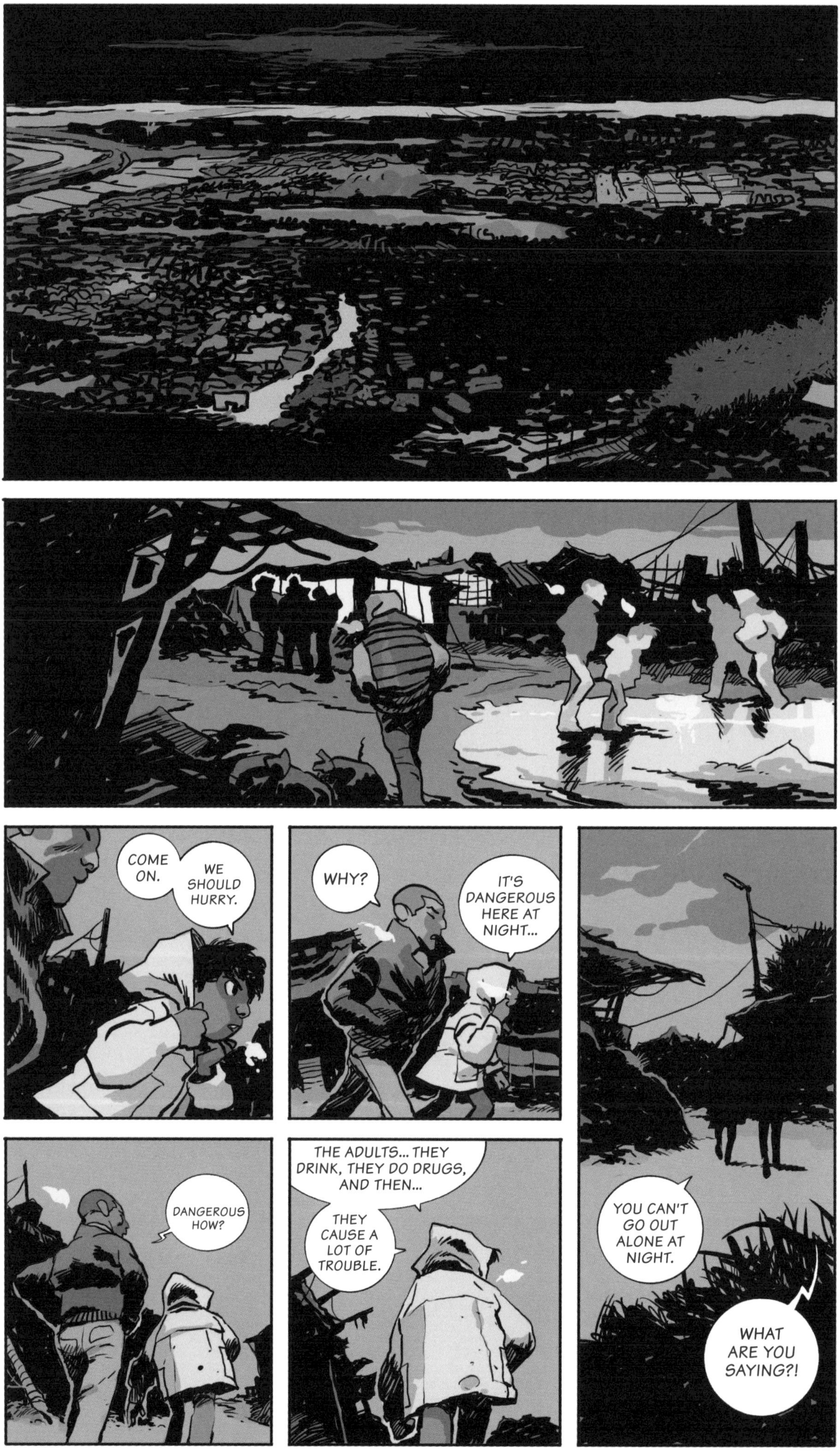

COME ON.
WE SHOULD HURRY.
WHY?
IT'S DANGEROUS HERE AT NIGHT...
DANGEROUS HOW?
THE ADULTS... THEY DRINK, THEY DO DRUGS, AND THEN...
THEY CAUSE A LOT OF TROUBLE.
YOU CAN'T GO OUT ALONE AT NIGHT.
WHAT ARE YOU SAYING?!

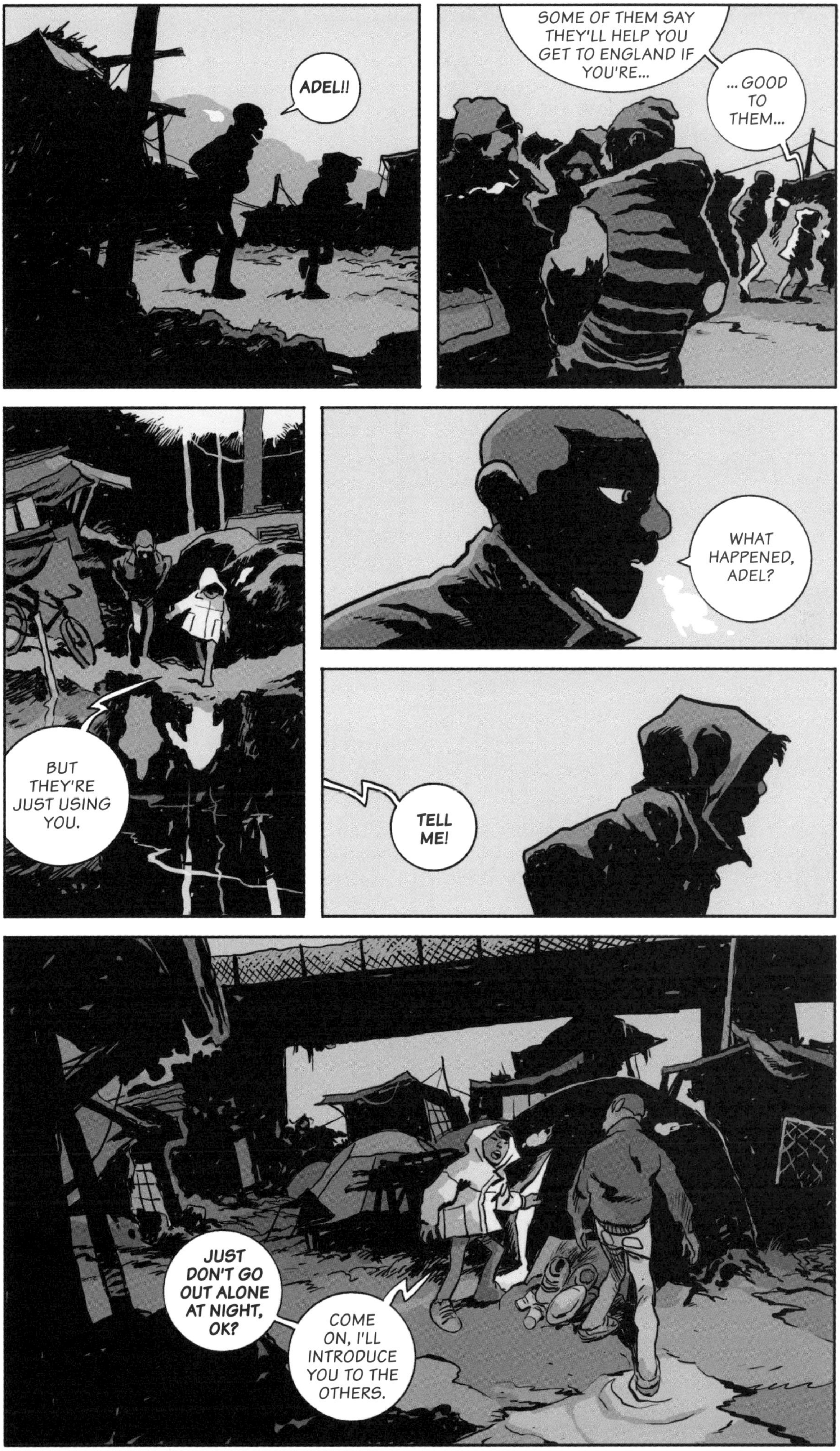
ADEL!!
SOME OF THEM SAY THEY'LL HELP YOU GET TO ENGLAND IF YOU'RE...
...GOOD TO THEM...
BUT THEY'RE JUST USING YOU.
WHAT HAPPENED, ADEL?
TELL ME!
JUST DON'T GO OUT ALONE AT NIGHT, OK?
COME ON, I'LL INTRODUCE YOU TO THE OTHERS.

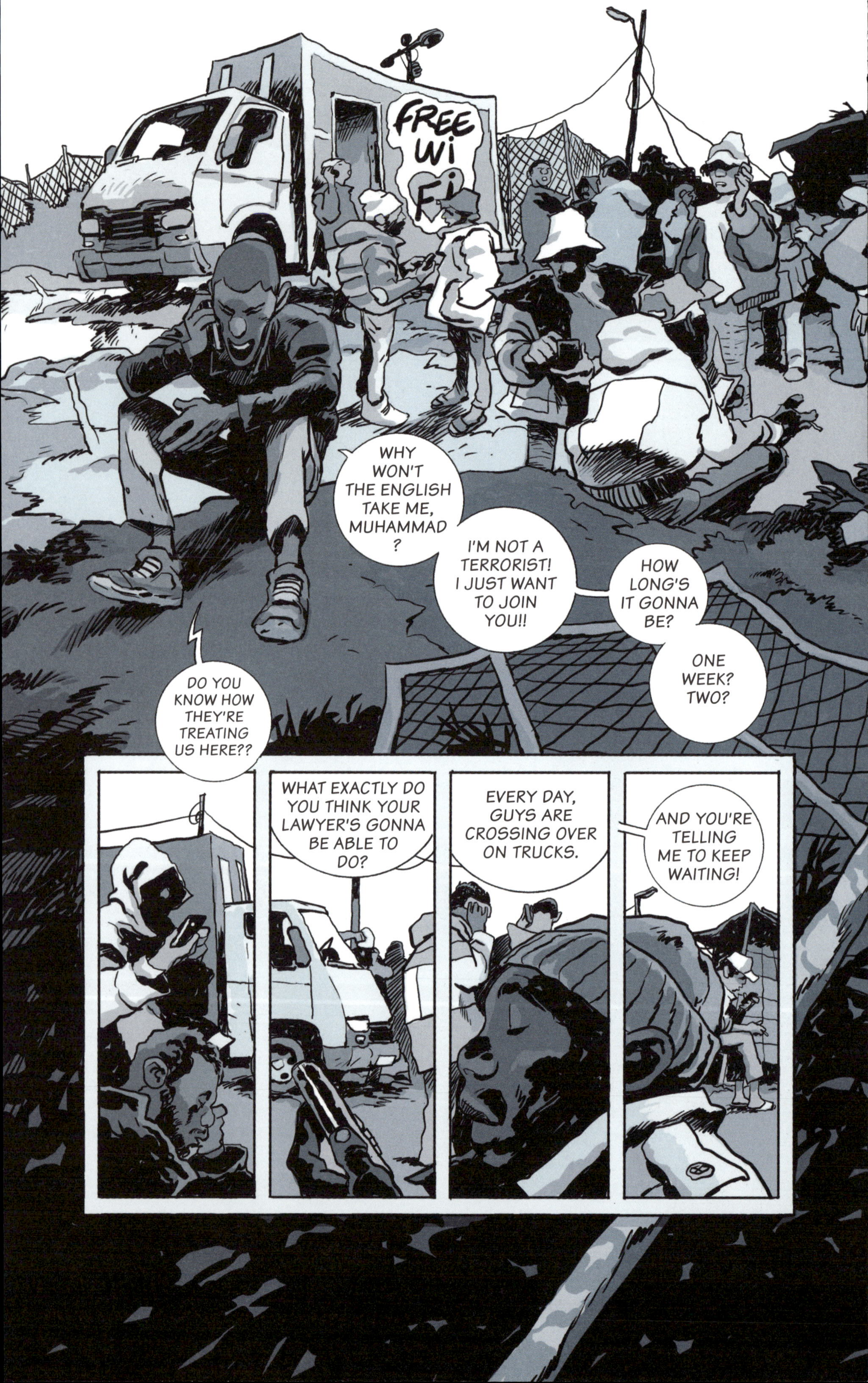
FREE Wi Fi
WHY WON'T THE ENGLISH TAKE ME, MUHAMMAD?
I'M NOT A TERRORIST! I JUST WANT TO JOIN YOU!!
HOW LONG'S IT GONNA BE?
ONE WEEK? TWO?
DO YOU KNOW HOW THEY'RE TREATING US HERE??
WHAT EXACTLY DO YOU THINK YOUR LAWYER'S GONNA BE ABLE TO DO?
EVERY DAY, GUYS ARE CROSSING OVER ON TRUCKS.
AND YOU'RE TELLING ME TO KEEP WAITING!

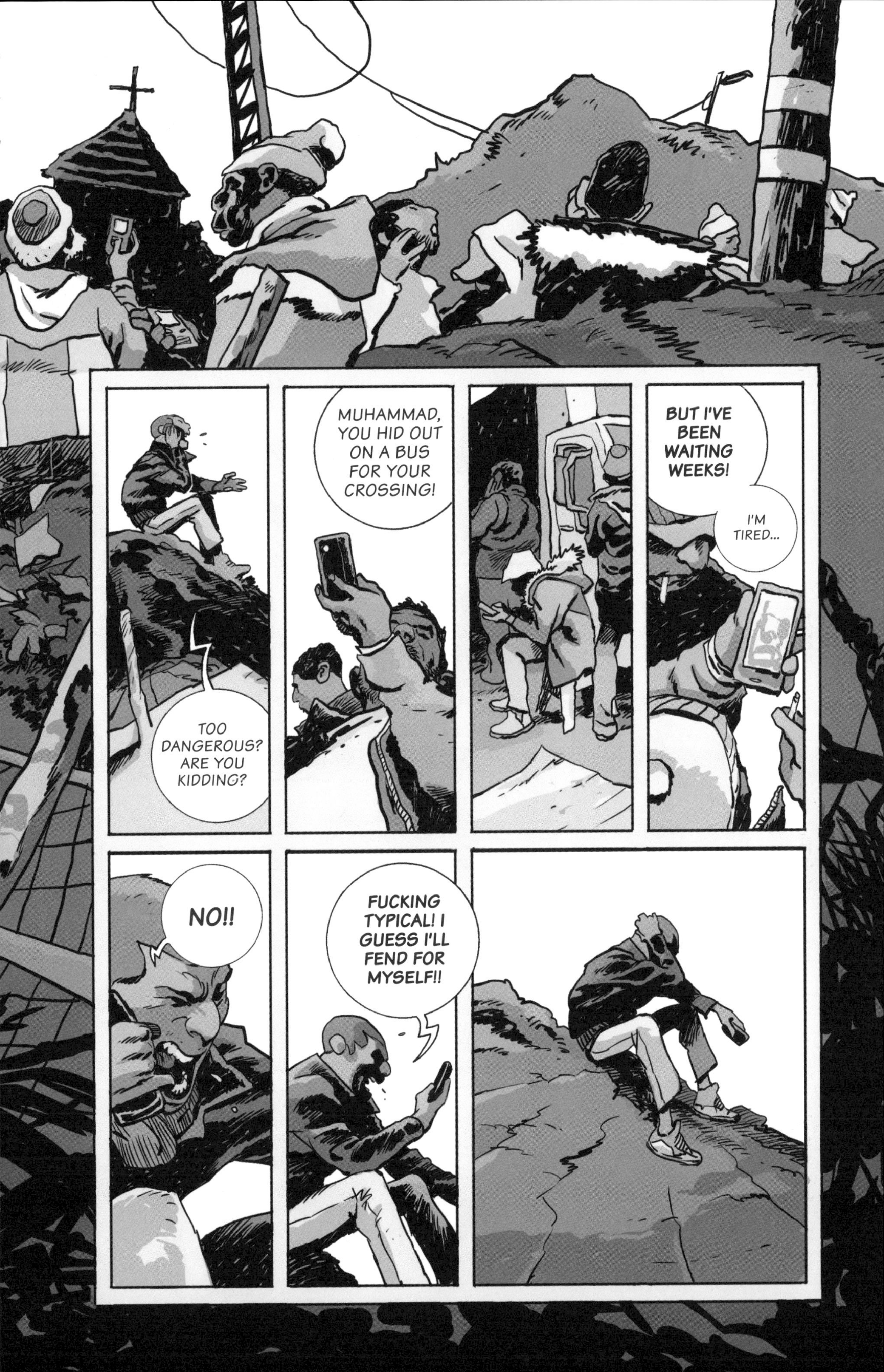
TOO DANGEROUS? ARE YOU KIDDING?
MUHAMMAD, YOU HID OUT ON A BUS FOR YOUR CROSSING!
BUT I'VE BEEN WAITING WEEKS!
I'M TIRED...
NO!!
FUCKING TYPICAL! I GUESS I'LL FEND FOR MYSELF!!

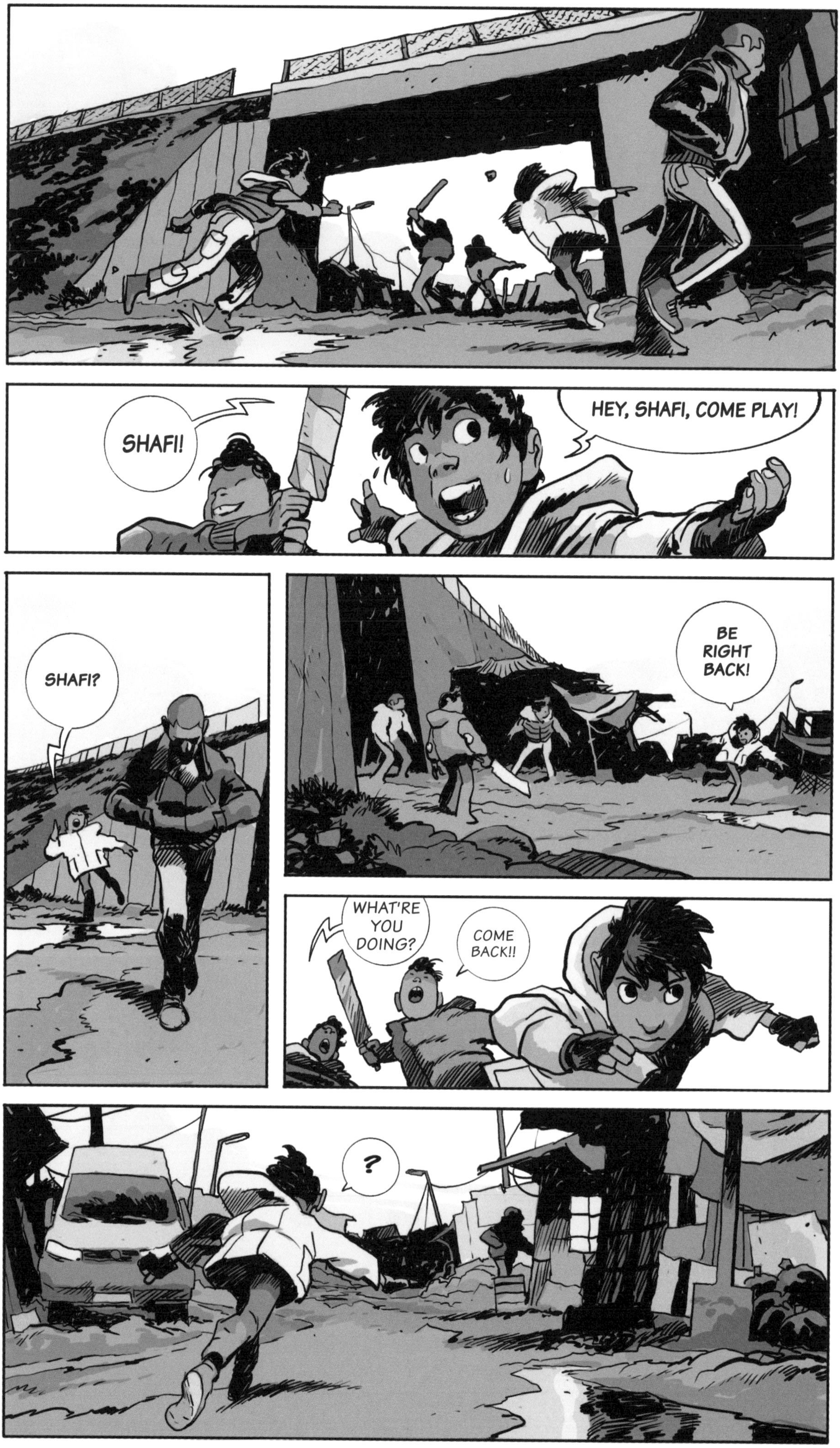
SHAFI!
HEY, SHAFI, COME PLAY!
SHAFI?
BE RIGHT BACK!
WHAT'RE YOU DOING?
COME BACK!!
?

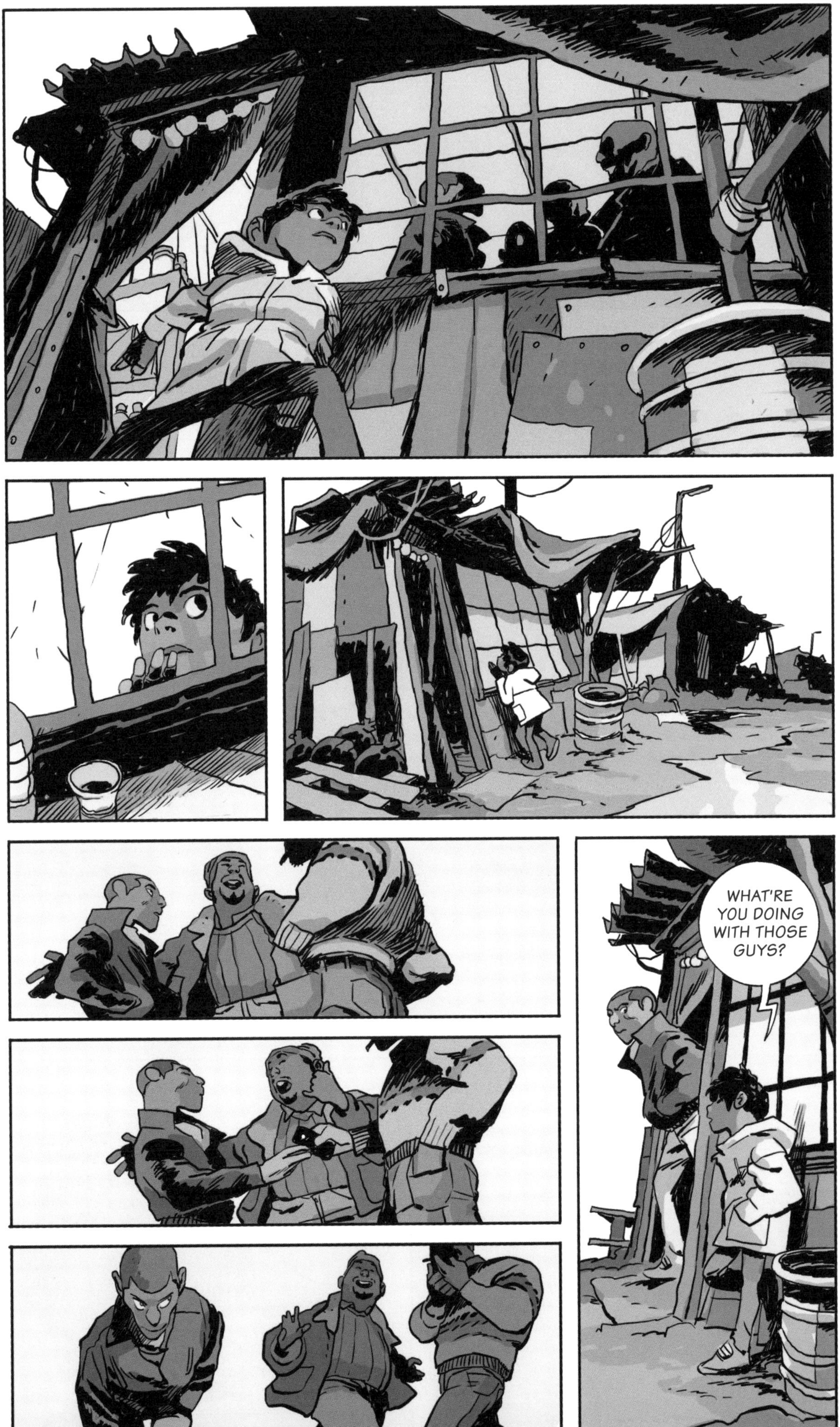
WHAT'RE YOU DOING WITH THOSE GUYS?

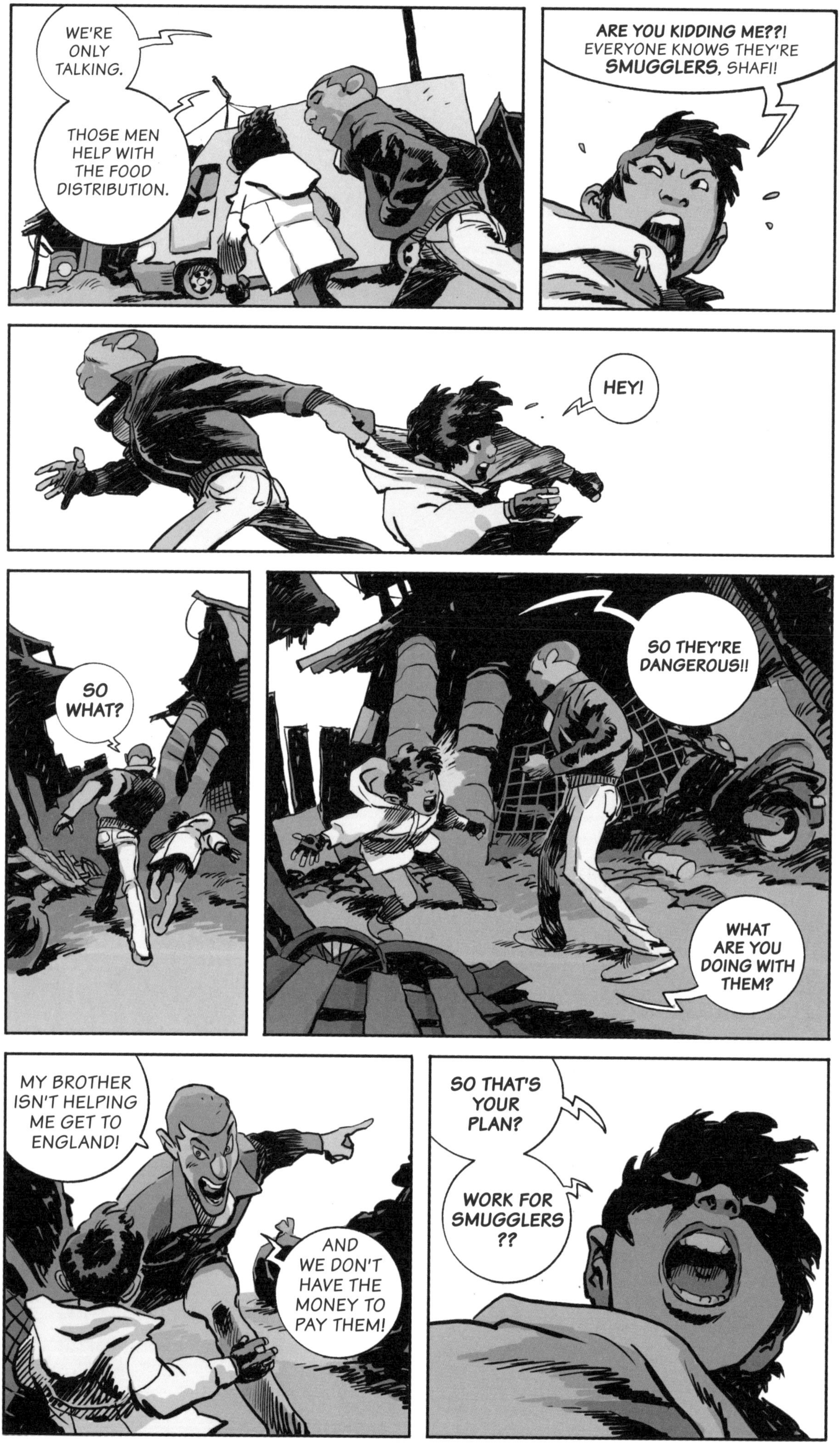
WE'RE ONLY TALKING.
THOSE MEN HELP WITH THE FOOD DISTRIBUTION.
ARE YOU KIDDING ME??! EVERYONE KNOWS THEY'RE **SMUGGLERS**, SHAFI!
HEY!
SO WHAT?
SO THEY'RE DANGEROUS!!
WHAT ARE YOU DOING WITH THEM?
MY BROTHER ISN'T HELPING ME GET TO ENGLAND!
AND WE DON'T HAVE THE MONEY TO PAY THEM!
SO THAT'S YOUR PLAN?
WORK FOR SMUGGLERS ??

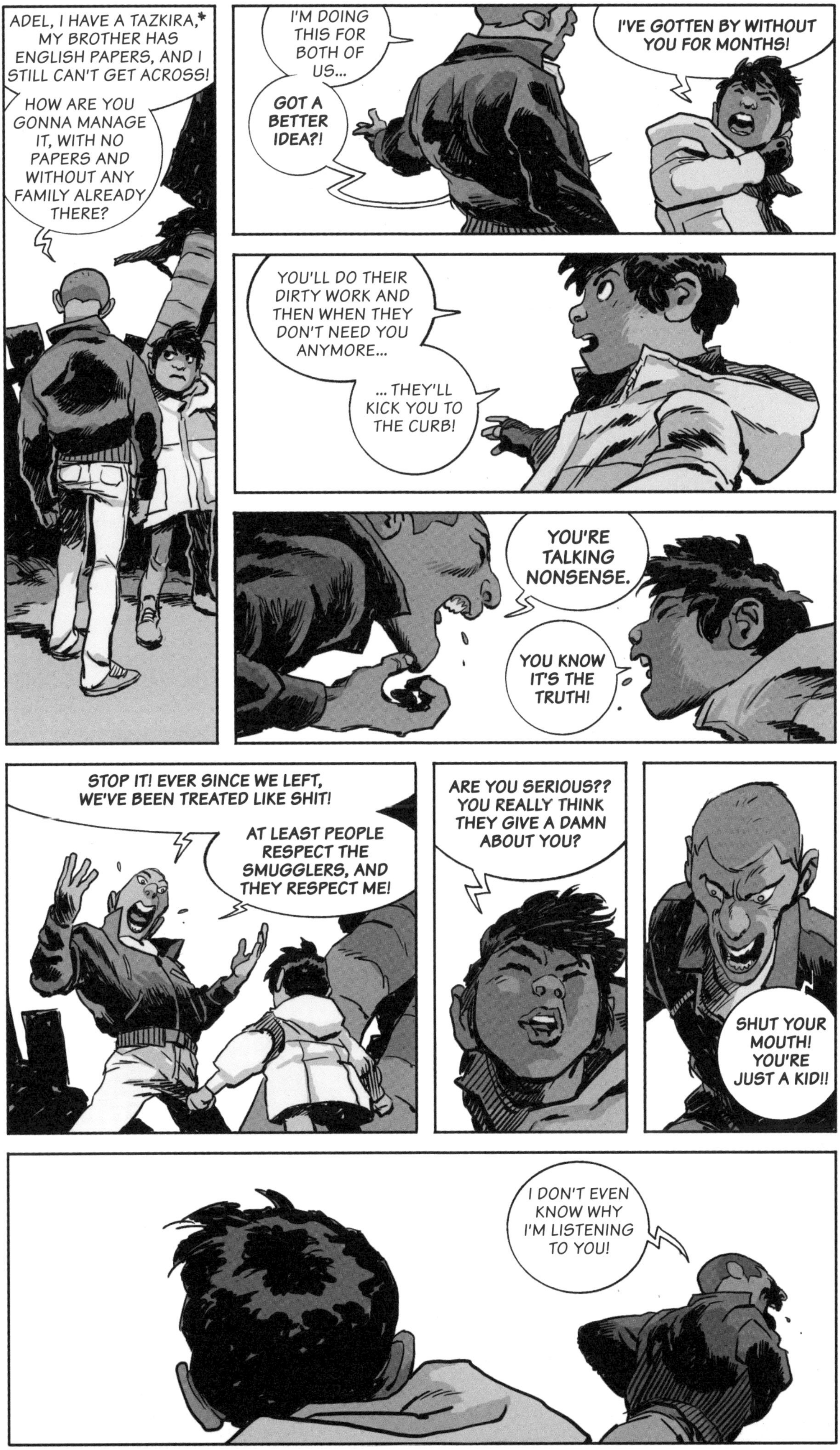
ADEL, I HAVE A TAZKIRA,* MY BROTHER HAS ENGLISH PAPERS, AND I STILL CAN'T GET ACROSS!
HOW ARE YOU GONNA MANAGE IT, WITH NO PAPERS AND WITHOUT ANY FAMILY ALREADY THERE?
I'M DOING THIS FOR BOTH OF US...
GOT A BETTER IDEA?!
I'VE GOTTEN BY WITHOUT YOU FOR MONTHS!
YOU'LL DO THEIR DIRTY WORK AND THEN WHEN THEY DON'T NEED YOU ANYMORE...
... THEY'LL KICK YOU TO THE CURB!
YOU'RE TALKING NONSENSE.
YOU KNOW IT'S THE TRUTH!
STOP IT! EVER SINCE WE LEFT, WE'VE BEEN TREATED LIKE SHIT!
AT LEAST PEOPLE RESPECT THE SMUGGLERS, AND THEY RESPECT ME!
ARE YOU SERIOUS?? YOU REALLY THINK THEY GIVE A DAMN ABOUT YOU?
SHUT YOUR MOUTH! YOU'RE JUST A KID!!
I DON'T EVEN KNOW WHY I'M LISTENING TO YOU!

*AFGHAN IDENTITY CARD.

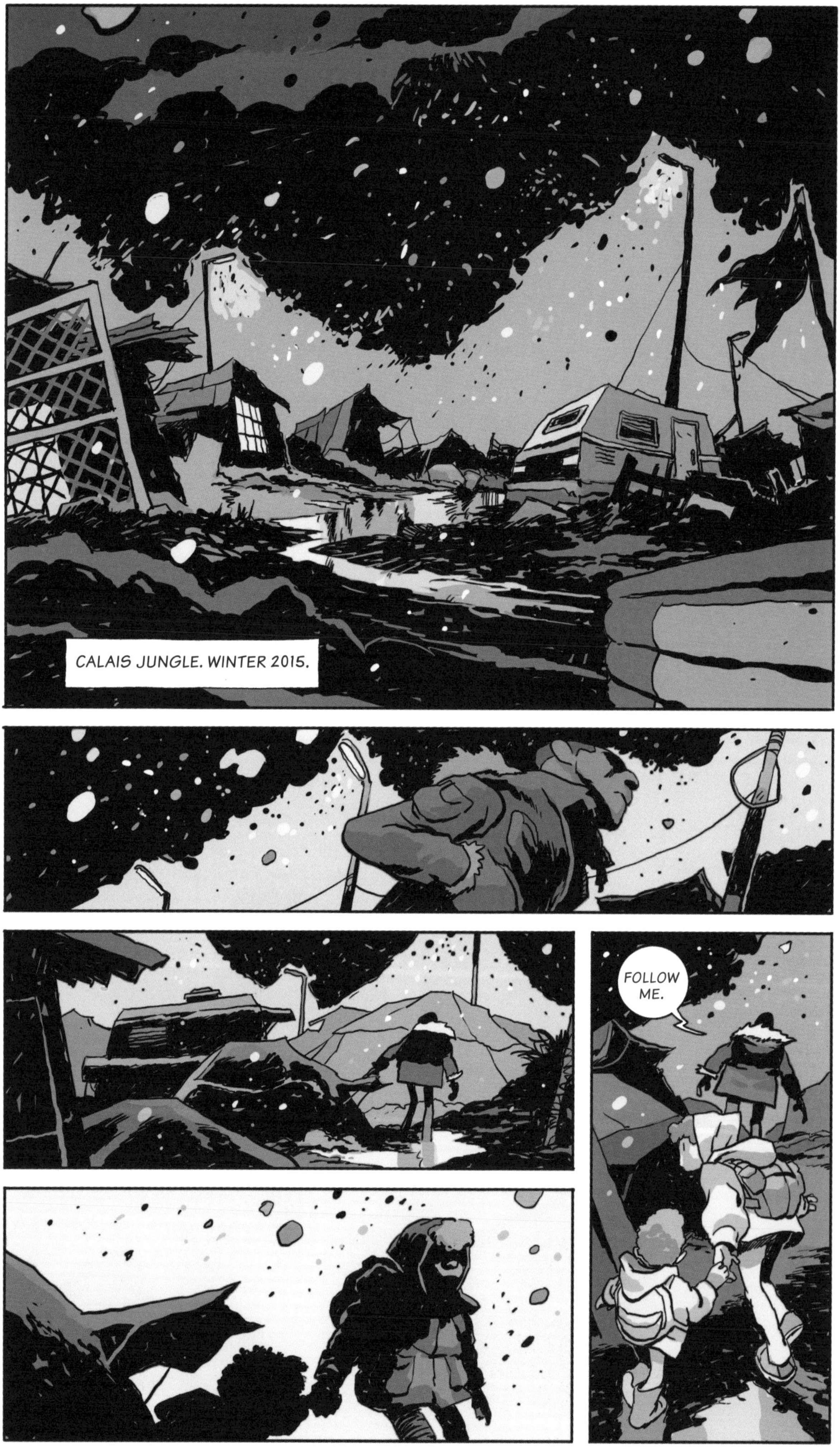
CALAIS JUNGLE. WINTER 2015.
FOLLOW ME.

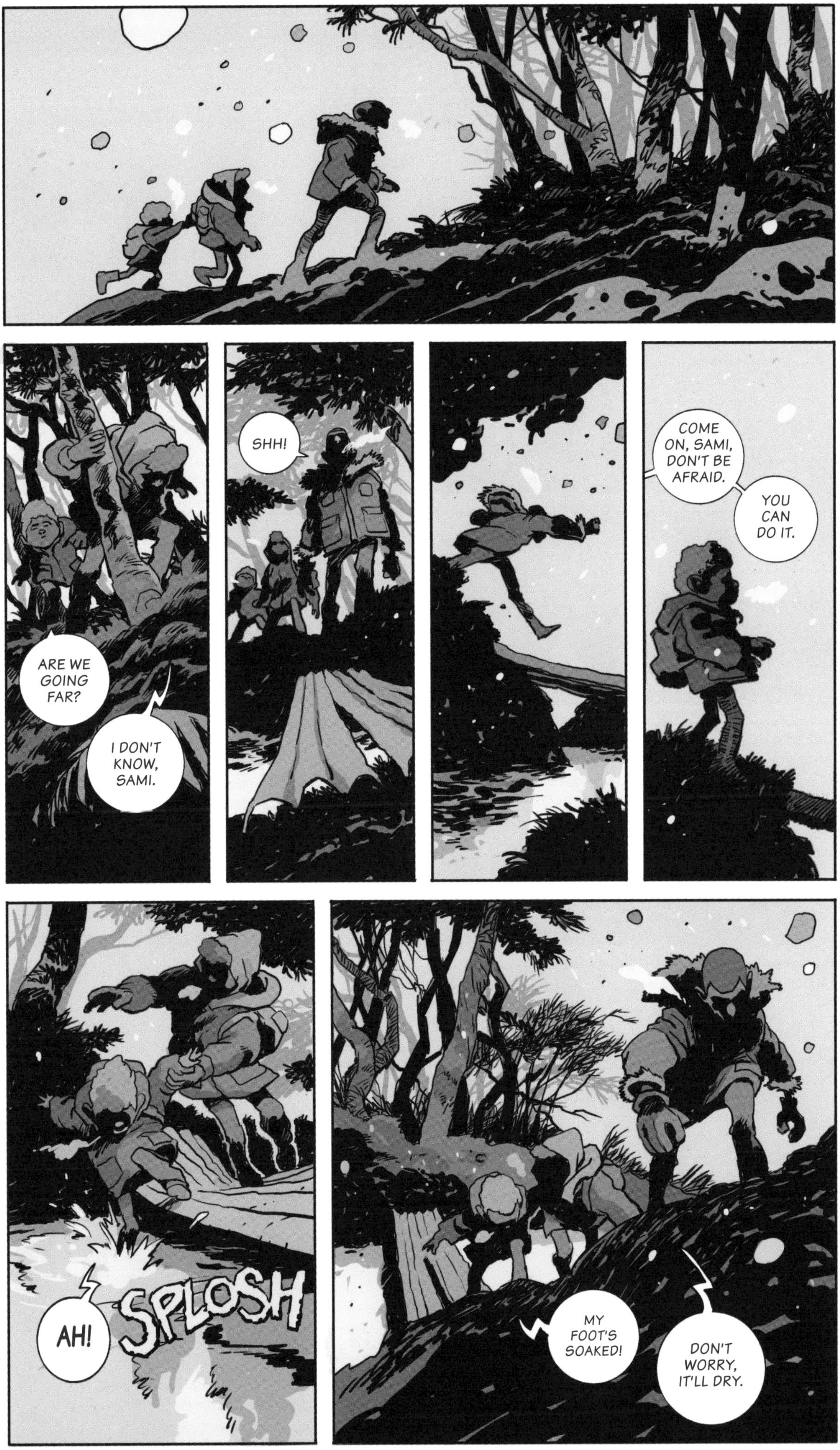

ARE WE GOING FAR?
I DON'T KNOW, SAMI.
SHH!
COME ON, SAMI, DON'T BE AFRAID.
YOU CAN DO IT.
AH!
SPLOSH
MY FOOT'S SOAKED!
DON'T WORRY, IT'LL DRY.

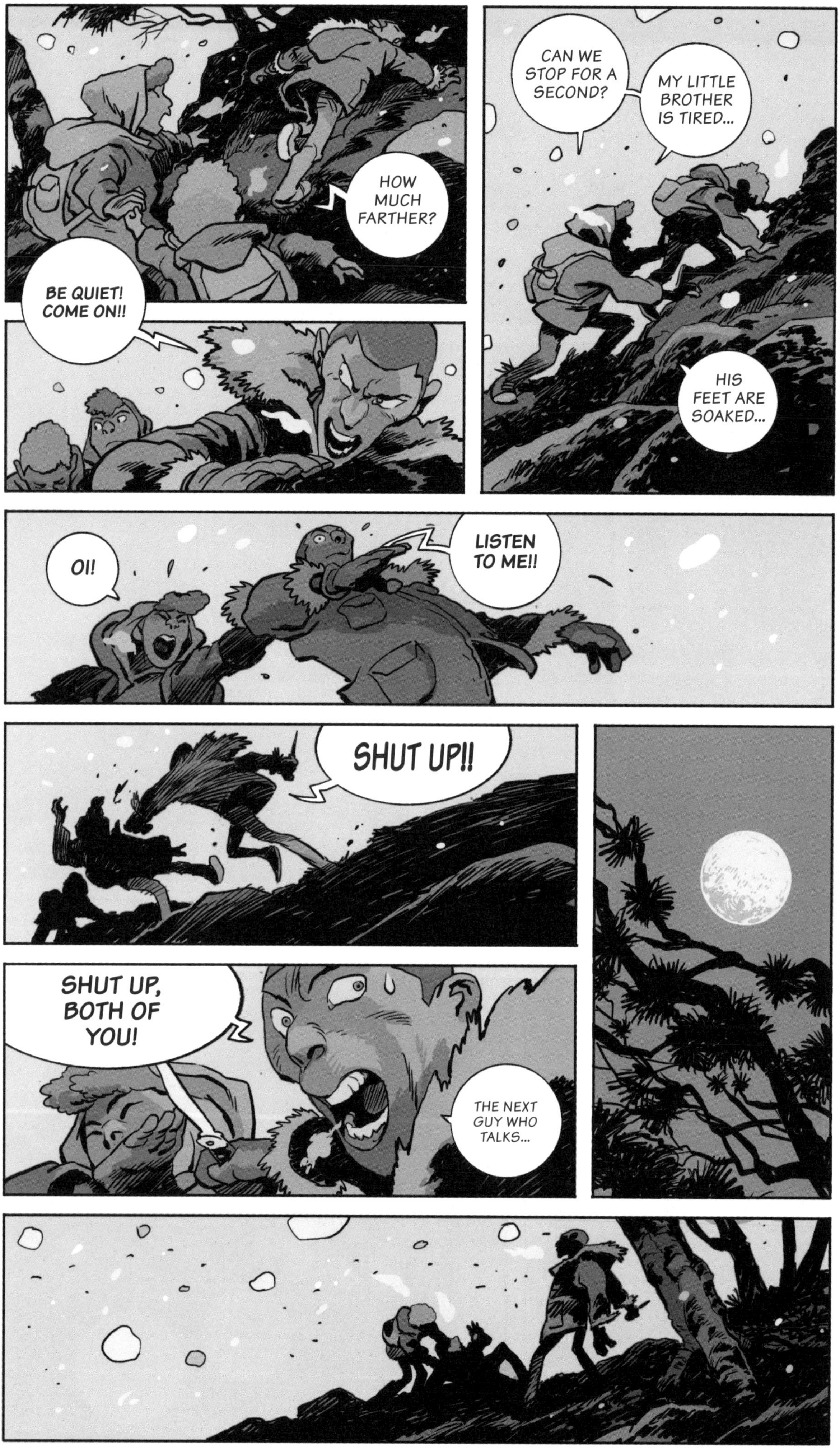
HOW MUCH FARTHER?
BE QUIET! COME ON!!
CAN WE STOP FOR A SECOND?
MY LITTLE BROTHER IS TIRED...
HIS FEET ARE SOAKED...
OI!
LISTEN TO ME!!
SHUT UP!!
SHUT UP, BOTH OF YOU!
THE NEXT GUY WHO TALKS...

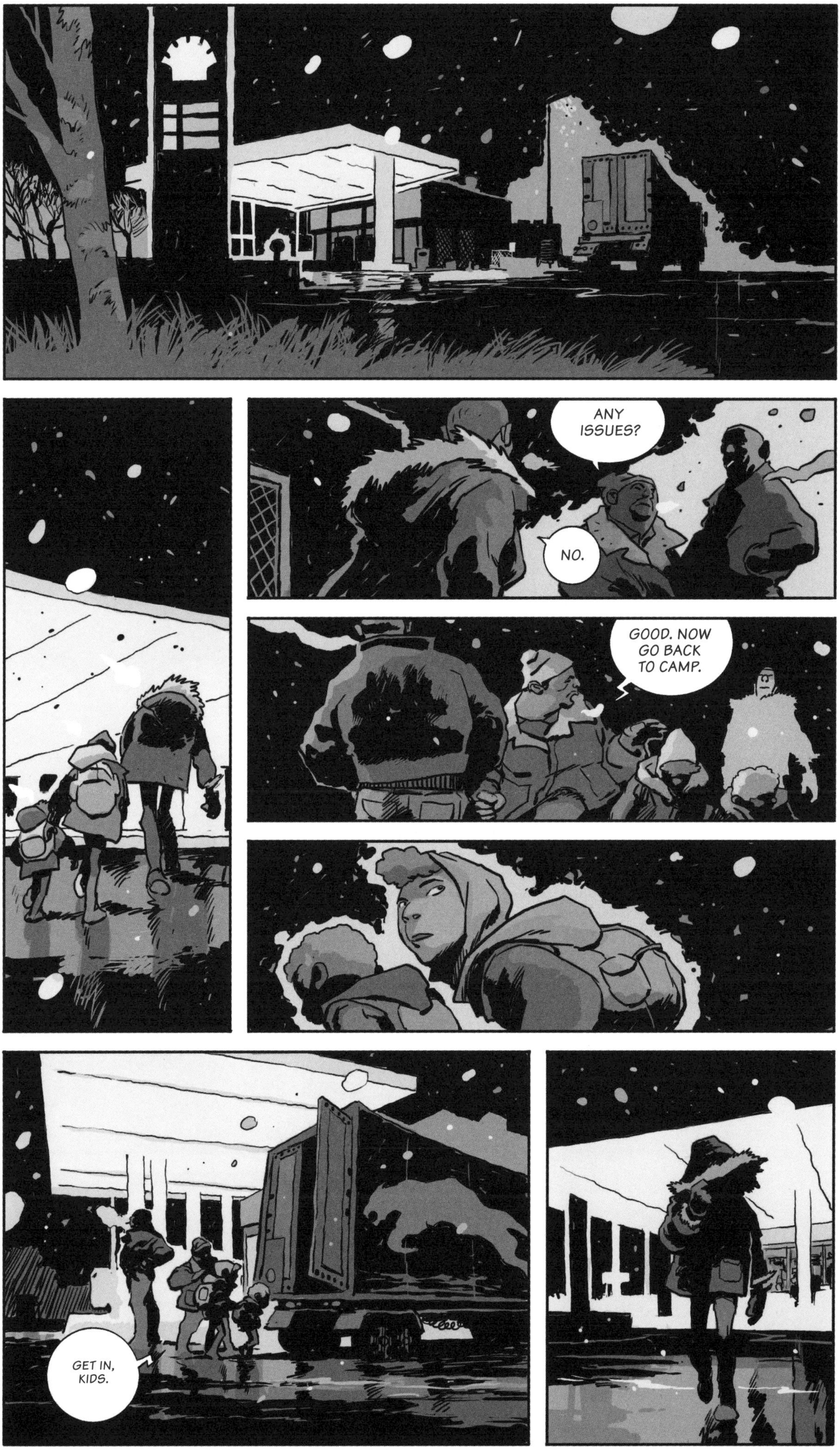
ANY ISSUES?
NO.
GOOD. NOW GO BACK TO CAMP.
GET IN, KIDS.

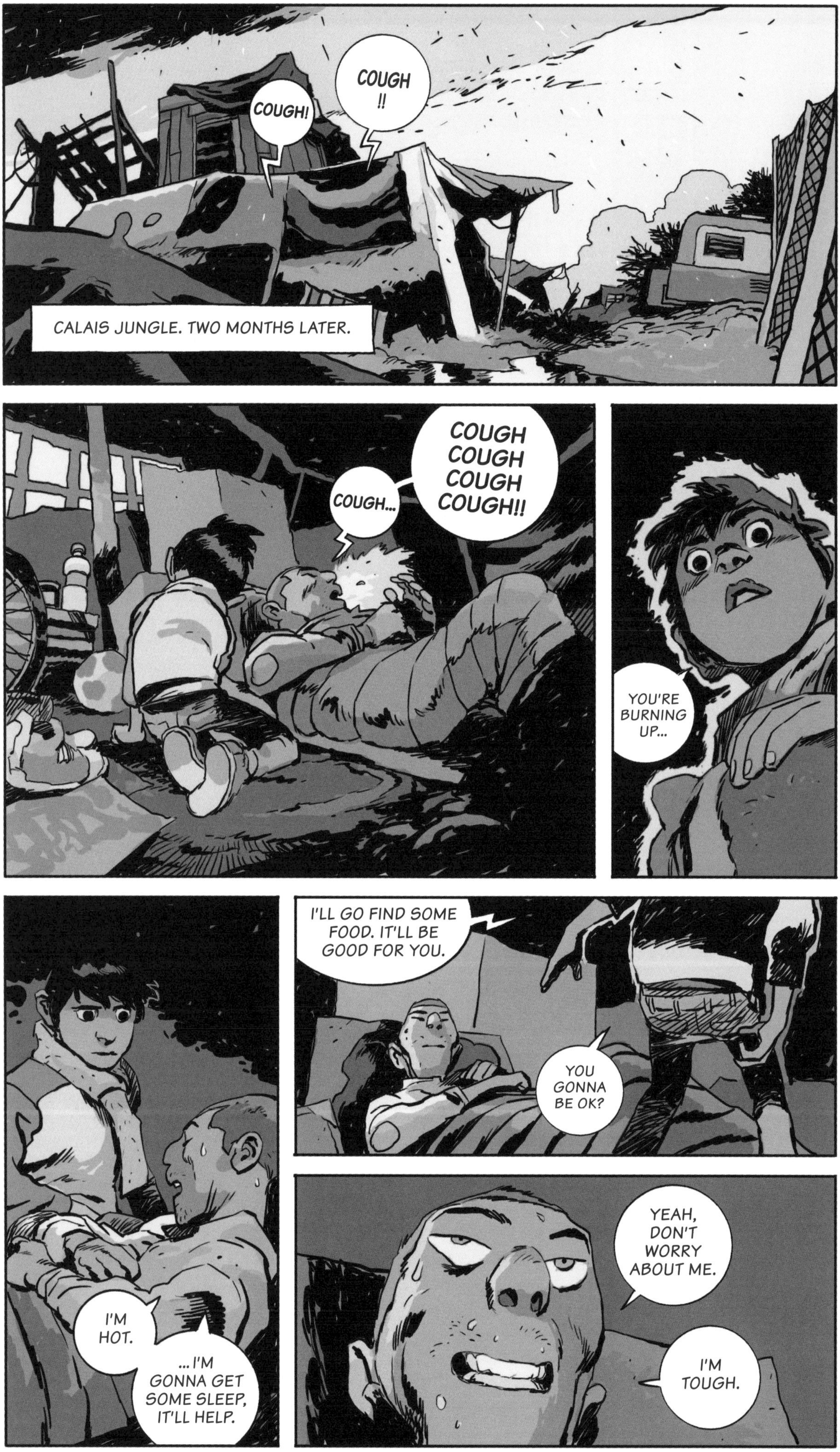
COUGH!
COUGH !!
CALAIS JUNGLE. TWO MONTHS LATER.
COUGH...
COUGH COUGH COUGH COUGH!!
YOU'RE BURNING UP...
I'M HOT.
...I'M GONNA GET SOME SLEEP, IT'LL HELP.
I'LL GO FIND SOME FOOD. IT'LL BE GOOD FOR YOU.
YOU GONNA BE OK?
YEAH, DON'T WORRY ABOUT ME.
I'M TOUGH.

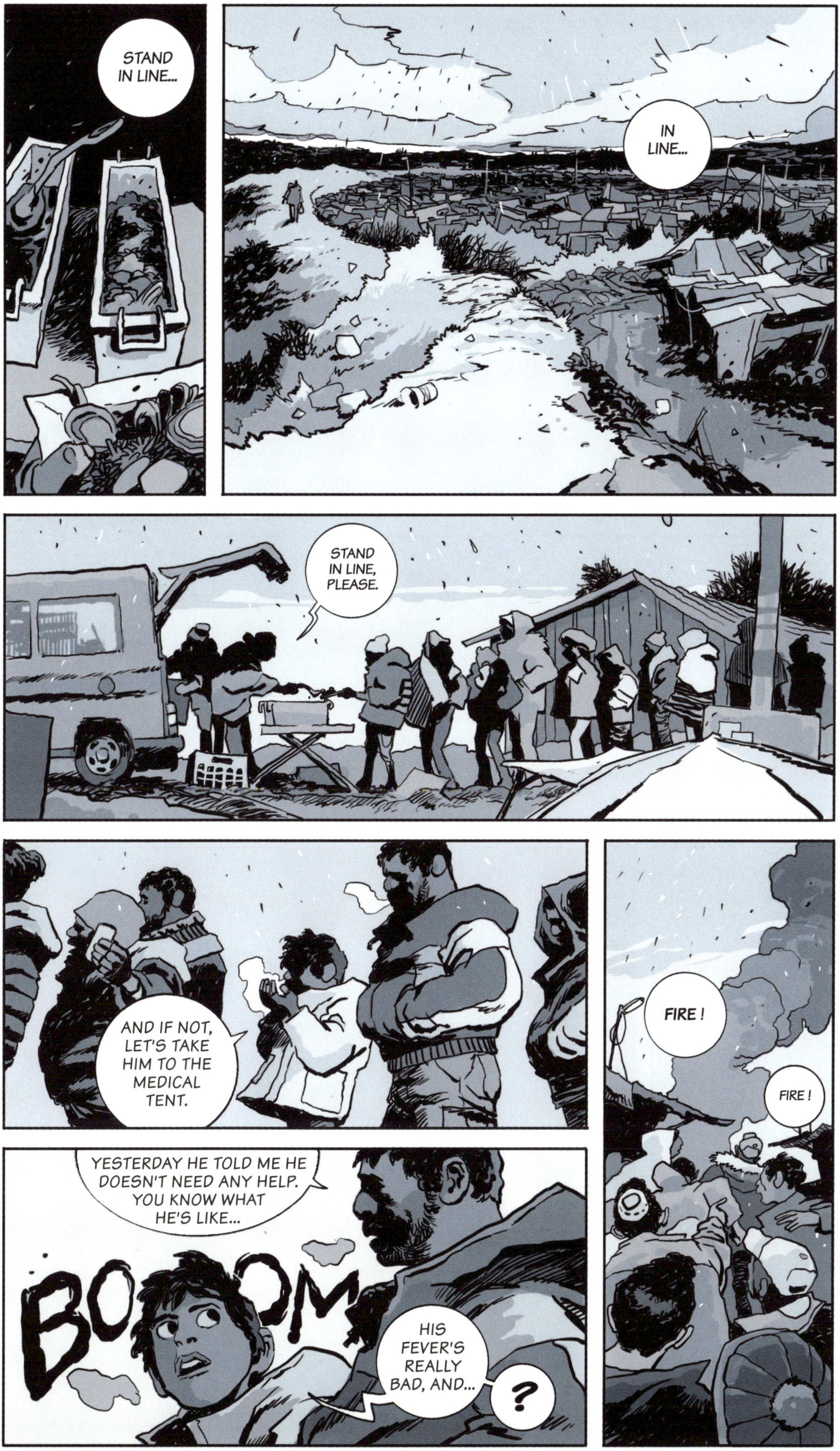
STAND IN LINE...
IN LINE...
STAND IN LINE, PLEASE.
AND IF NOT, LET'S TAKE HIM TO THE MEDICAL TENT.
YESTERDAY HE TOLD ME HE DOESN'T NEED ANY HELP. YOU KNOW WHAT HE'S LIKE...
BOOM
HIS FEVER'S REALLY BAD, AND...
?
FIRE !
FIRE !

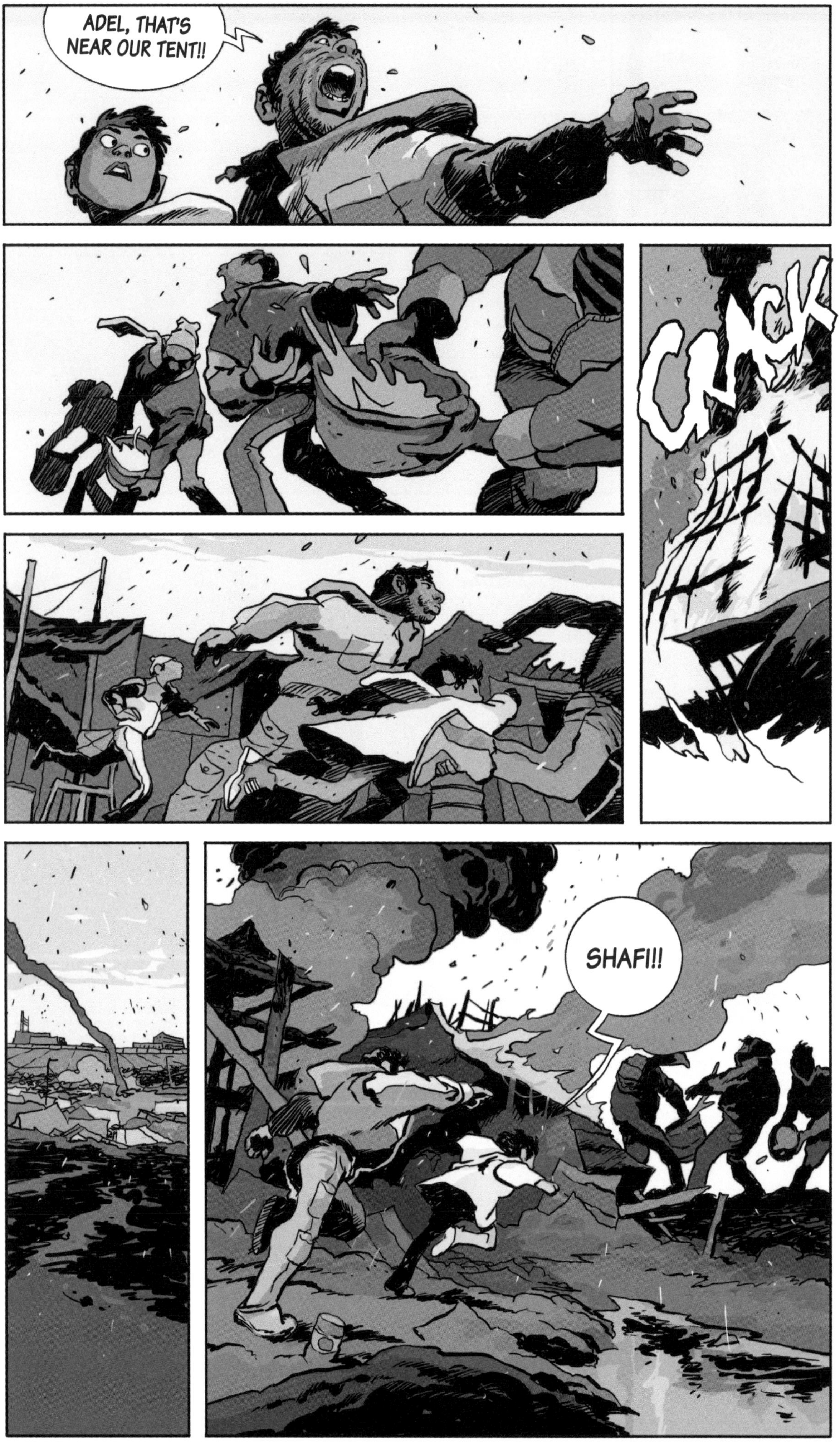
ADEL, THAT'S NEAR OUR TENT!!
CRACK
SHAFI!!

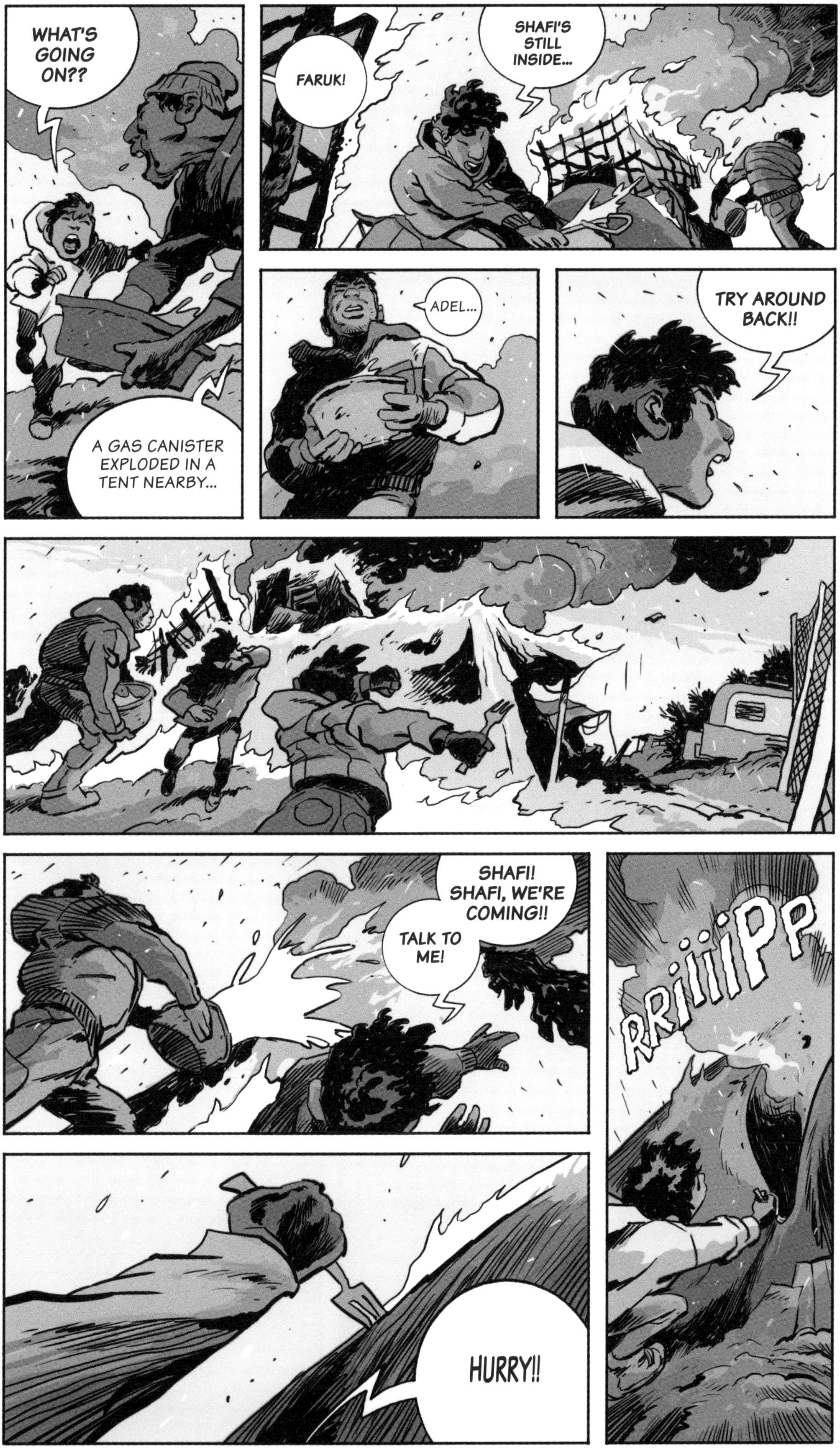
WHAT'S GOING ON??
A GAS CANISTER EXPLODED IN A TENT NEARBY...
FARUK!
SHAFI'S STILL INSIDE...
ADEL...
TRY AROUND BACK!!
SHAFI! SHAFI, WE'RE COMING!!
TALK TO ME!
HURRY!!
RRiiiiPP

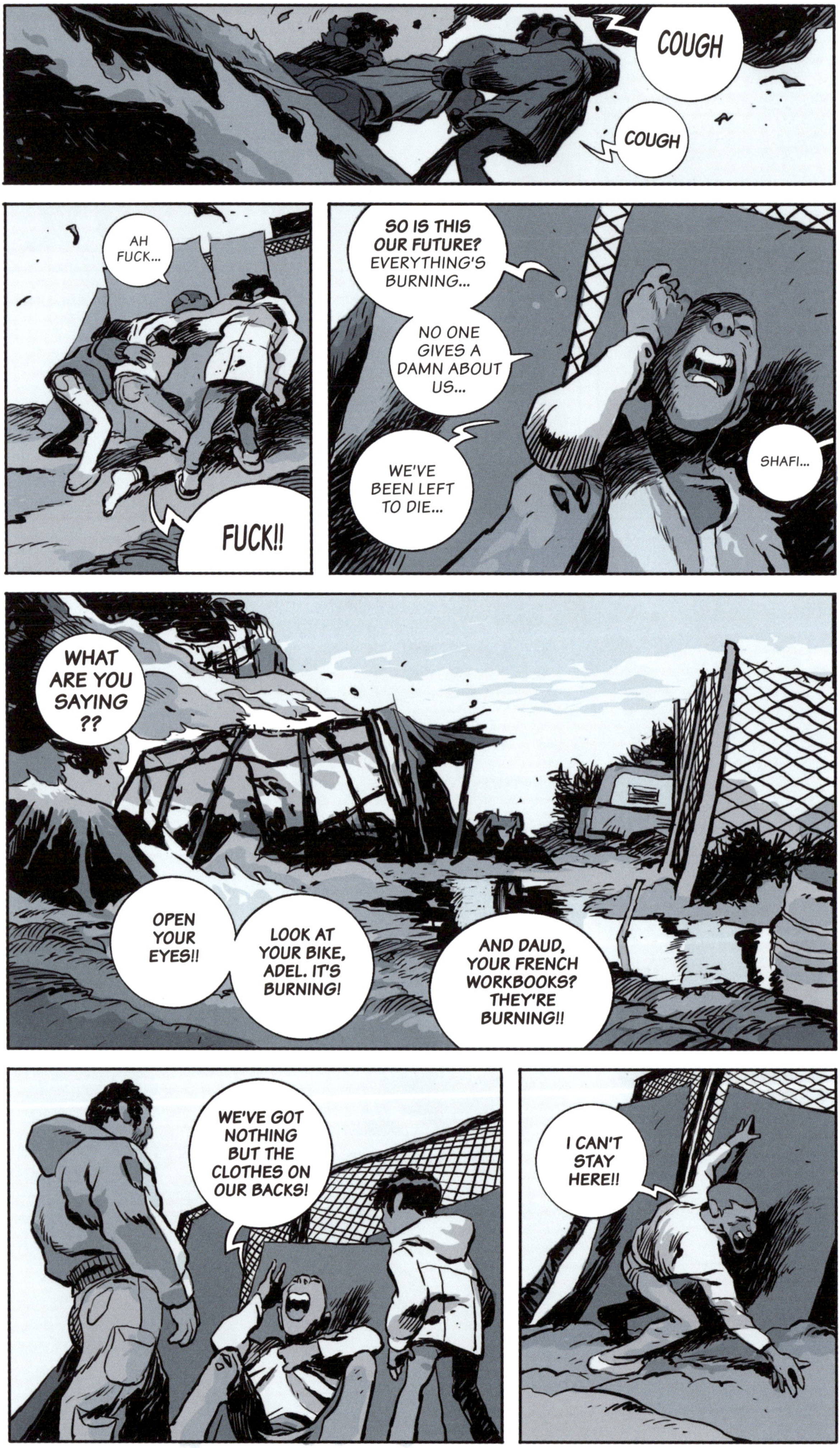
COUGH
COUGH
AH FUCK...
FUCK!!
SO IS THIS OUR FUTURE? EVERYTHING'S BURNING...
NO ONE GIVES A DAMN ABOUT US...
WE'VE BEEN LEFT TO DIE...
SHAFI...
WHAT ARE YOU SAYING ??
OPEN YOUR EYES!!
LOOK AT YOUR BIKE, ADEL. IT'S BURNING!
AND DAUD, YOUR FRENCH WORKBOOKS? THEY'RE BURNING!!
WE'VE GOT NOTHING BUT THE CLOTHES ON OUR BACKS!
I CAN'T STAY HERE!!

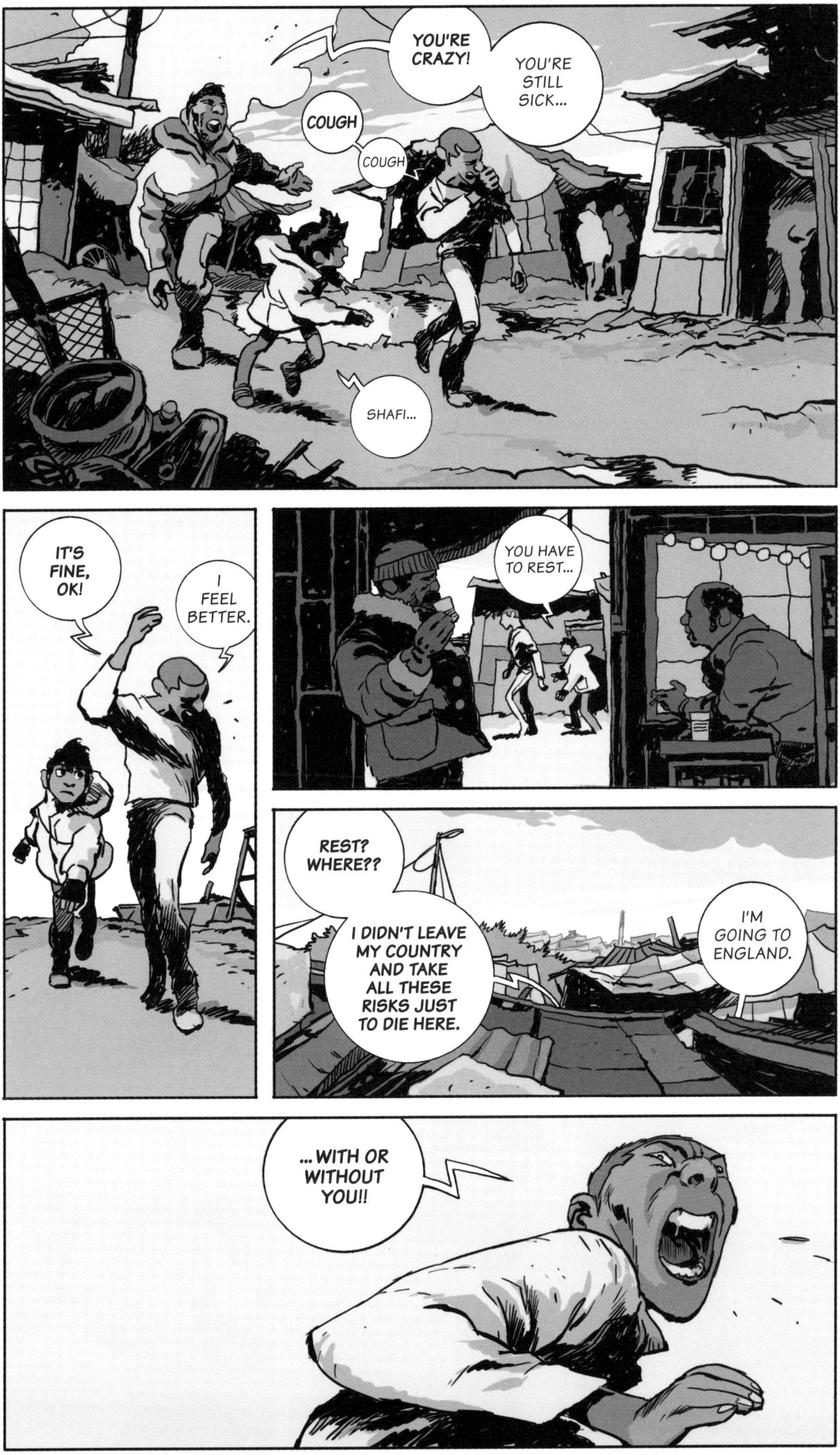
YOU'RE CRAZY!
YOU'RE STILL SICK...
COUGH
COUGH
SHAFI...
IT'S FINE, OK!
I FEEL BETTER.
YOU HAVE TO REST...
REST? WHERE??
I DIDN'T LEAVE MY COUNTRY AND TAKE ALL THESE RISKS JUST TO DIE HERE.
I'M GOING TO ENGLAND.
...WITH OR WITHOUT YOU!!

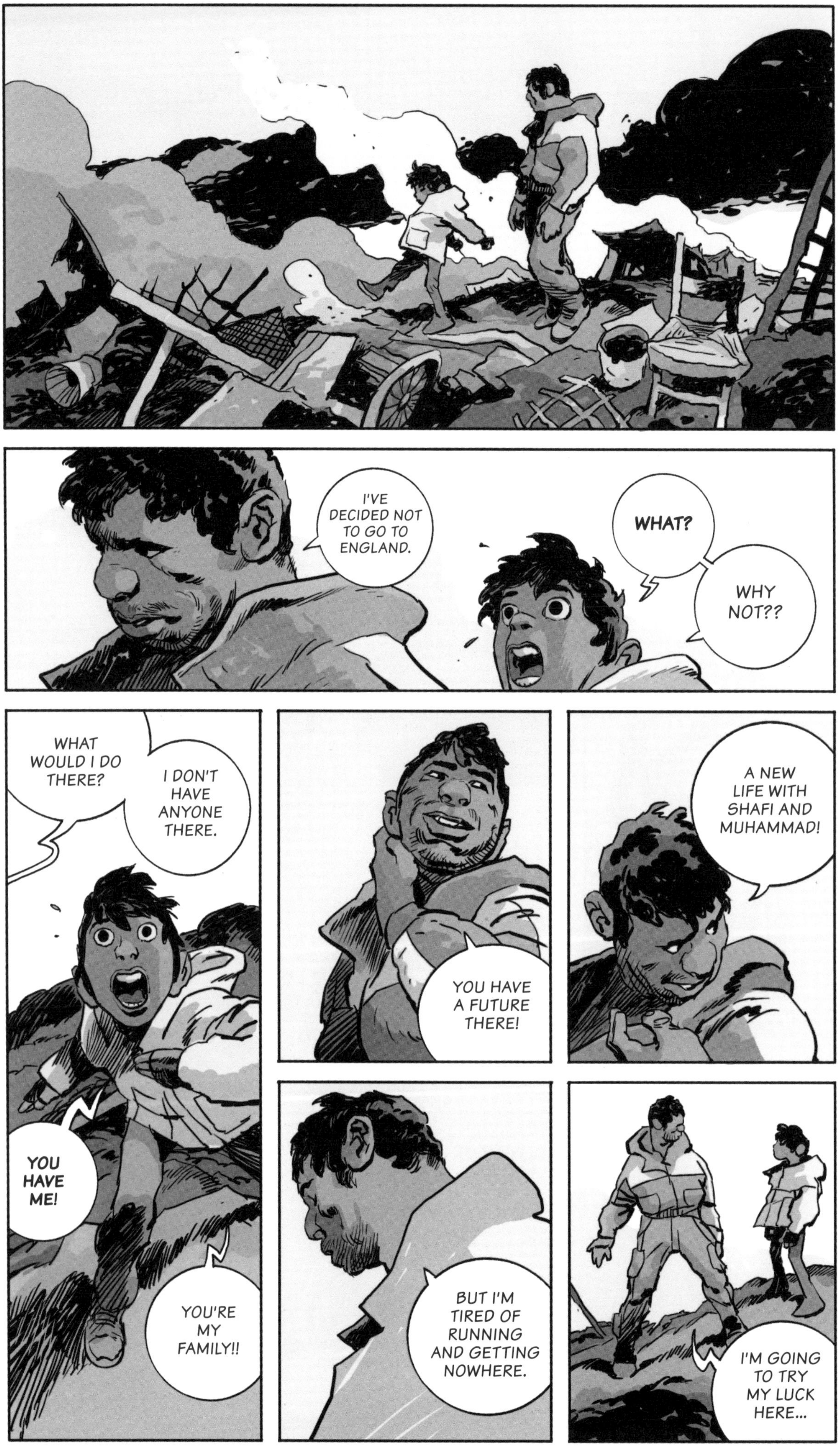
I'VE DECIDED NOT TO GO TO ENGLAND.
WHAT?
WHY NOT??
WHAT WOULD I DO THERE?
I DON'T HAVE ANYONE THERE.
YOU HAVE A FUTURE THERE!
A NEW LIFE WITH SHAFI AND MUHAMMAD!
YOU HAVE ME!
YOU'RE MY FAMILY!!
BUT I'M TIRED OF RUNNING AND GETTING NOWHERE.
I'M GOING TO TRY MY LUCK HERE...

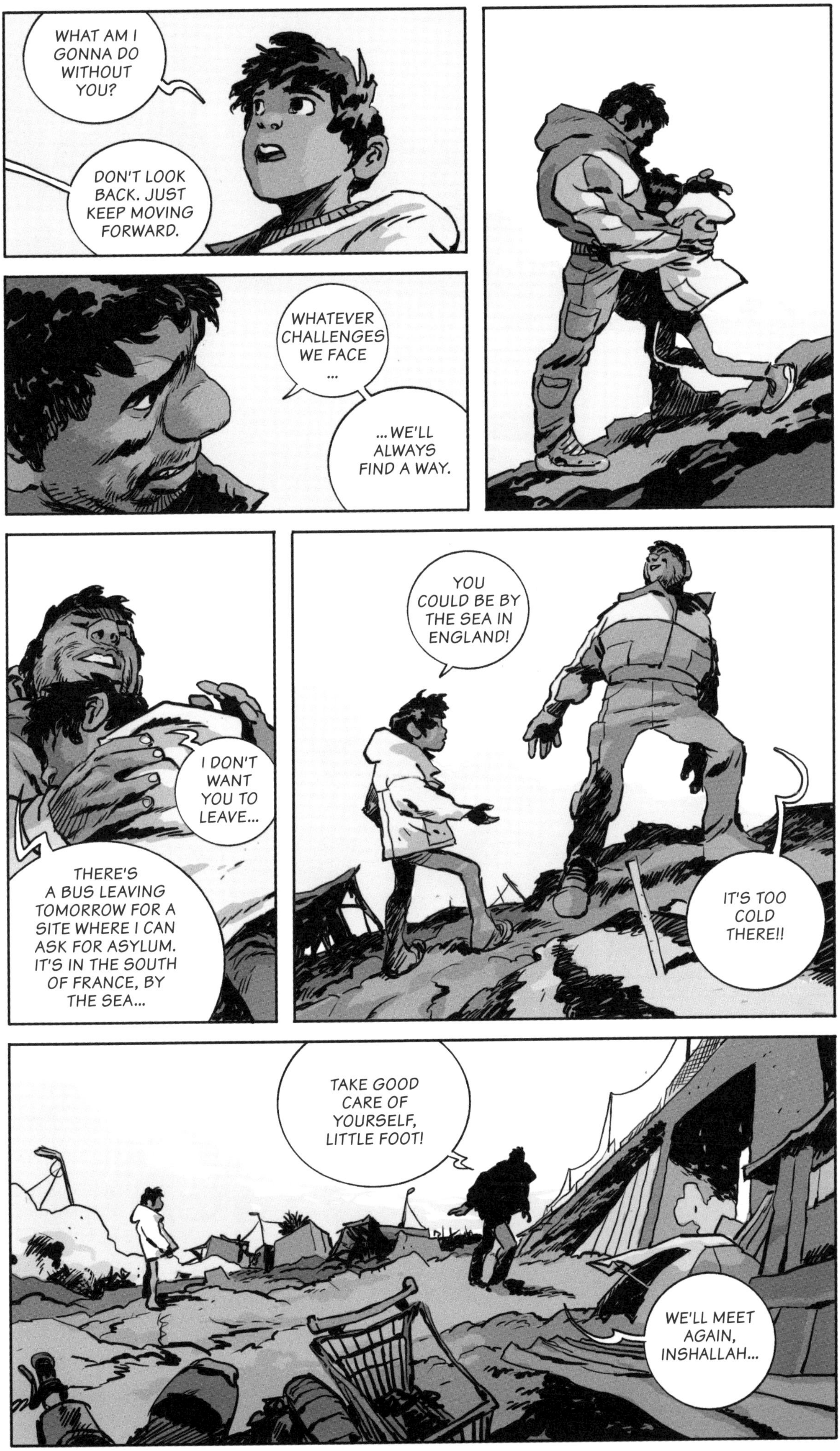
WHAT AM I GONNA DO WITHOUT YOU?
DON'T LOOK BACK. JUST KEEP MOVING FORWARD.
WHATEVER CHALLENGES WE FACE ...
...WE'LL ALWAYS FIND A WAY.
I DON'T WANT YOU TO LEAVE...
THERE'S A BUS LEAVING TOMORROW FOR A SITE WHERE I CAN ASK FOR ASYLUM. IT'S IN THE SOUTH OF FRANCE, BY THE SEA...
YOU COULD BE BY THE SEA IN ENGLAND!
IT'S TOO COLD THERE!!
TAKE GOOD CARE OF YOURSELF, LITTLE FOOT!
WE'LL MEET AGAIN, INSHALLAH...

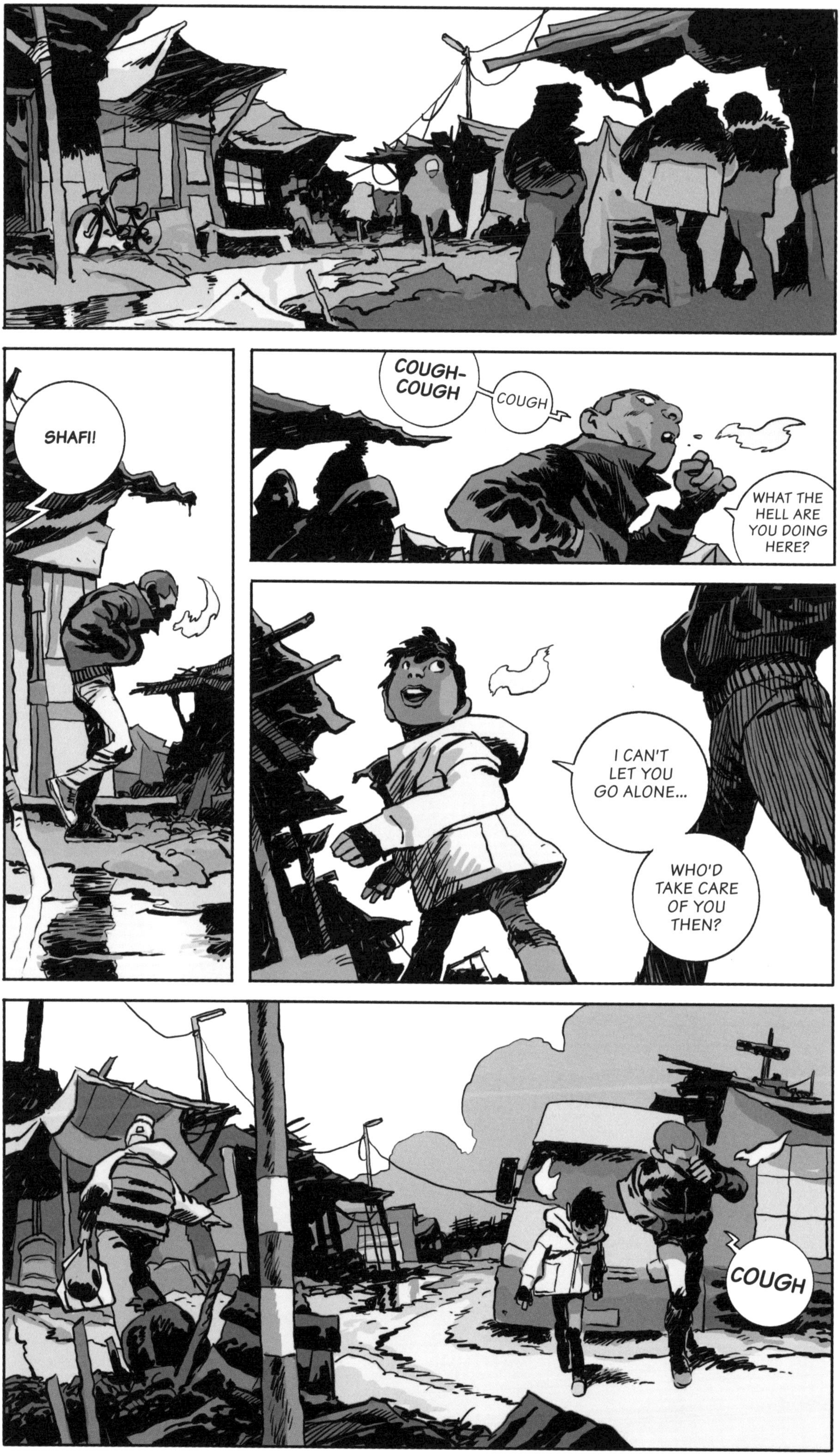
SHAFI!
COUGH-COUGH
COUGH
WHAT THE HELL ARE YOU DOING HERE?
I CAN'T LET YOU GO ALONE...
WHO'D TAKE CARE OF YOU THEN?
COUGH

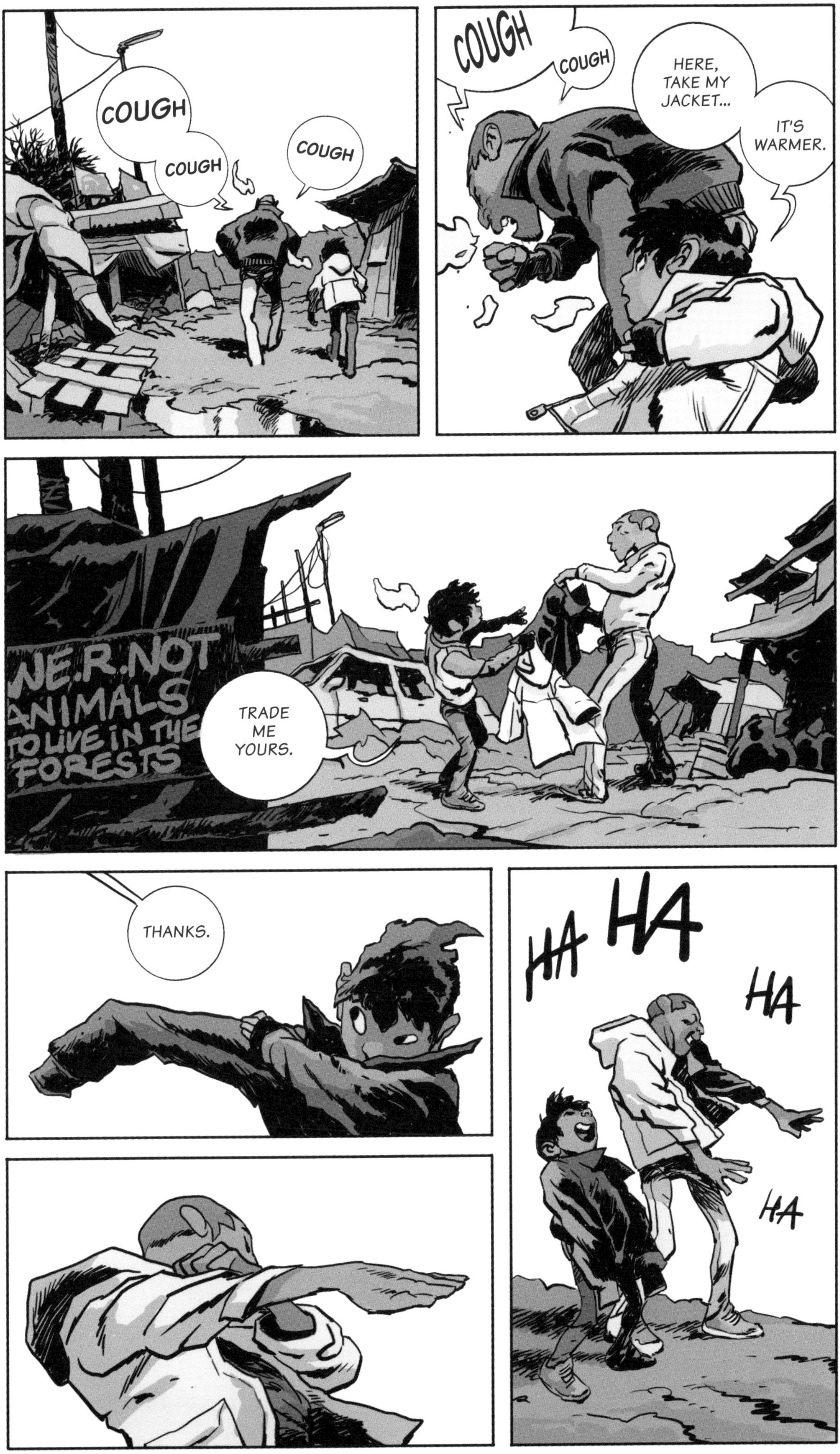
COUGH
COUGH
COUGH
COUGH
COUGH
HERE, TAKE MY JACKET...
IT'S WARMER.
W.E.R. NOT ANIMALS TO LIVE IN THE FORESTS
TRADE ME YOURS.
THANKS.
HA HA
HA
HA

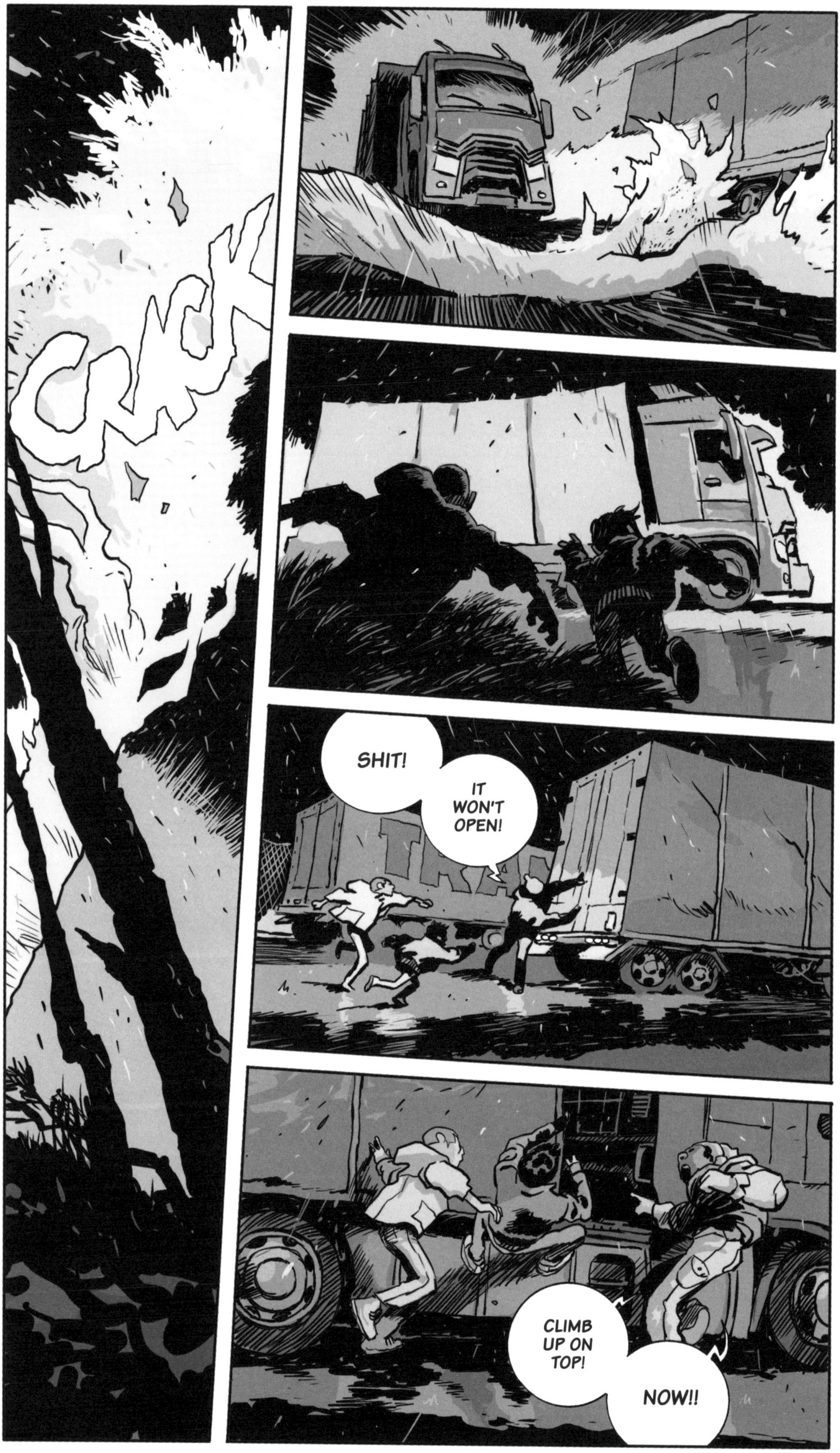
CRACK
SHIT!
IT WON'T OPEN!
CLIMB UP ON TOP!
NOW!!

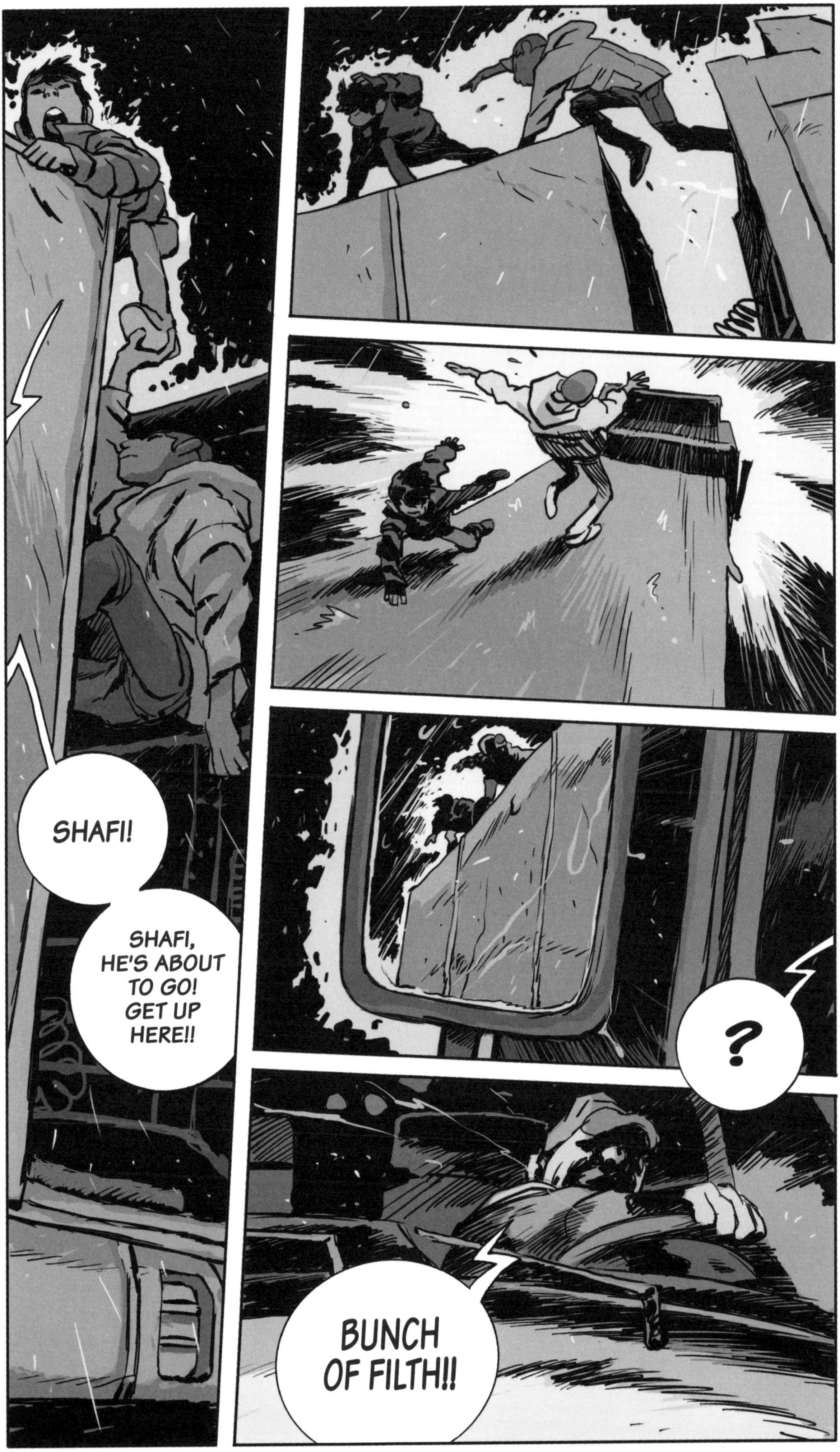
SHAFI!
SHAFI, HE'S ABOUT TO GO! GET UP HERE!!
?
BUNCH OF FILTH!!

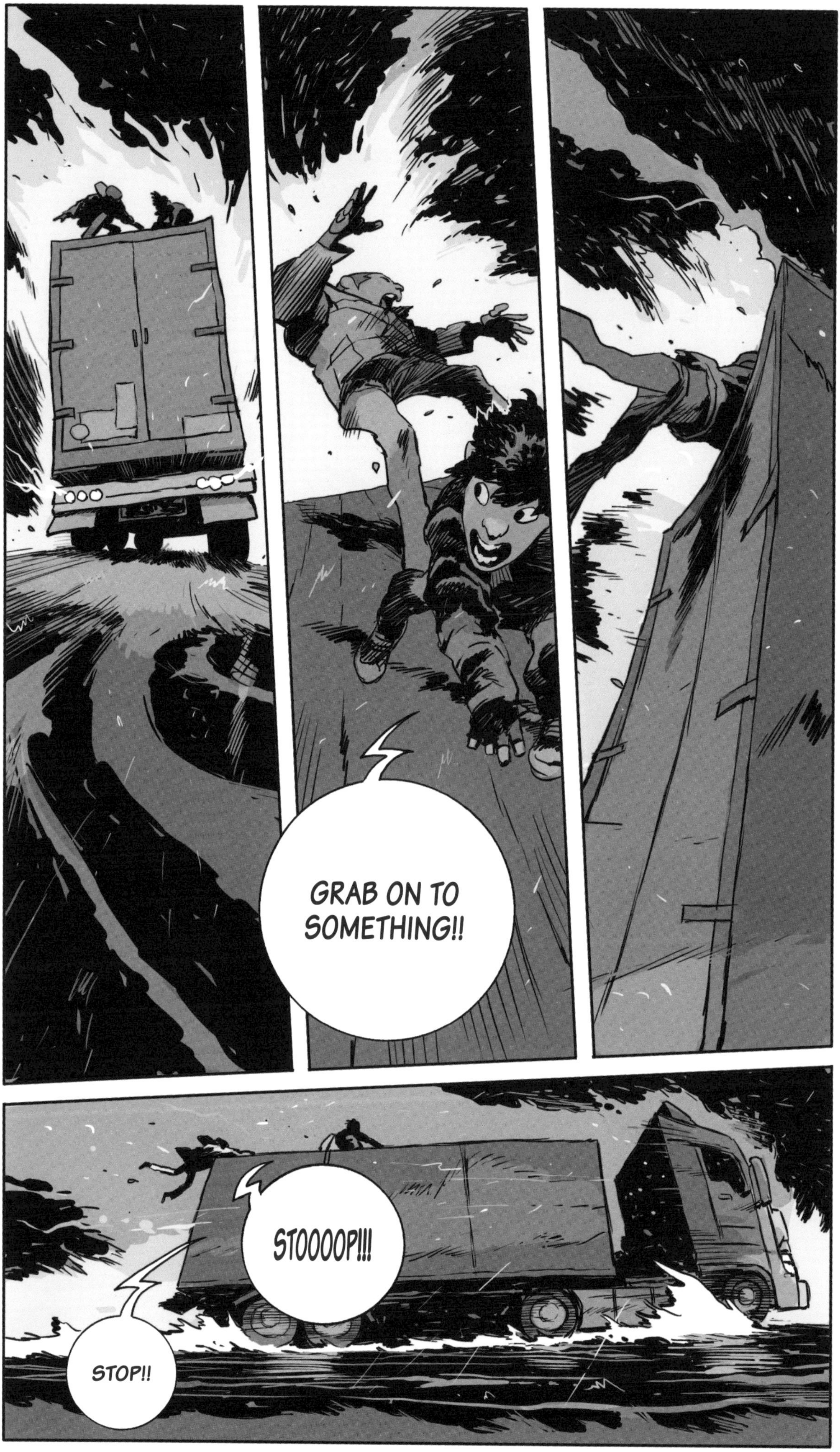
GRAB ON TO SOMETHING!!
STOOOOP!!!
STOP!!

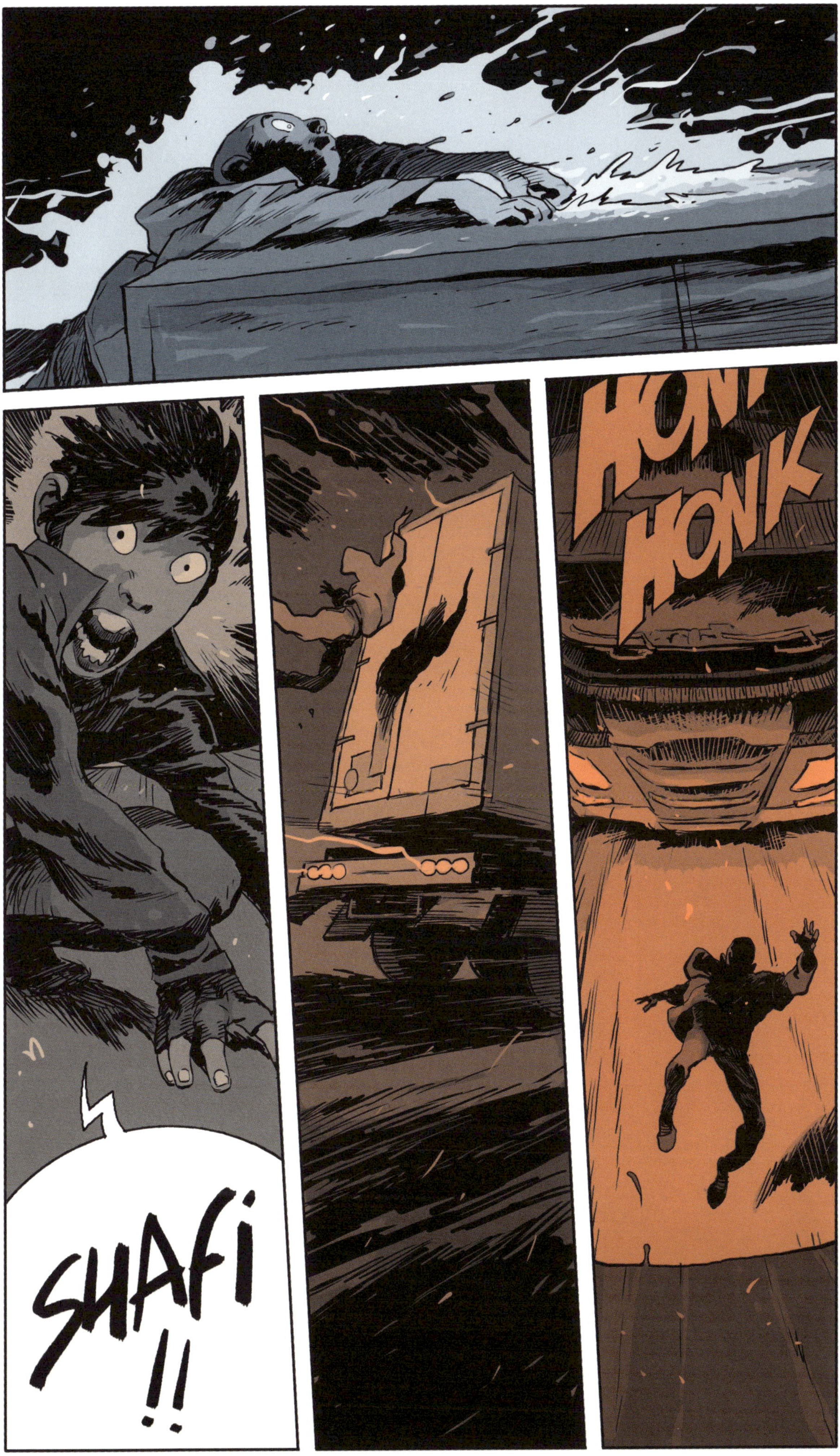
SHAFI !!
HONK HONK

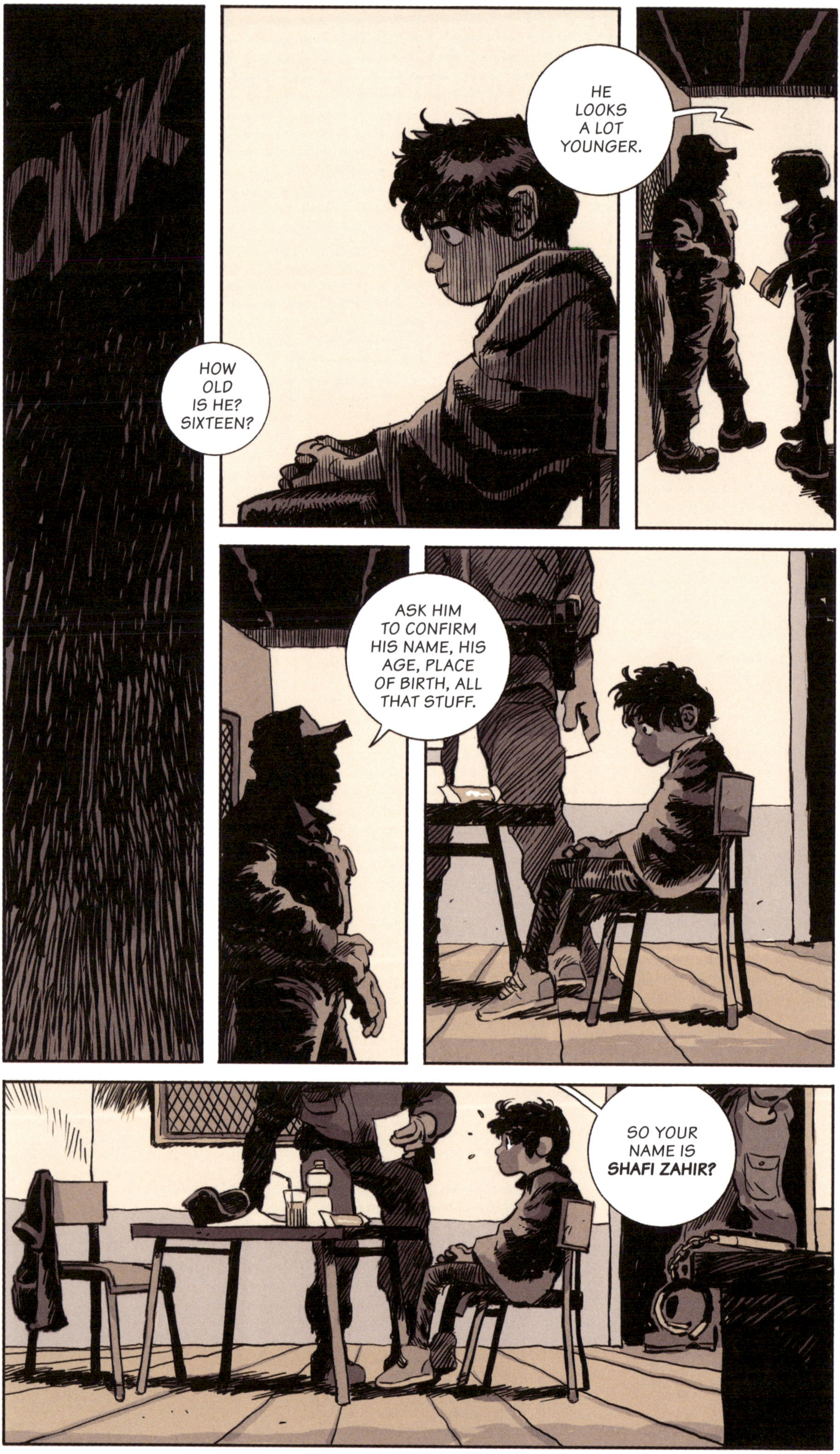
HE LOOKS A LOT YOUNGER.
HOW OLD IS HE? SIXTEEN?
ASK HIM TO CONFIRM HIS NAME, HIS AGE, PLACE OF BIRTH, ALL THAT STUFF.
SO YOUR NAME IS **SHAFI ZAHIR?**

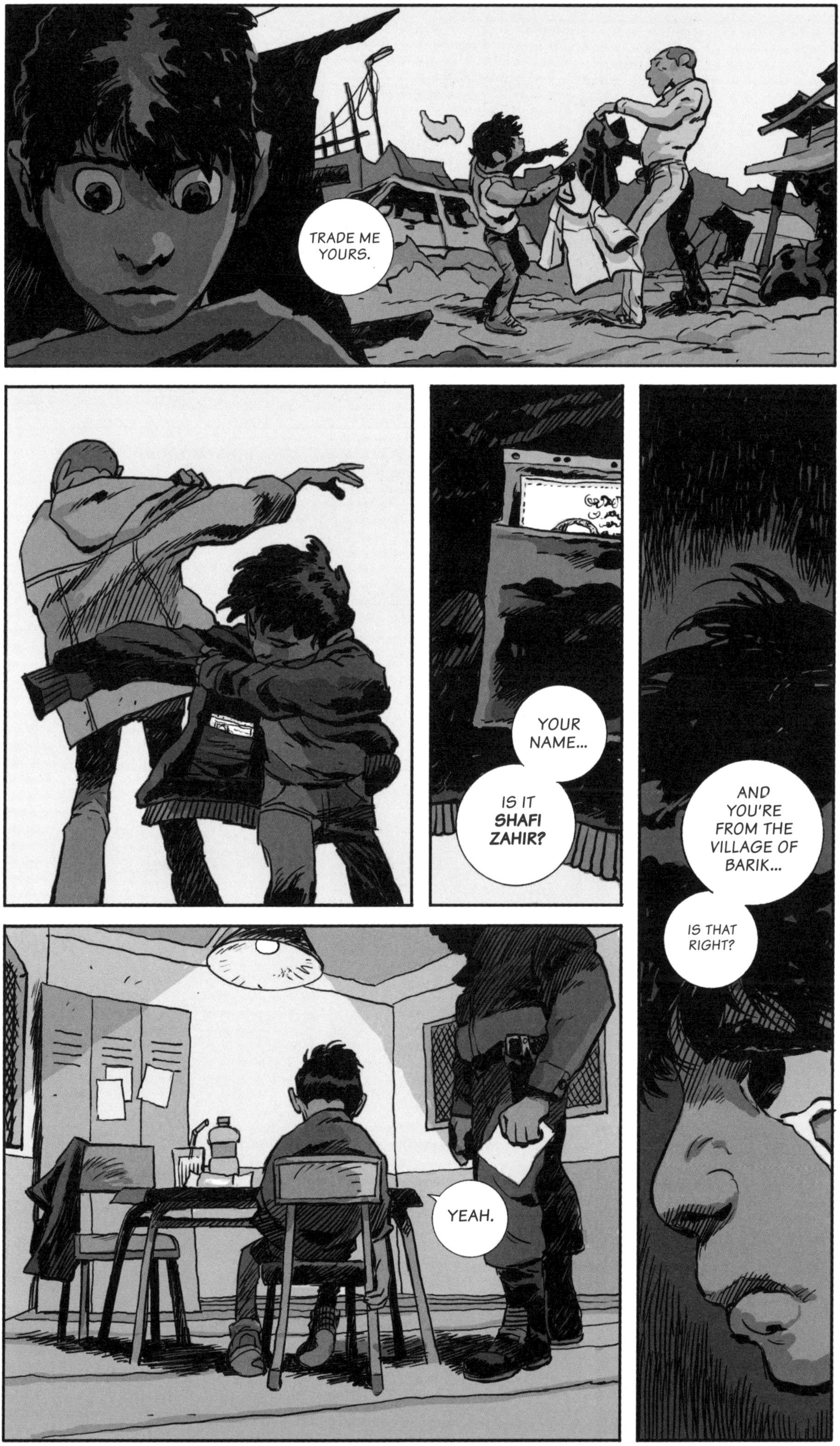
TRADE ME YOURS.
YOUR NAME...
IS IT **SHAFI ZAHIR?**
AND YOU'RE FROM THE VILLAGE OF BARIK...
IS THAT RIGHT?
YEAH.

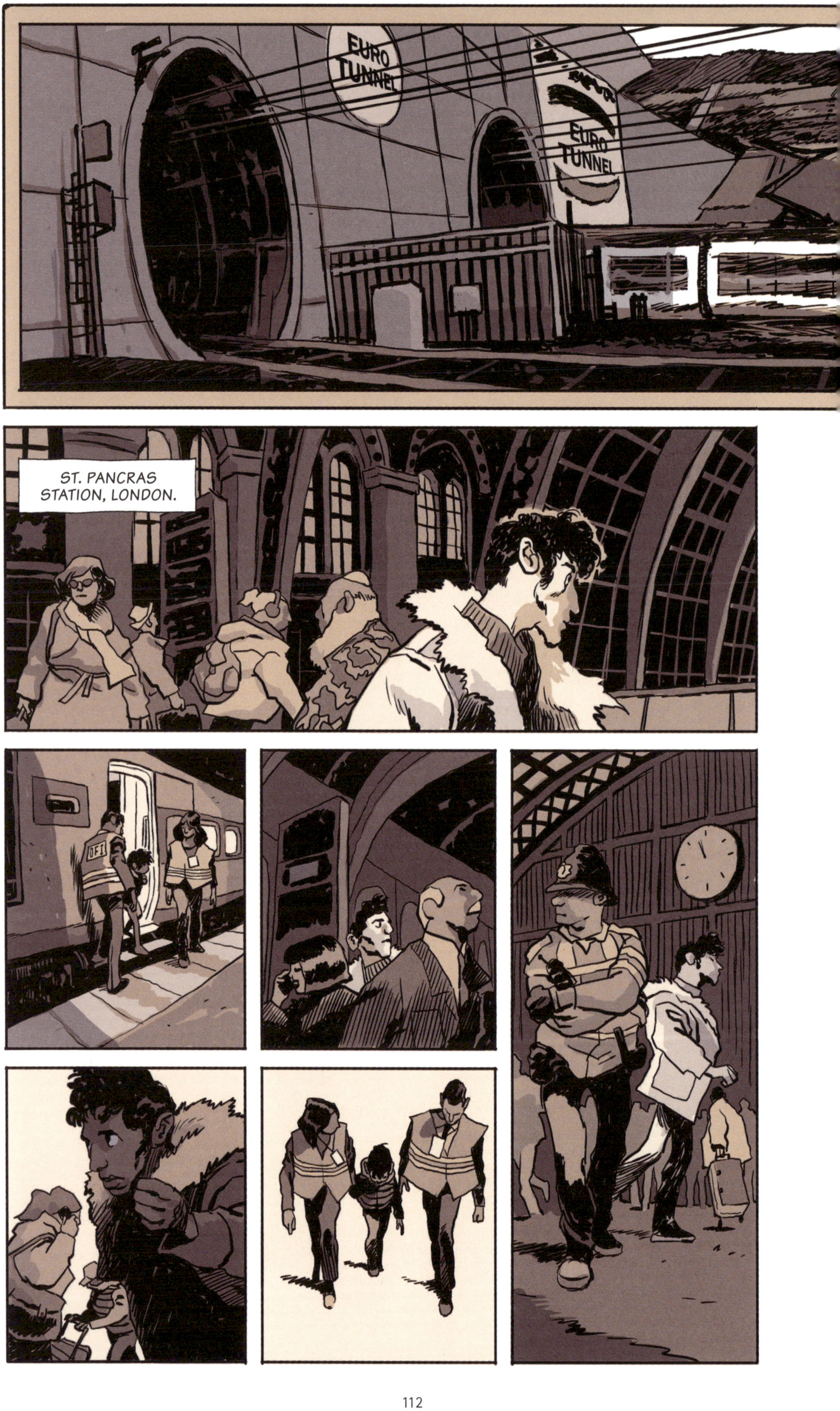
EURO TUNNEL
EURO TUNNEL
ST. PANCRAS STATION, LONDON.
OFI

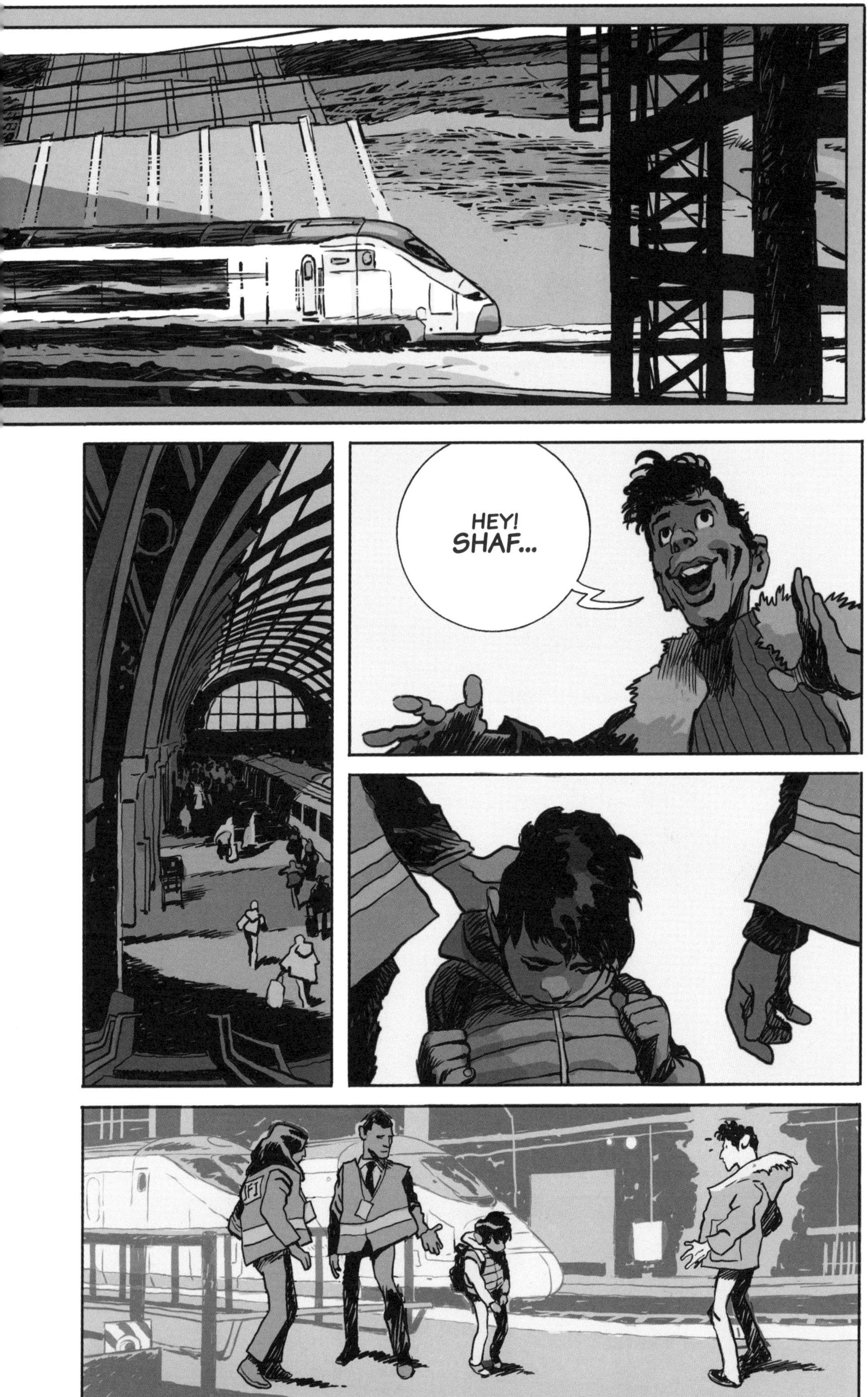
HEY! SHAF...

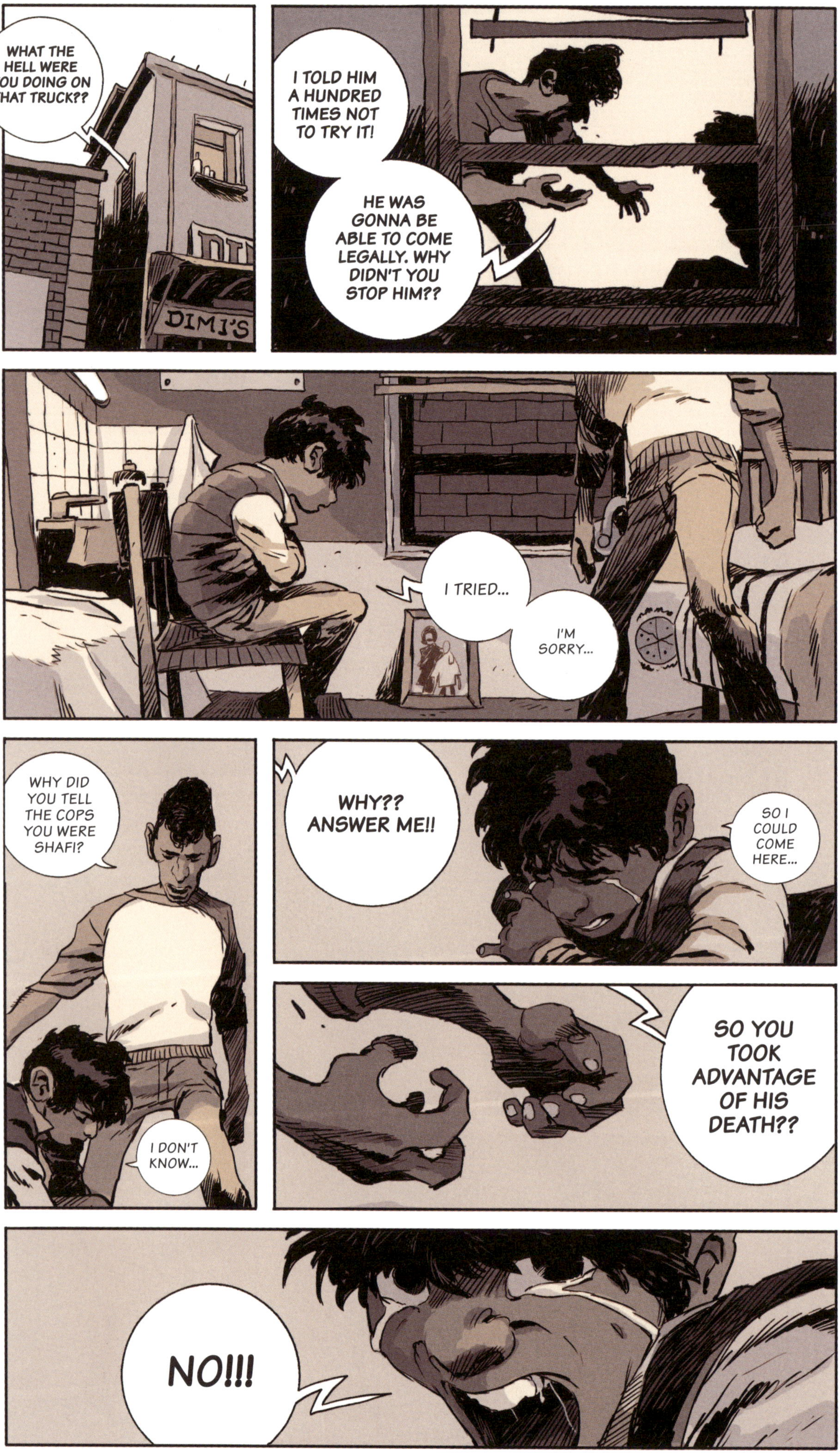
WHAT THE HELL WERE YOU DOING ON THAT TRUCK??
DIMI'S
I TOLD HIM A HUNDRED TIMES NOT TO TRY IT!
HE WAS GONNA BE ABLE TO COME LEGALLY. WHY DIDN'T YOU STOP HIM??
I TRIED...
I'M SORRY...
WHY DID YOU TELL THE COPS YOU WERE SHAFI?
I DON'T KNOW...
WHY?? ANSWER ME!!
SO I COULD COME HERE...
SO YOU TOOK ADVANTAGE OF HIS DEATH??
NO!!!

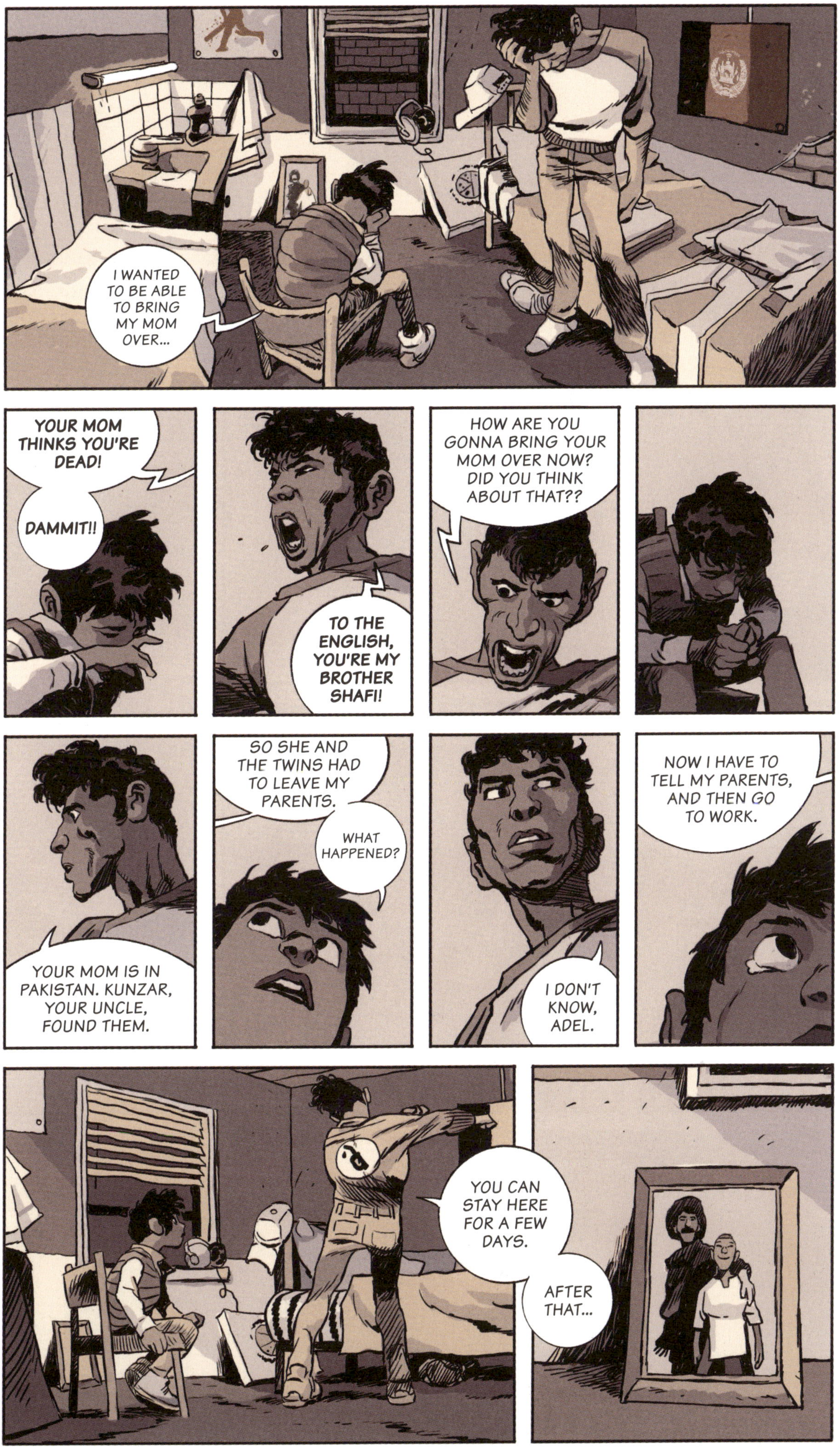
I WANTED TO BE ABLE TO BRING MY MOM OVER...
YOUR MOM THINKS YOU'RE DEAD!
DAMMIT!!
TO THE ENGLISH, YOU'RE MY BROTHER SHAFI!
HOW ARE YOU GONNA BRING YOUR MOM OVER NOW? DID YOU THINK ABOUT THAT??
YOUR MOM IS IN PAKISTAN. KUNZAR, YOUR UNCLE, FOUND THEM.
SO SHE AND THE TWINS HAD TO LEAVE MY PARENTS.
WHAT HAPPENED?
I DON'T KNOW, ADEL.
NOW I HAVE TO TELL MY PARENTS, AND THEN GO TO WORK.
YOU CAN STAY HERE FOR A FEW DAYS.
AFTER THAT...

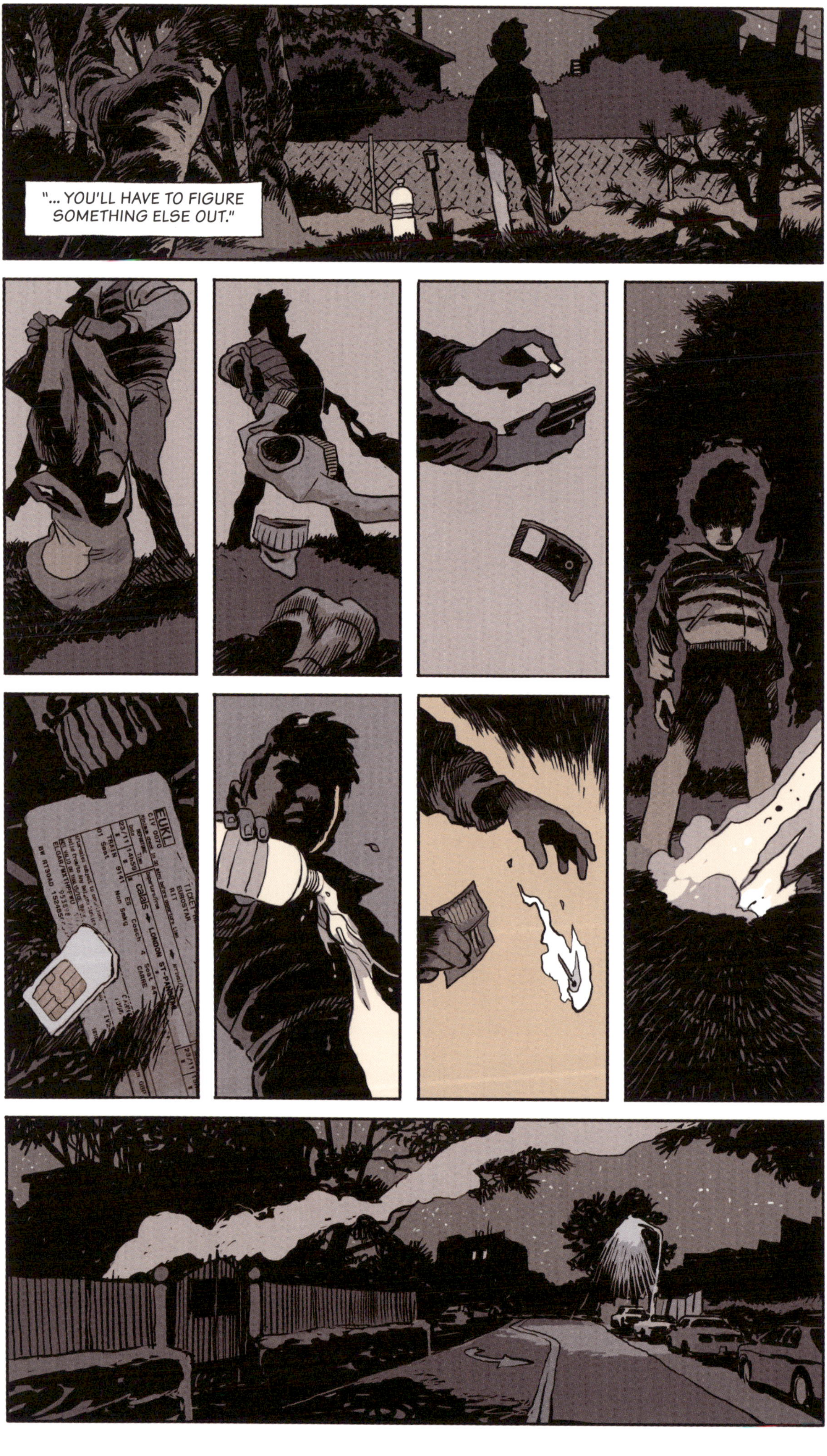
"... YOU'LL HAVE TO FIGURE SOMETHING ELSE OUT."

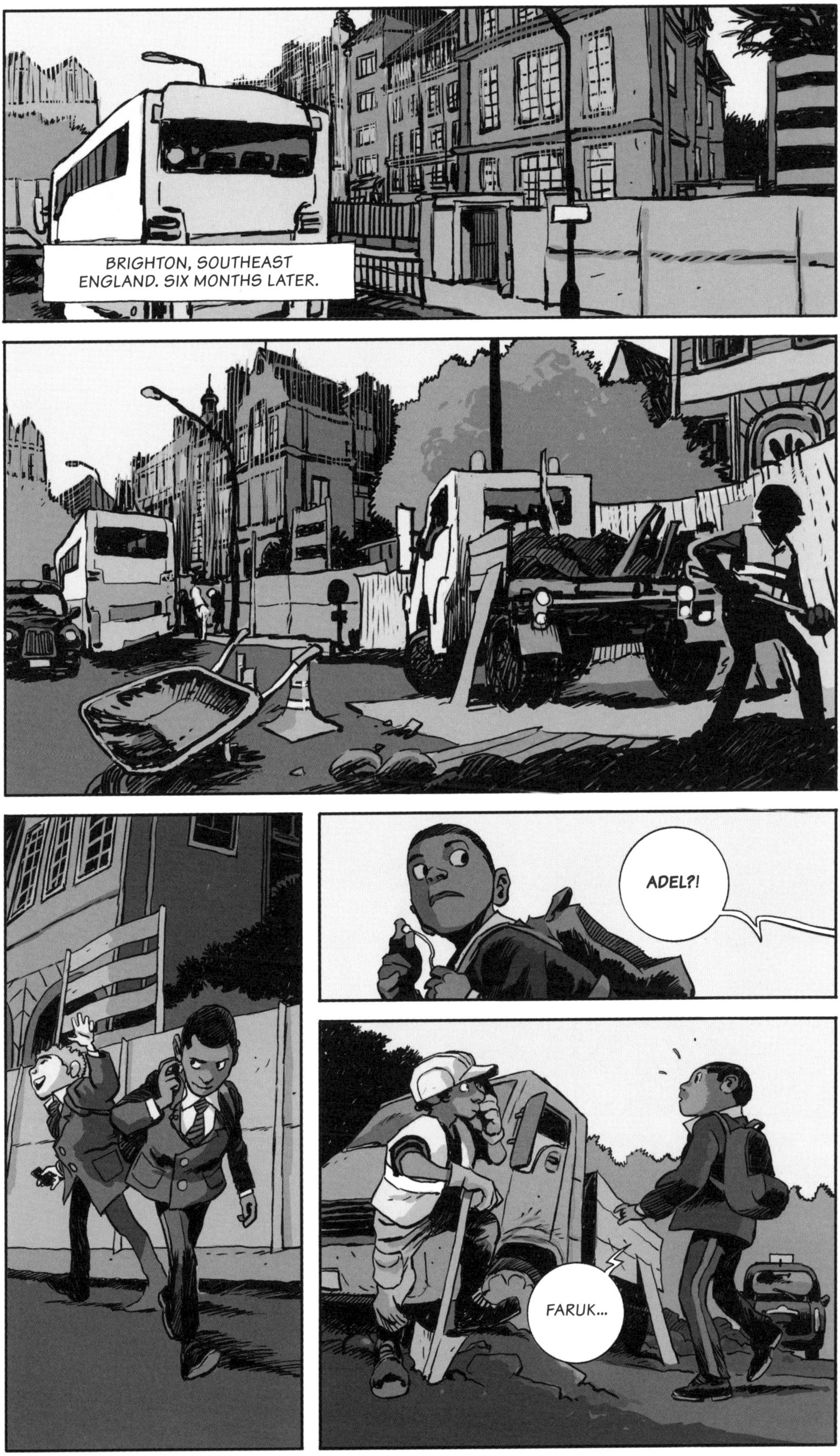
BRIGHTON, SOUTHEAST ENGLAND. SIX MONTHS LATER.
ADEL?!
FARUK...

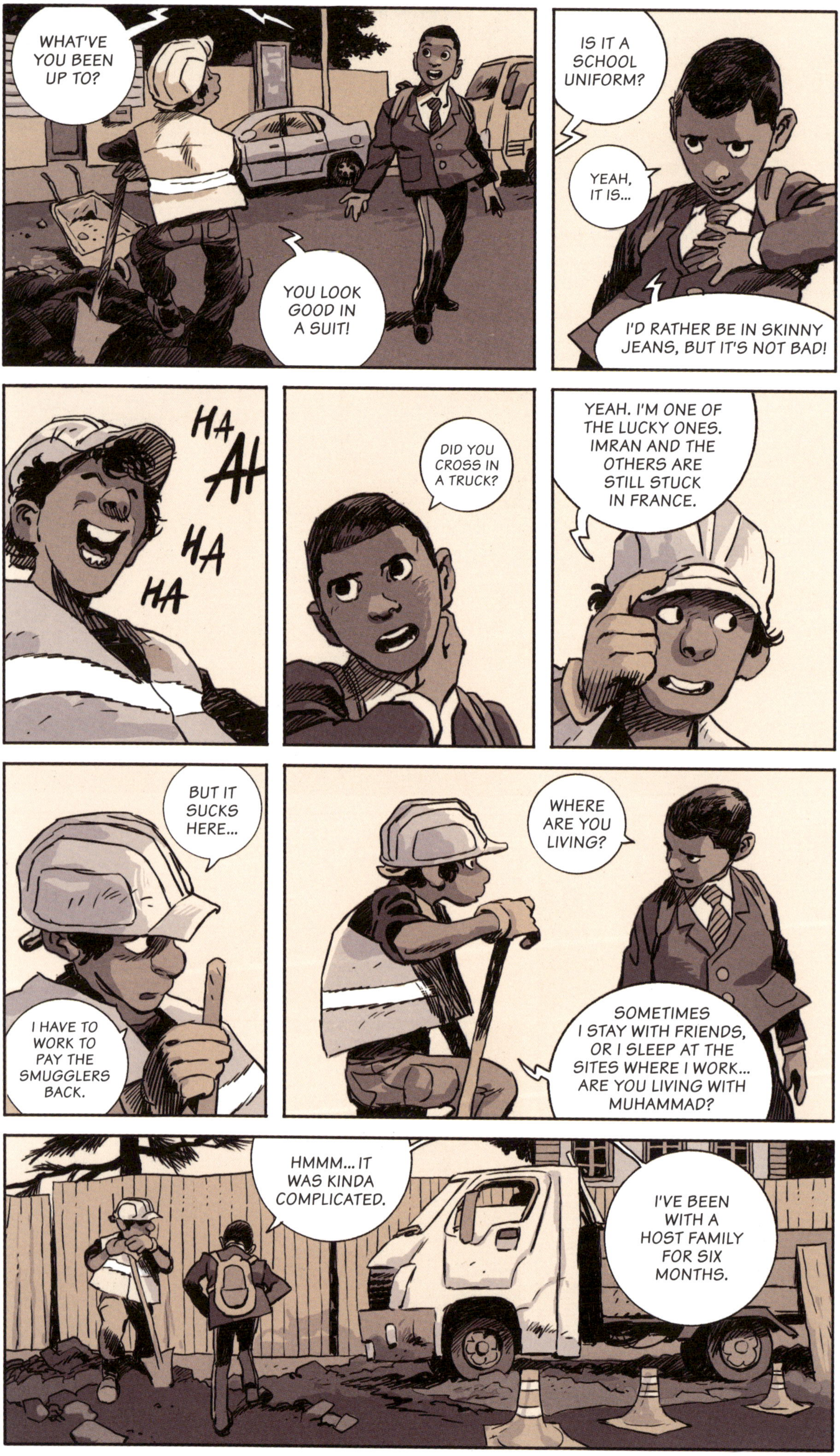
WHAT'VE YOU BEEN UP TO?
YOU LOOK GOOD IN A SUIT!
IS IT A SCHOOL UNIFORM?
YEAH, IT IS...
I'D RATHER BE IN SKINNY JEANS, BUT IT'S NOT BAD!
HA AH HA HA
DID YOU CROSS IN A TRUCK?
YEAH. I'M ONE OF THE LUCKY ONES. IMRAN AND THE OTHERS ARE STILL STUCK IN FRANCE.
BUT IT SUCKS HERE...
I HAVE TO WORK TO PAY THE SMUGGLERS BACK.
WHERE ARE YOU LIVING?
SOMETIMES I STAY WITH FRIENDS, OR I SLEEP AT THE SITES WHERE I WORK... ARE YOU LIVING WITH MUHAMMAD?
HMMM... IT WAS KINDA COMPLICATED.
I'VE BEEN WITH A HOST FAMILY FOR SIX MONTHS.

YOU KNOW...
ALL OF US IN CALAIS WERE SORRY ABOUT SHAFI...
THANKS, FRIEND...
MAY GOD WATCH OVER HIM.
HEY!
WHAT ARE YOU DOING? GET BACK TO WORK!!
PFFF...
SOME DAYS I WISH I'D BEEN KILLED BY A BOMB BACK HOME...
...INSTEAD OF DYING SLOWLY HERE...
SORRY, I GOTTA GO.
IT WAS GOOD TO SEE YOU AGAIN, ADEL...
YOU TOO, FRIEND.
MAY GOD BE WITH YOU.

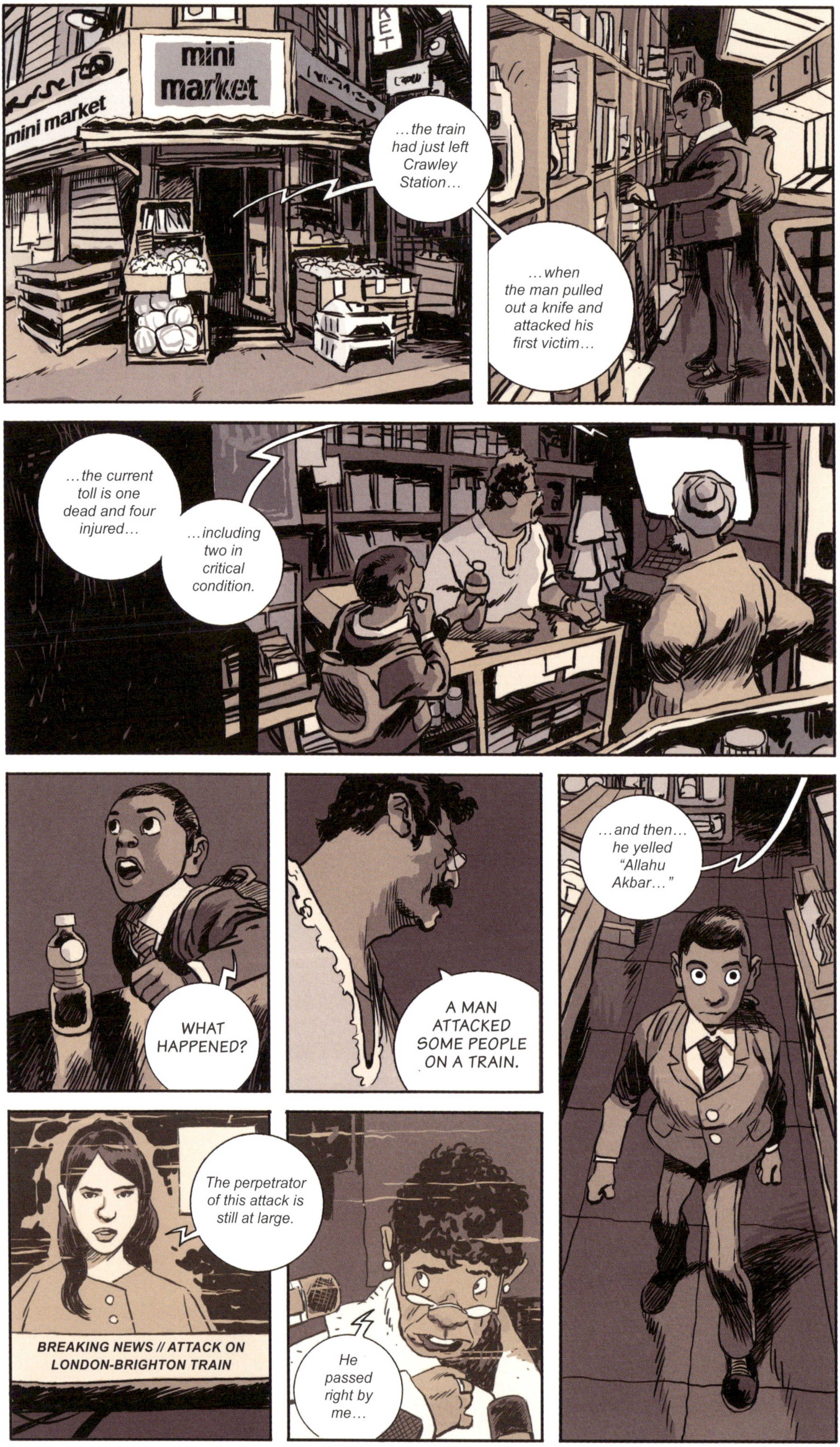
mini market
mini market
…the train had just left Crawley Station…
…when the man pulled out a knife and attacked his first victim…
…the current toll is one dead and four injured…
…including two in critical condition.
WHAT HAPPENED?
A MAN ATTACKED SOME PEOPLE ON A TRAIN.
…and then… he yelled "Allahu Akbar…"
BREAKING NEWS // ATTACK ON LONDON-BRIGHTON TRAIN
The perpetrator of this attack is still at large.
He passed right by me…

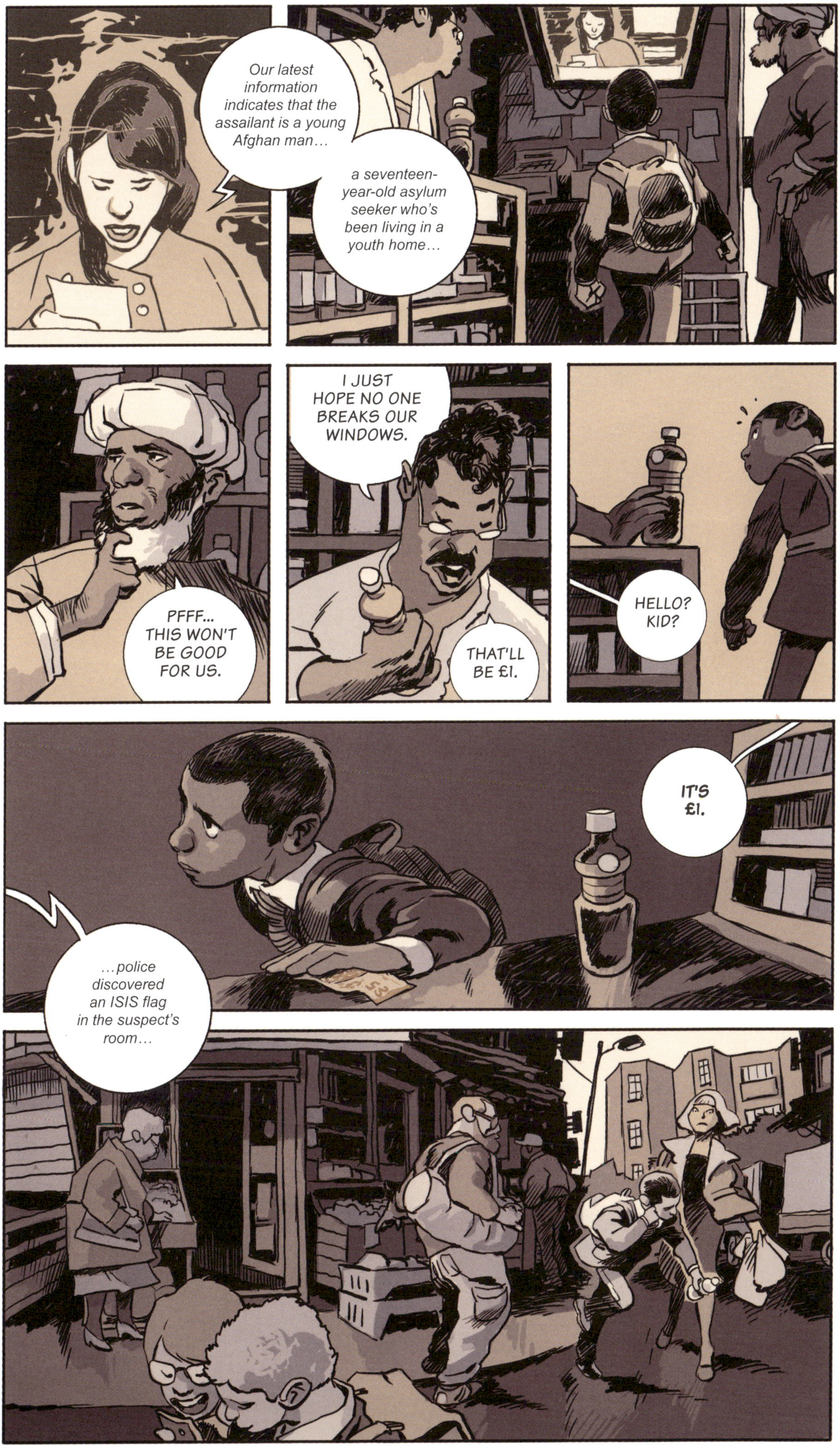
Our latest information indicates that the assailant is a young Afghan man…
a seventeen-year-old asylum seeker who's been living in a youth home…
PFFF… THIS WON'T BE GOOD FOR US.
I JUST HOPE NO ONE BREAKS OUR WINDOWS.
THAT'LL BE £1.
HELLO? KID?
IT'S £1.
…police discovered an ISIS flag in the suspect's room…

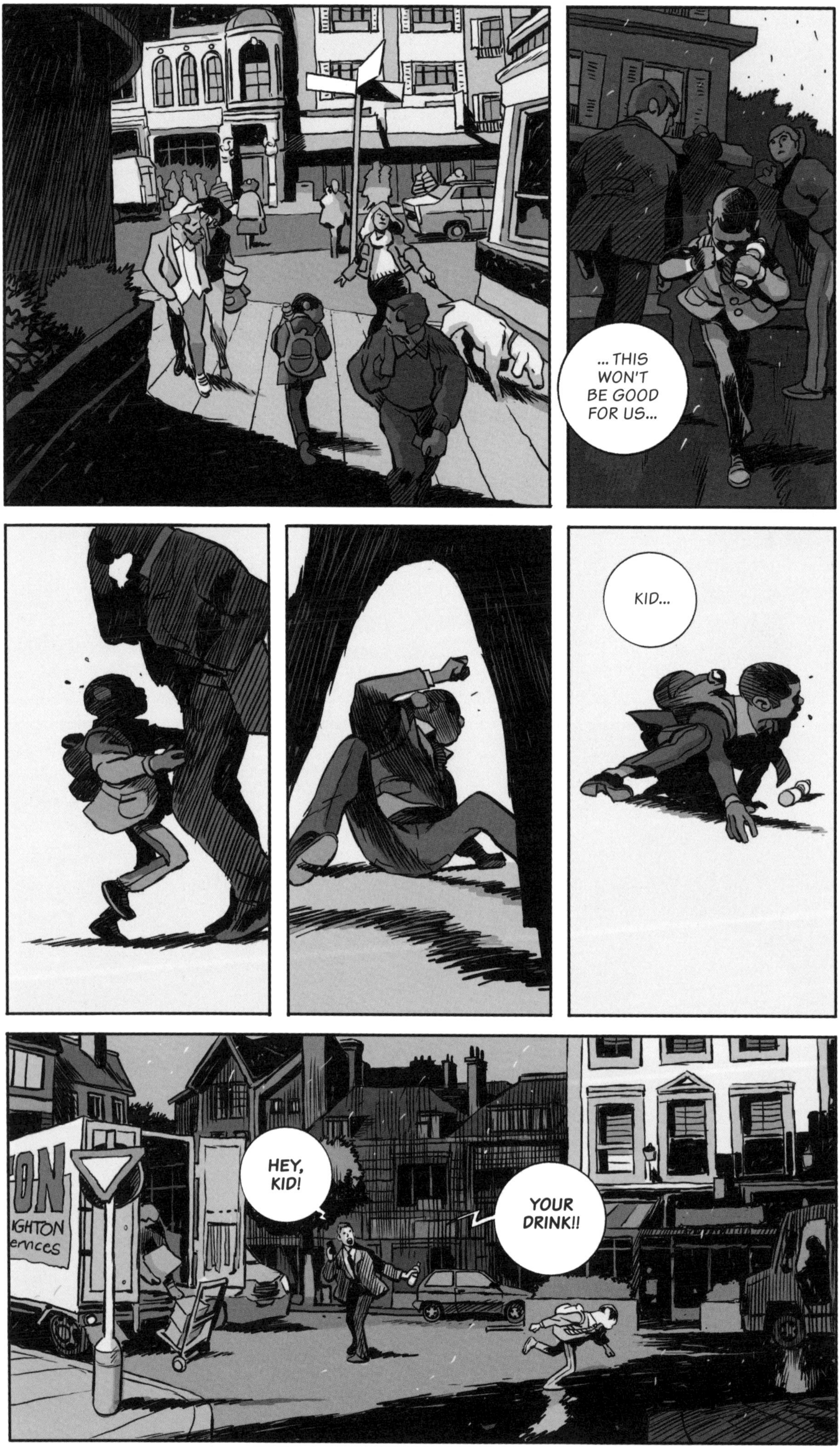
...THIS WON'T BE GOOD FOR US...
KID...
HEY, KID!
YOUR DRINK!!
ON
IGHTON
ervices

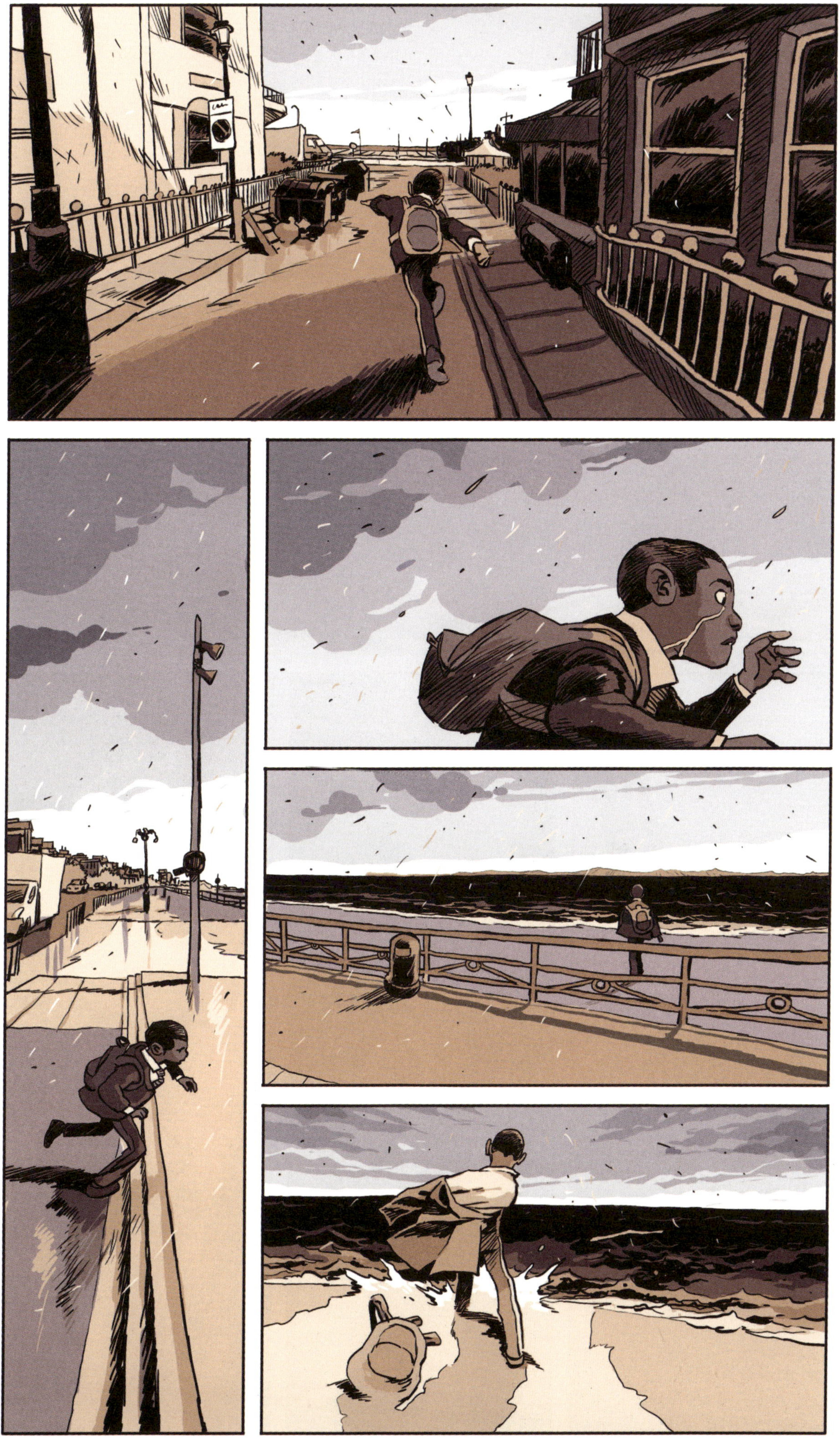

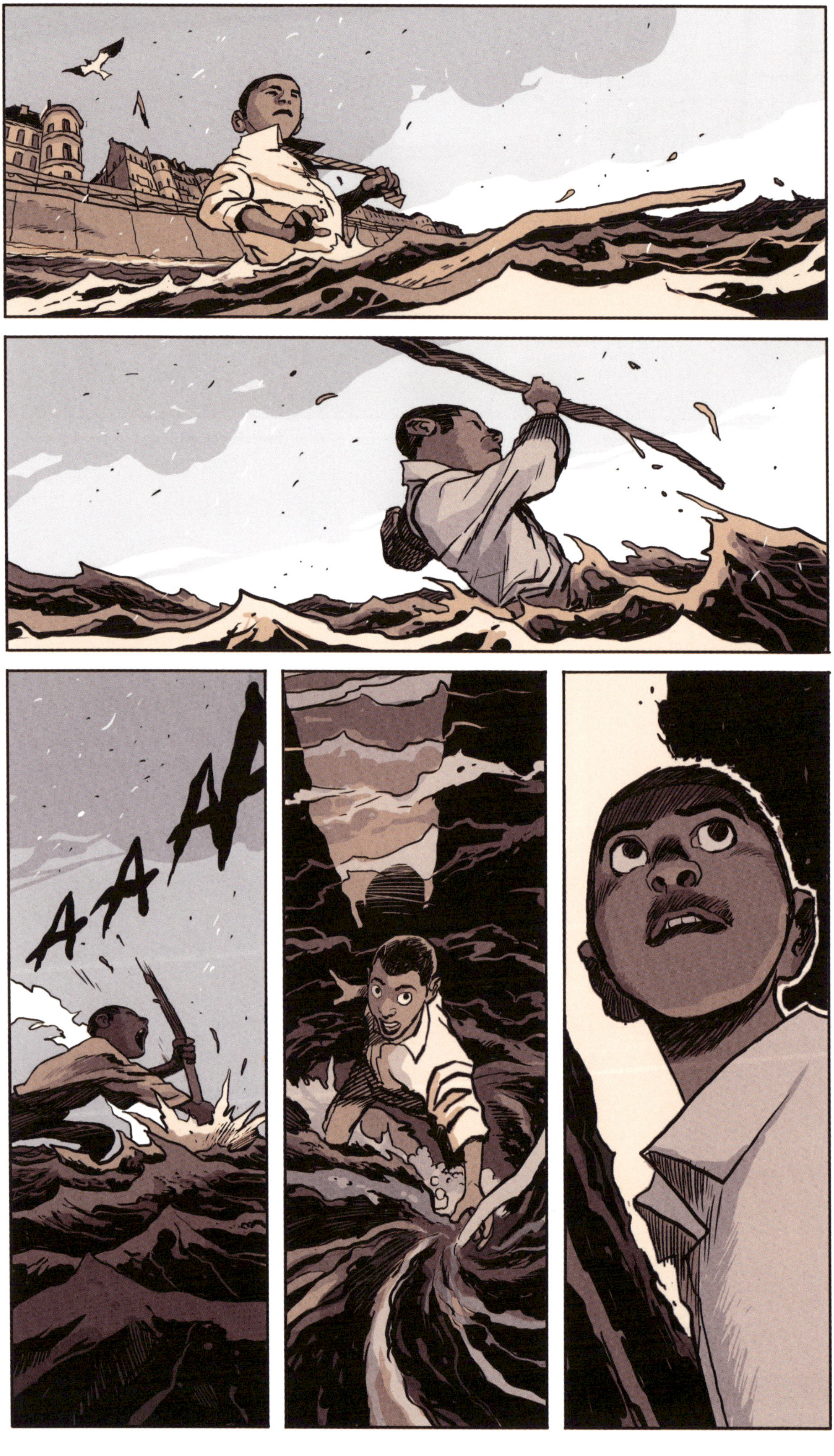
AAAA

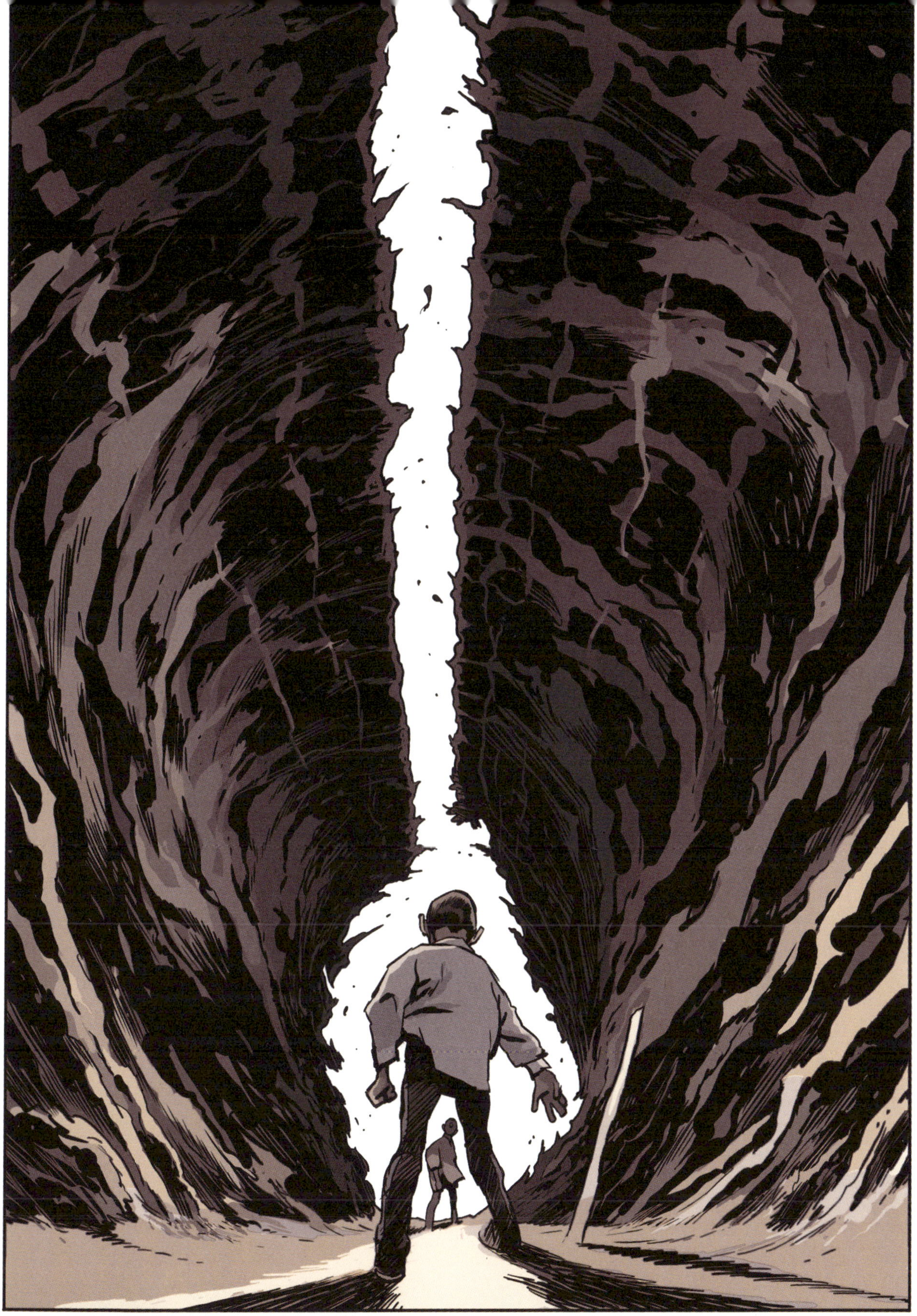

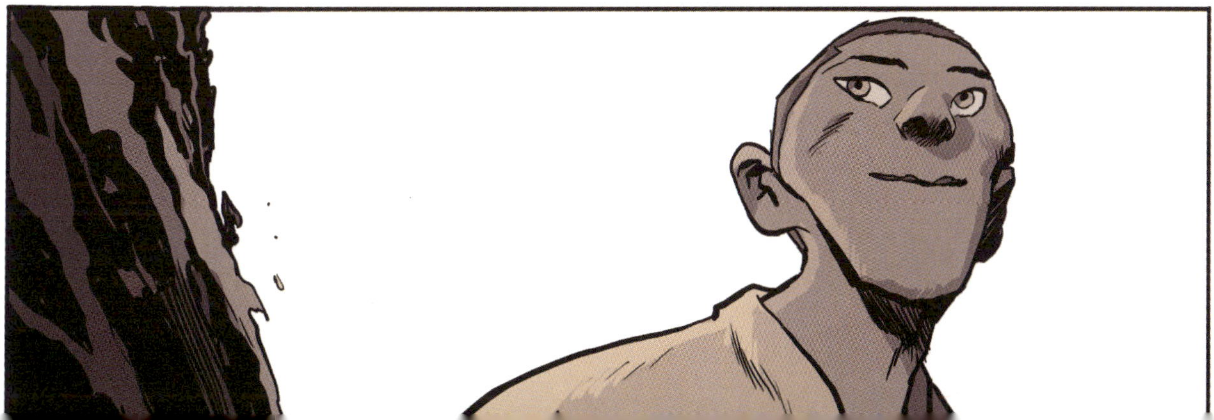